THE MiFID REVOLUTION

The Market in Financial Instruments Directive (MiFID) is nothing short of a revolution. Introduced on 1 November 2007, it will have a profound, long-term impact on Europe's securities markets. It will see banks operating as exchanges for certain activities, offering alternative execution services for equities that more closely resemble the structure of OTC markets, and will lead to the decentralization of order execution in an array of venues previously governed by concentration rules. Crucially, MiFID will also have a profound impact on the organization and business strategies of investment firms, exchanges, asset managers and other financial market intermediaries. Until now, analysis has focused on the directive's short-term implementation issues. This book focuses on the long-term strategic implications associated with MiFID, and will be essential reading for anybody who recognizes that their firm will need to make constant dynamic readjustments in order to remain competitive in this challenging new environment.

JEAN-PIERRE CASEY is a Vice-President in Product and Technical Compliance at Barclays Wealth in London. He was previously Head of Research at the European Capital Markets Institute (ECMI) and Research Fellow at the Centre for European Policy Studies (CEPS).
Any views expressed in this book are only personal, and cannot necessarily be taken to represent the views of Barclays Wealth or any entity in the Barclays Group.

KAREL LANNOO is Chief Executive of the Centre for European Policy Studies (CEPS) in Brussels and directs the European Capital Markets Institute (ECMI). He has published extensively on European financial regulation matters.

THE MiFID REVOLUTION

J.-P. CASEY AND K. LANNOO

preface by
DAVID WRIGHT

CAMBRIDGE
UNIVERSITY PRESS

CAMBRIDGE UNIVERSITY PRESS
Cambridge, New York, Melbourne, Madrid, Cape Town, Singapore, São Paulo, Delhi, Dubai, Tokyo

Cambridge University Press
The Edinburgh Building, Cambridge CB2 8RU, UK

Published in the United States of America by Cambridge University Press, New York

www.cambridge.org
Information on this title: www.cambridge.org/9780521518635

First published 2009

Printed in the United Kingdom at the University Press, Cambridge

A catalogue record for this publication is available from the British Library

ISBN 978-0-521-51863-5 hardback

TABLE OF CONTENTS

LIST OF ILLUSTRATIONS

PREFACE

The Markets in Financial Instruments Directive (MiFID) entered into force on 1 November 2007. The outcome of extensive consultation and many years' work, MiFID represents a significant regulatory overhaul of investment services and securities markets in Europe. Competition in trading various financial instruments is opened up among traditional stock exchanges, multilateral trading facilities (MTFs) and investment firms, and is done so throughout Europe by way of the right to 'passport' these services across borders. Investors benefit from a greater number of trading venues as well as a robust and comprehensive framework ensuring high levels of investor protection. Together with the other parts of the EU Financial Services Action Plan (FSAP), MiFID is expected, over time, to lower the cost of capital and to bring major benefits for the European economy. MiFID has also demonstrated that the Lamfalussy process can work well.

Before 1 November 2007, much ink had been spilled on the likely effects of MiFID for Europe's capital markets. Yet noticeably little of this work took a long-term view, combining both theoretical and empirical perspectives. Pessimists were threatening that the costs of complying with MiFID would far outweigh its benefits. Since the date of implementation, these voices have been muted and the consensus has become more positive.

Despite its young life, MiFID has proven to be largely supportive of how markets and technology were already changing the face of investment services in Europe for the better. Moreover, by introducing important safeguards for investors and extending the scope of activities subject to regulation, it has made valuable improvements to how and which products may be sold to clients. MiFID thus both fosters innovation in financial markets and buffers new entrants and less experienced investors from their more complex and risky features.

This book is a timely contribution to a view of the post-MiFID landscape. The initial dust has settled; the scepticism has died down; so policy-makers and stakeholders can once again take the long view. This book will help us do just that. Where did MiFID get it right? Where might problems emerge? What do we need to focus on next? The European Commission is committed to a careful and continuous evaluation of the consistency and efficiency of the existing framework.

From its origins and various key provisions to its anticipated impacts and potential international implications, this work provides a comprehensive look at MiFID as well as the market reality it serves. It analyses its subject material with clarity, criticism and rigour. It will prove a valuable companion, as the 'MiFID revolution' continues to play out.

David Wright
Deputy Director General
DG MARKT
European Commission

Introduction

MiFID was formally adopted by the EU legislator on 30 April 2004, but until now, a systematic overview and discussion of the impact of the directive and its different provisions has not existed. The European Directive 2004/39/EC, better known as the Market in Financial Instruments Directive (MiFID), is nothing short of a revolution. This directive represents the cornerstone of the Commission's Financial Services Action Plan and was recently transposed into national law and implemented by investment services providers.

MiFID will fundamentally alter the structure of European securities markets, in a way that possibly not many other pieces of EU financial services legislation have so far done. Much of the available analysis surrounding MiFID has focused on compliance, on building the supporting IT infrastructure and on upgrading procedures within financial institutions. Yet the regulatory impact of MiFID extends far beyond short-term implementation for investment firms. The unprecedented scope of harmonization of securities markets legislation and the resulting open architecture ushered in by MiFID, especially in trade execution and reporting, will cause a profound upheaval within existing market structures.

MiFID is indeed revolutionary; its role and impact can be considered ground-breaking from the competitive, economic and legislative points of view. MiFID came into force in the EU and European Economic Area (EEA) countries on 1 November 2007, but as there were serious delays at the level of the member states and firms in adapting to this, a full appreciation of the changes brought about by this process can still be expected to take some time.

MiFID is revolutionary from the competitive point of view, as it dramatically changes the conditions for operators in capital markets. It abolishes the monopoly of exchanges and allows systematic internalizers and Multilateral Trading Facilities (MTFs) as trade execution venues. On the other hand, it radically upgrades the operating conditions for service providers in capital markets, through 'best execution', client suitability and appropriateness, and conflict of interest criteria. The combination of market opening measures and tightening of conduct of business rules will have profound implications for the structure of European capital markets, the competitive position of investment services providers, the design of investment products and the attitude of investors.

The seismic shifts brought about by MiFID will also have long-lasting implications for the strength of financial services sectors in EU countries, leading to a re-positioning of European financial centres. The huge delays which many member states experienced in transposing the directive in time have led some to argue that the 'variable geometry' concept, used to refer to the different degrees of institutionalized cooperation which exist between EU member states, could also be applied to MiFID. The diversity in preparedness of member states will exacerbate differences between financial centres in the EU, and strengthen the well organized, leading to a consolidation of EU financial centres.

MiFID is revolutionary from a legislative point of view, too, as it is the first EU financial services directive to make ample use of the provisions for secondary legislation, initiated under the 'Lamfalussy' approach. The MiFID directive allows for implementing measures for a whole set of provisions in the directive, by which legislators can agree on swift adaptations to the basic rules. MiFID also introduces a series of new concepts in much detail in EU law, which either did not exist at EU level or were not previously spelled out. Concepts such as 'best execution', conflicts of interest, and client suitability will fundamentally alter the way of doing financial business in the EU. These requirements will not remain limited to the area of investment firms, but will become standard principles for all retail investment products and investment services providers.

The implementation of MiFID was largely overshadowed by the financial crisis. Yet MiFID could be seen to be well adapted to the post-crisis regulatory landscape. Detailed regulation of concepts such as best-execution, know your customer rules and conflict of interest provisions was forward looking and is what is needed to convince investors that regulators were attuned to market developments. Its correct and strong implementation is what supervisors need to ensure to bring them back to the markets. With the large possibilities for adaptation to market developments in secondary legislation, MiFID can also sustain pressure of the times.

This book is intended as a handbook for practitioners, markets operators, financial services industry professionals, regulators, investors and students. It gives an in-depth understanding of this new EU directive in its multifaceted implications for the different business lines in financial markets. The individual chapters are designed to be read either independently or in combination.

Chapter 1 paints a portrait of the likely EU securities market landscape post-MiFiD. Much of the available analysis on MiFID has focused on short-term adjustment and compliance costs. Yet MiFID represents a revolution in European securities markets that is likely to lead to deep and long-lasting structural changes. The analysis in this chapter concentrates on ten predictions that the authors make about the likely impact of MiFID on market structures, and the likely strategic responses of financial services firms.

The second chapter traces the origins of MiFID, starting with the review of the 1993 Investment Services Directive (ISD), the formal Commission proposals for an ISD II (November 2002) and the decision-making process within the European institutions. It gives a broad overview of the structure of the text and discusses the most important principles.

Chapter 3 focuses on the new conduct of business regime introduced by MiFID, which set forth new powerful investor protection tools in the suitability and the appropriateness assessments, aiming at guarding the investors' interests. These devices, however, have been perceived as a threat by the industry, as they represent not only an additional compliance burden, but even a tricky teaser to be better solved in time before the entry into force of the directive. Suitability and appropriateness, in fact, have the potential to lead to an unpleasant situation for the industry: if not clearly understood in their distinctive scope and purpose, they may turn themselves into 'terrible twins', whose features risk overlapping. Even though suitability and appropriateness share the same goal of enhancing investor protection, they are subject to two different regimes, applicable when the situations described in the chapter occur.

Chapter 4 sheds light on the complex 'best execution' requirements introduced by MiFID. Interestingly, very few member states had formalised best execution provisions in place before. At most, some had vaguely defined fiduciary duty obligations. Best execution not only implies that firms have adopted and published a policy that takes into account several intertwined criteria, that they get a specific consent from the clients to the policy itself and that they review it annually, but also that they have adapted their IT systems to ensure that orders are executed in accordance to what is stated in the written policy and that the latter is constantly effective. This may force firms to outsource certain activities, as they may not be able to provide best execution in-house. Hence, MiFID is in this sense not only a burden for smaller firms, but also a threat for large integrated financial services groups.

Another change brought about by MiFID, the opening up of the market for equity market data, raises the question of whether data will be sufficiently consolidated and of high enough quality post-MiFID, or whether it will become too fragmented, thereby hindering price transparency and the implementation of best execution policies. **Chapter 5** discusses the market for financial market data, the provisions of MiFID and the implementing measures regarding financial data and data consolidation. It compares the approaches taken by the Committee of European Securities Regulators (CESR), the UK Financial Services Authority (FSA) and the US authorities on the organization of the market for market data. It concludes that markets should be capable of adapting and that additional licensing requirements, such as those proposed by the FSA, are in fact premature and act as a barrier to the single market. Nor would a US-style monopoly consolidator be needed in this case.

Chapter 6 addresses the issue of conflicts of interest as a tool to promote investors' protection and to enhance market integrity. It is based on the assumption that conflicts of interest are ubiquitous in the financial services industry, but this does not mean that regulators are prepared to accept conflicts as an unavoidable fact of life. The chapter focuses mainly on the MiFID provisions on investment research.

Strongly linked to the previous chapter, **Chapter 7** looks at the MiFID rules on inducements. It argues that while the policy objectives underpinning the rules are valid and necessary, the instruments regulators have chosen for achieving those objectives are in need of fine-tuning, and especially clarification, if the objectives are to be met without inflicting collateral damage on the European fund industry.

Chapter 8 addresses the interaction between the MiFID and the Undertakings for Collective Investments in Transferable Securities (UCITS) regime, identifying two main areas where MiFID impacts most on the asset management business: best execution, on the one side, and conflicts of interest and inducements, on the other. As UCITS are mostly distributed by institutions subject to MiFID, these new rules will have a far-reaching impact on the organization of the fund management business. MiFID, on the other hand, may also provide a platform for the distribution of non-harmonized funds. However, the national application of these provisions may differ, which calls for a consistent interpretation.

Chapter 9 aims at contributing to the ongoing policy debate on MiFID art. 65.1, which tasks the Commission with conducting a study to report on whether the trade transparency requirements that currently apply to share trading ought to be extended to non-equity markets. It presents the pros and cons of introducing greater transparency into non-equity markets, especially bonds. The chapter highlights the insufficient level of data available to market participants and regulators on volumes and aggregate bond market activity, as well as the lack of appropriate information made available to retail investors, suggesting that dealers may have little time to come up with a solution, and that an industry code of conduct may be an appropriate avenue – and one preferable to legislative initiatives – for introducing more transparency uniformly (within each fixed income asset class) across the EU.

Chapter 10 on the supervisory architecture introduced by MiFID sheds light on the technical issue of allocation of responsibilities between the competent authorities of the home and the host member state in the cross-border provision of financial services. The chapter also analyses the role played and to be played by CESR in the overall supervisory convergence.

Chapter 11 explores the transatlantic context, investigating whether MiFID and the US Regulation National Marketing System (Reg NMS) could be accepted as equivalents by regulators on both sides of the Atlantic. Apart from many similarities, the most important one being that the main purpose of both measures is to enforce best execution in equity trading, there are many differences as well in the definition of best execution, the structures of the markets, and the role and powers of supervisory authorities. The chapter calls upon the European Commission to make a detailed comparison between both measures and to take the opportunity to negotiate a mutual recognition agreement with the US.

The book ends with a general bibliography and a glossary. Specific references are kept at the end of each chapter.

The authors would like to express their thanks to the European Capital Markets Institute (ECMI), an independent non-profit making organization established in 1993, for having provided the context to write this book. Back in 1996 ECMI produced a standard work on Europe's capital markets and the ISD, entitled *The European Equity Markets*. With this book, we hope to set the standard for MiFID.

Special thanks go to Piero Cinquegrana, Guilia Gobbo, Gregor Pozniak, Geert Vander Beken, Fabio Recine and Carlo Comporti for comments on parts of this book; to Anne Harrington and Els Van den Broeck for editorial assistance and to Giovanni Candigliota and Mark Rothemund for research assistance.

1

The MiFID revolution

The Markets in Financial Instruments Directive (MiFID) has essentially been seen as a compliance and IT exercise for financial services firms. As a result, much of the analysis surrounding MiFID compliance and the development of business strategies for the new regulatory landscape has focused on upgrading internal procedures and building the supporting IT infrastructure.

The impact of MiFID extends far beyond mere compliance and IT alone, however. The unprecedented scope of harmonization of securities markets legislation and the resulting open architecture ushered in by MiFID, especially in trade execution and reporting, will cause a profound upheaval within existing market structures.

MiFID is nothing short of a revolution: it will see banks operating as exchanges for some activities, exchanges offering alternative execution services that more closely resemble the structure of OTC markets than traditional organized markets, and the decentralization of order execution among a panoply of venues in markets previously governed by concentration rules: *le monde à l'envers*. MiFID has a profound impact on the organization, day-to-day operations and business strategies not only of investment firms – which have tended to be the focus thus far – but also of exchanges, asset managers and other financial markets intermediaries, such as brokers, data consolidators and business solutions providers. Overall market design and functioning are likely to be heavily impacted, not least because the implementation of MiFID is not a static event necessitating only one-off sunk costs; rather, it requires firms to make constant dynamic readjustments to remain competitive.

In light of this reality, insufficient analysis has been devoted to the strategic implications of MiFID, even though these are far-reaching – even more so, we believe, than what Basel II represented for banks – because of the profound market restructuring that is expected. The accompanying uncertainties as to how market participants are to position themselves strategically in the new regulatory landscape and respond to newly emerging threats will shake up the status quo.

As with all revolutions, the shock to the status quo represents a profitable opportunity for those who are well prepared – and a death sentence for those who cannot adapt to the new environment. The well prepared are the actors who in the post-MiFID world will generate higher revenue streams, steal market share from the less well prepared, and begin to compete in areas lying outside their traditional scope of service provision – areas previously closed to them, or deemed to be unprofitable prior to MiFID. On the other hand, the less well prepared will have been startled, soon after November 2007, to find themselves competing in business lines against actors from whom they previously faced little or no competition, including actors whom they may not even have viewed as natural competitors prior to MiFID.

1. Ten key predictions on the impact of MiFID

MiFID accelerates some important ongoing changes in European financial markets that are driven primarily by technological improvements and enhanced competition in the provision of financial services arising from globalization. Greater recourse to electronic trading, the facilitation of straight-through processing, the continued disintermediation of brokering through direct market access and algorithms and the 'exchangization' of Over-The-Counter (OTC) markets are but a few examples of ongoing structural shifts in financial markets that are reinforced or precipitated by MiFID.

MiFID leads to a higher degree of harmonization for investment services and securities transactions in the EU, by extending the reach of services and products covered as compared to the Investment Services Directive (ISD), and by imposing more detailed performance rules on exchanges and investment firms. As such, it should lead to more integrated European capital markets, but will also have significant impacts on market structure and development.

MiFID directly touches four distinct groups of actors within the financial services industry: investment firms (which may have fairly different organizational models across countries); exchanges and quasi-exchanges (multilateral trading facilities (MTFs)); data vendors; and specialized IT firms and solution providers, such as third-party algorithm developers. It affects equity markets, commodity and derivatives markets, and to a lesser extent bond markets.[1] This represents a considerable upgrade as compared to the Investment Services Directive, which it replaces. The analysis therefore starts with a discussion of the main developments in European capital markets over the past decade and reviews the effects of the ISD. We next rehearse the key points of MiFID and discuss the issues raised by its implementation for the various markets affected. A final section offers a brief outlook for the future of European securities markets. While numerous papers have already been published on how to prepare for MiFID, there has been much less consistent analysis of its impact on the market and the industry.

In our view, MiFID will bring about the following fundamental changes:

1. As a result of high compliance costs and greater operational complexity, MiFID will lead to a further consolidation phase in the brokerage industry, although smaller firms will continue to have a niche, essentially because of the proximity to clients. MiFID will lead to a tighter competition between financial centres, as a result of the abolition of the monopoly of the status symbol of financial centres, the stock exchange, and because of large differences in the preparedness of member states and firms.
2. Although investment firms and MTFs are able to compete with exchanges on order execution as a result of the abolition of the concentration rule, exchanges are expected to remain the main source of liquidity and price formation for the time being, but they will be subject to more competition in their market data and settlement activities. Despite a misconception that they will only face more competition from market-makers in the trading function, exchanges will also face enhanced competition from other exchanges. On the post-trading side, exchanges will be impacted by the European Central Bank's (ECB's) Target 2 Securities initiative and the European Commission's Code of Conduct on Clearing and Settlement.
3. OTC markets are going to be more heavily regulated than in the past under MiFID, meaning that the heydays of market opacity and cosy execution arrangements between providers are over: the distance

[1] Under MiFID art. 65, national regulatory authorities are free to extend the strict MiFID pre- and post-trade information requirements to non-equity markets. Some already do so, such as those in Denmark, owing to the large retail investor presence in its mortgage bond market. See Chapter 9.

between OTC markets and regulated markets will be narrowed as the former become more competitive, more transparent and more closely monitored.

4. A significant rise in algorithmic trading is almost a certainty. The need to rapidly search prices available on a variety of execution venues *ex-ante* and to verify the quality of execution *ex-post* will stimulate demand for business solutions such as algorithms. As execution venues proliferate, traders will rely more on smart order-routing systems to provide best execution.
5. Trading volumes should increase as a result of greater competition between execution venues and enhanced market transparency. More competition means lower transaction costs, which should feed into higher volumes. More transparency means more confidence in the quality of price discovery, enhancing market efficiency, which should also generate higher volumes. Greater transparency will contribute to the parcelization of block trades into a more continuous stream of orders, since it will increase the market impact of large trades.
6. Connectivity is a central feature of the post-MiFID trading landscape that will be characterized by the fragmentation of liquidity pools as trading is decentralized. Connectivity necessitates the acceleration of efforts to arrive at common standards to facilitate straight-through processing in an accelerated and more competitive trading environment, as well as to ensure seamless order transmission and data retrieval, across the spectrum of business lines in a decentralized trading environment.
7. A massive market for market data arises out of MiFID. In countries where the concentration rule was applied, the local stock exchange acted as the sole execution venue, meaning that market data revenues of equity trading essentially accrued to exchanges. The more execution venues there are, the greater is the need to gather data. MiFID's strict best execution and order-handling rules heavily increase the need for reliable analysis in both the pre- and post-trade periods to ascertain the venues that will most likely perform a successful execution pre-trade and the self-imposed quality of execution tests MiFID requires post-trade.
8. MiFID necessitates a response on the part of buy-side firms. Most analysis has focused on the impact of MiFID on sell-side institutions. The buy side will be faced with the challenge of ensuring efficient data management, as market data are likely to increase significantly

post-MiFID. The challenge is to monitor the quality of execution buy-side firms obtain for their clients.

9. Although MiFID is much more detailed and harmonizing in scope than its predecessor and the European Commission has tried to restrict the loopholes in the Implementing Directive, 'goldplating' will continue, as suggested by the emergence of initial indications in this direction. In addition, contract law and consumer protection remain national. The European Commission thus faces a heavy policing role in the post-MiFID era to ensure correct implementation, tight enforcement and a level playing field.
10. Given the heavy conduct of business regime of MiFID, the search for less stringent regimes can be expected, but also new non-passportable national regimes may emerge. On the other hand, MiFID is so all-encompassing that its rules will spill over into related sectors, such as asset management under the UCITS regime. MiFID may well set the standard for the conduct of business regime for all forms of retail investment products, frustrating attempts to further harmonize product regimes in the EU.

2. Delayed implementation by the member states

Overall, the preparation by European authorities of the MiFID implementation went smoothly, but the problem lay with the member states. Although the directive was adopted by the EU in April 2004, it took most member states more than three years to be ready! Almost all member states failed to meet the deadline for transposing the text into national law, 1 February 2007. In June 2007, the European Commission sent warning letters to twenty-two member states for their dereliction – Ireland, Lithuania, Slovakia and Romania the being the exceptions. On the deadline of application of MiFID, 1 November 2007, at least 7 member states were not ready, representing 1/3 of the EU population (Italy, Spain, The Netherlands, Poland, Czech Republic, Hungary and Finland). By the end of January 2008, the Czech Republic, Hungary and Spain had still not implemented MiFID, which led the European Commission to refer the cases to the European Court of Justice.

Given this diversity in preparedness by the member states, it is no wonder that firms are also late with their preparations. In some member countries, financial institutions had been regularly informed by their authorities, from about two years ahead of the November 2007 deadline, what it was going to take to plan for MiFID. In other states, however, nothing – but *absolutely* nothing – was circulated until a few months before the implementation deadline. How, then, could firms be expected to be MiFID compliant, if they had to inform themselves during the preparation phase with guidance provided by regulatory authorities of other member states, and their own national implementing legislation was not ready by 1 November 2007? It can thus be expected that MiFID will exacerbate differences between financial centres in the EU, and that it will strengthen the well prepared.

This diversity in preparation has important strategic implications for banks. Delays in preparation also prevent firms from appreciating the strategic impact of MiFID, because they see only the regulatory burden. The City of London, for example, which was initially critical about MiFID, abandoned this attitude more than a year before the implementation deadline and started to see it as a strategic opportunity. The local regulator, the UK FSA, published many papers about how to prepare for MiFID, and many of the local blue chip banks have made a point of being fully compliant in time. On the other hand, the UK's authorities have also been the first to report four areas where they superimpose EU rules with national rules, applicable to all those which are doing business on UK territory.

The road ahead is not easy, either. With these delays in implementation, the European Commission was delayed in its enforcement work as well. It could only continue to send warning letters to the member states which are behind, but was delayed in starting the detailed scrutiny of the national enacting legislation. The European Commission will need to make sure it does not repeat the mistakes of the post-ISD period (the 1993 Investment Services Directive, precursor of MiFID), during which it failed to give firm guidance on the implementation of certain provisions, such as on the home/host distinction for conduct of business rules. Although, this time, conduct of business rules have been much more harmonized, the confusion about who is in charge of enforcement remains. MiFID art. 32.7 says that the host country – i.e. the country where the branch of an investment firm is located – is in charge of enforcing the conduct of business rules, whereas the home country is in charge of prudential control (see Chapter 10 below).

3. Delayed preparedness with firms

Most surveys with firms conducted before the entry into force of MiFID found limited and delayed preparedness for MiFID. Although not many systematic and consistent surveys exist, early surveys made in 2006 and later surveys conducted in 2007, when the directive was already in force, essentially came to that same conclusion. Late preparedness has an impact on the strategic implications of MiFID, and on the competition between financial centres.

An extensive survey of investment firms based in Germany carried out by the University of Frankfurt in early 2006, found that only 14 per cent of the firms concerned were very familiar with the new rules, and only about half had started the necessary internal preparations (on a sample of fifty-five). Most firms had foreseen the implementation in 2007, also from a budgetary perspective. A survey of financial institutions Europe-wide by KMPG, carried out around the same time, found about the same degree of preparation (48 per cent on a sample of 199), and that only 29 per cent of the surveyed firms had assigned a project manager. A survey carried out for the UK FSA during the summer of 2006 continued to find the same degree of preparedness (score of 4 out of 10) (LECG 2006). The same message emerged from surveys conducted in 2007, when the directive should already have been implemented. Surveys by the technology provider Sungard indicated that in April 2007 only 40 per cent of the firms were on track or ahead of schedule with their plans. The last survey on the subject, published in July 2007, showed only a limited improvement in the preparedness of firms to 55 per cent.

The interesting finding of the first two studies mentioned above is that MiFID is primarily seen as an IT and compliance exercise. Surprisingly, less thinking seems to have been invested in developing a MiFID strategy across the business. This was the main message of a KPMG report (KPMG 2006), which found a blatant lack of awareness in top management on the strategic implications of MiFID. A University of Frankfurt study (Gomber and Reininger 2006) found that only 30 per cent of surveyed firms had thought about the strategic implications, and among those, the theme of 'best execution' seemed to be the most important. The degree of awareness differed from country to country and may result from the fact that some national regulators, such as the German BaFin, had given markets very little feedback on the national regulatory strategy, nature, scope and impact of MiFID implementation, at least until a few months before the directive had to be applied by firms. On the other hand, others, such as the UK FSA, have been very forthcoming and transparent, and have preceded national MiFID implementation exercises by extensive consultations with the industry.

The most wide-ranging findings concerned the cost of implementation, suggesting considerable confusion and little consensus as to the real impact of MiFID. The Frankfurt University study (Gomber and Reininger 2006) comes up with relatively low figures, which are proportional to the size of the firm: most of the surveyed firms expect compliance costs to range from €500,000 to €1 million. Some 16 per cent of firms expected costs of between €1 and €5 million and only 4 per cent anticipated that costs would exceed €20 million. The implementation of the best execution provisions is considered the most important cost element. On the other hand, in its analysis on the impact of MiFID (JPMorgan 2006), JPMorgan estimated that implementation costs for very large institutions would reach €106 million (largely due to IT investments and disclosure requirements), with proportionally larger costs for the smaller institutions in their sample. The technology company Vhayu (Vhayu 2006) estimated the cost of compliance to be between €6 and €36 million per institution, affecting small banks proportionally more. In its cost/ benefit analysis, the FSA estimated that, to be in line with the rules on internalization alone, the cost to dealer firms would be between £8 and £40 million (FSA 2006). Another study for the FSA estimated the one-off cost of implementation for the UK investment industry, excluding internalization, at £90,000 for small firms, £2.15 million for mid-sized firms and £4.75 million for large firms (LECG 2006, p. 67).

4. Market impact

The consensus is that the biggest impact of MiFID falls essentially on investment firms; exchanges would be less affected. However, it could be more appropriate to say that, in the short term, the impact of MiFID is most likely to be felt by investment firms, but in the long term the implications of MiFID will probably be more profound for exchanges. We expect this result because of the combination of internalization by investment firms and increased competition to exchanges from new entrants and actors in specialized business lines such as data vendors, such that the traditional business model of the established exchanges is going to be challenged as never before. Although investment firms will initially feel the impact of MiFID more directly in terms of the one-off costs associated with compliance with the new best execution, systematic internalization, client (re-)classification requirements, exchanges will feel the impact as they reposition themselves strategically in response to investment firms' and other market participants' moves. Exchanges may also choose not to wait to react to competitive threats but might opt instead to anticipate them by taking an aggressive proactive approach to the new reality, as some have done in consolidating their operations with other market participants.

It is curious to note that a radical shift of stance towards MiFID has emerged from the City and large financial players. Whereas, initially, MiFID was seen as an enemy to be beaten back, an example of regulatory burden, today large banks view it not only as a *fait accompli*, but also as an opportunity to be seized. The directive is seen not just as incurring costs, but also as an important source of new revenues, at least for the well prepared.

4.1 Investment firms

The expectation is that the implementation of MiFID will lead to a further consolidation process in the brokerage industry. This view emanates not only from reports of analysts and consultants, but also from those of regulatory authorities, such as the FSA. The implementation cost figures, mentioned above, are a case in point. In addition, the growing complexity of the legislation and the heavy compliance requirements are burdens that can hardly be absorbed by small brokerage firms, which were widely present in many continental European countries until a decade ago. Moreover, MiFID could exacerbate the differences between the larger and smaller players. Large firms already have much of the required IT infrastructure and capacity in place to deal with MiFID relatively well, whereas the cost for smaller firms will be more pronounced (JPMorgan 2006, p. 24). However, the surveys of firms in the German and British markets (Gomber and Reininger 2006; LECG 2006) imply that the cost factor should not be exaggerated, and that it is proportional to the size of the firm. Smaller brokers are reported to have said that they have already brought their operations in line with many of the provisions of the directive, and that they are already providing 'best execution'. The client suitability requirements are much easier to implement for smaller firms than for large ones, or are already complied with, since they know their customers much better, and they do not have the same need for expensive computer solutions. Thus, even if most observers expect consolidation to continue, niche players with a strong client focus may continue to thrive. Very large players are expected to face significant compliance costs as well. A report by JPMorgan analysts expected that as much as €19 billion could be wiped off the market capitalization of eight leading European wholesale banks as a result of MiFID. This effect is predicted to be driven by a mixture of increased competition (lower profits) and the costs of implementing the detailed client suitability arrangements, higher transparency and strict best-execution requirements resulting from MiFID. The JPMorgan analysts expect the directive to represent above all a threat to the integrated banking model, whereby the retail distribution network will subsidize the investment banking division to a lesser extent as a result of outsourcing to cheaper third-party providers. The loss of captive private banking volumes (i.e. private banking trades which are executed on the investment bank's internal platform) could lead to a 20 per cent decline in margins.

To what extent will banks internalize? We would maintain that, because of the constraints on internalization and the associated costs for banks in implementing it, *systematic internalization*, as defined by the directive, will remain limited. The JPMorgan study estimates that the potential savings of an internal exchange would be just 2 per cent of the overall cost of trading. This result is based on the assumption that 20 per cent of trades are settled internally, whereas most large banks today settle a maximum of 5 per cent of trades internally. Exchanges are therefore expected to remain the main source of liquidity for shares. However, the trades to which the rules on systematic internalizers apply are limited to retail trades in some 900 blue chip shares, and thus a bank that is dealing above a retail market size is not bound by the rules.[2] While internalization was already tolerated in markets such as Germany and the UK, it was not allowed, or only allowed to a (very) limited extent, in France, Italy, Spain and (to an even lesser extent) in the Netherlands. A study on the impact of MiFID on the French market expects that 10 per cent of the annual turnover in CAC40 securities, mostly large block trades, could be lost to the regulated market in the medium term, but dynamic effects are difficult to predict, as thirty securities on Euronext Paris account for 80 per cent of the transactions, and are concentrated in the hands of ten investment firms.[3] Apart from challenging exchanges on trading activities, internalizing banks are no longer requested to pass the trade information obtained on to the exchanges for publication. Under MiFID, they are free to publish data reports through a Multilateral Trading Facility (MTF) or a data vendor instead of an exchange if they so prefer, which will affect this income flow of exchanges (see Chapter 5).

[2] The systematic internalization requirements apply to trades below the 'standard market size threshold', i.e. the average of the value of retail trade transactions. CESR keeps the list of liquid shares updated on its website.

[3] See Cherbonnier and Vandelanoite (2008), pp. 84–5, who expect that this volume will be more or less equally shared between SIs and MTFs.

The complexity of the regulatory regime will certainly drive firms to look into alternatives. The regime for investment fund companies (UCITS III), which was adopted in 2002, introduced the single licence for fund management companies, broadening the 1985 UCITS product directive.[4] It is a valuable, although more constrained, alternative to MiFID. It grants the 'single licence' to fund management companies in the broad sense of the word, allowing the management of investment funds, the 'core services', but also other forms of portfolio management, such as pension funds for individuals, investment advice, safekeeping (custody) and administration of investment funds, which are seen as 'non-core' or ancillary. In the latter case, certain MiFID provisions apply to UCITS management companies, more especially capital and organizational requirements, and conduct of business obligations (see Chapter 8). However, elements of MiFID, such as increased transparency, best execution and cost unbundling, could also spill over into the UCITS regime, which is currently under review. Whether MiFID would also lead member states to create new non-passportable regimes, as was done as a result of the 2003 Prospectus Directive, is also a possibility, albeit a rather theoretical one at this stage.

4.2 Exchanges

The regulatory changes resulting from MiFID are less profound at the outset for exchanges than investment firms. Apart from tighter organizational and governance requirements, the regime does not change that much from the ISD. However, two developments will have an important direct impact on European exchanges: (1) the increased competition on the trade information side from other channels; and (2) the impact of the ECB and EU initiatives on the settlement side. In addition, there is the increased competition from broker dealers as internalizers and MTFs, which can challenge exchanges for order flow.

Traditionally, exchanges were the predominant, almost exclusive, source of market data, not least due to the concentration of trading and data reporting imposed by regulatory authorities. With this breakdown will come increased opportunities for investment firms for recapturing revenue streams that were originally generated by their orders. The aggregate pan-

4 Directive 2001/107/EC amending Council Directive 85/611/ECC relating to undertakings for collective investment in transferable securities (UCITS), with a view to regulating management companies and simplified prospectuses, OJ L41 of 13/02/02.

European market for market data is estimated at about €2.3 billion per year (Wall Street and Technology 2006). This sizeable revenue pool is up for grabs by innovative firms and other financial market actors.

Investment firms have not been slow on the uptake. In September 2006, a group of nine London-based investment banks set up a joint effort called 'Project Boat', which is intended to capture back data revenue sources from trades where investment firms – and not the exchange – are the liquidity providers/facilitators. Prior to MiFID, investment firms paid exchanges a fee to report OTC trades, only to buy back the collated and repackaged information from information providers against a fee. This odd situation squeezed investment firm margins on both the revenue and cost sides. By opening up the architecture for trade reporting, MiFID challenges an important revenue source for exchanges and provides a valuable opportunity for investment firms to get in on the game. Even self-regulatory bodies such as the International Capital Markets Association (ICMA) are positioning themselves to use existing engines and technology to tap some of this expected revenue stream.

Income from the sale of trade information today accounts for about 12.5 per cent of the revenue of the six largest exchanges in the EU. For some exchanges, it is much higher, reaching 30.3 per cent for the London Stock Exchange (which also includes revenues from regulatory information services). Although the usefulness of the trade information gathered by exchanges is closely related to the degree to which exchanges are the main source of liquidity, the competition from new facilities or from data vendors, resulting from the 'open architecture' for market data introduced by the directive, may form a direct threat to this revenue stream for exchanges. Hence, the combined effect of more internalization by investment firms and more trades routed through MTFs could have a direct impact on the degree to which the trade information that exchanges collect and sell is representative. Exchange participation fees (commissions) will also come under pressure with the proliferation of execution venues and the breakdown of the traditional national trading environment. So will trading fees, which currently account for about 45 per cent of the largest European stock exchange revenues on average. Exchanges will not only face more competition from liquidity providers, but also from other exchanges, who can compete for liquidity in equities that are not necessarily cross-listed in their home market. For example, the SWX Swiss Exchange launched a 'sponsored segment', in July 2005, whereby Swiss Exchange members can trade foreign-listed equities on the SWX, even if these securities are not cross-listed on the SWX.

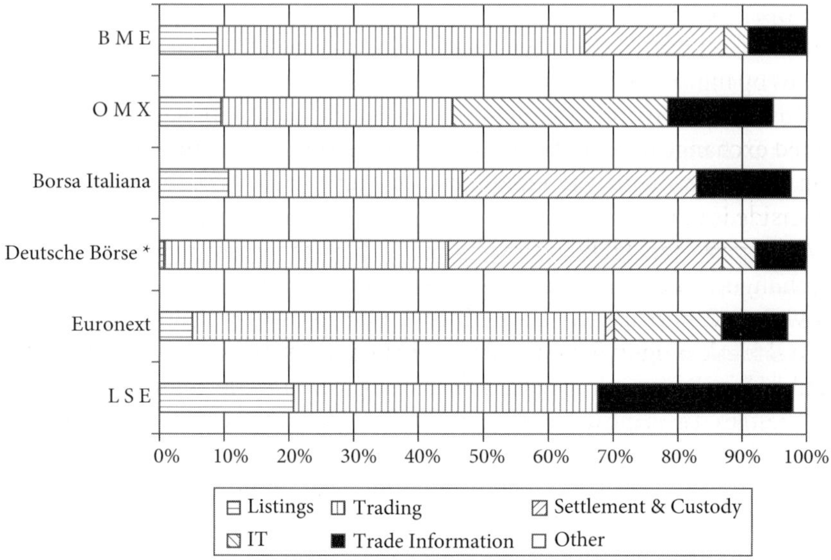

Source: Annual reports. Data for LSE are for book year closed on 31 March 2007.

Figure 1.1 Largest European stock exchanges revenue decomposed by activity (2006)

The threat to the revenue that exchanges earn from settlement services may be even more severe, at least for the vertically integrated exchanges. MiFID art. 46 requires clearing and settlement facilities to provide direct access to regulated markets from other member states. In itself, this article may not change much, as a similar provision already existed in the ISD, and some vertically integrated exchanges are already providing direct access. However, to the extent that MiFID allows internalization, it may lead to settlement occurring on platforms other than that of the home exchange. In addition, MTFs can obtain a European passport and settle where it is most cost-effective. Vertically integrated exchanges may be protected from some of these pressures for some time to come, as it will be difficult to organize settlement outside the home country of the securities issuer, owing to company and tax law requirements.

The main question in settlement revolves around the impact of initiatives by the European Central Bank and the EU on post-trading. In November 2006, the European Commission forced the back-office industry to adopt a European Code of Conduct for Clearing and Settlement to improve price transparency, advance access and interoperability, and unbundle services and separate accounts. The first experiences with the Code were considered to be positive, as it is a much faster and smoother way to open up markets than a harmonizing directive. Some have already stated that it will spell the beginning of the end for the vertically integrated exchange model. It has also led some groups to demand the extension of the scope of the Code beyond equity securities. However, the downside is that the Code remains a non-legal instrument.

As regards the ECB initiative, again, it is too early to say how far-reaching it will be and how likely it is to affect the activities of settlement providers. In principle, the ECB will provide settlement only against central bank money for euro-denominated government bonds or assets eligible for Eurosystem credit operations (meaning in practice all euro-denominated securities), but it will not manage corporate actions nor act as a custodian. This will, as the ECB indicated itself, 'eliminate the need for any other settlement platform for securities transactions denominated in euro at CSD level' (Godeffroy 2006). Although local CSDs may continue to provide straight-through processing (STP), and settle in the end on the Target 2 securities platform, there will be no technical justification to do so. The creation of a monopoly for settlement of euro-denominated securities will, according to the ECB, lead to post-market integration and to the exploitation of scale economies. This initiative could potentially have a serious detrimental impact on the settlement income of vertically integrated exchanges and bond settlement platforms, and lead banks to reconsider their relations with these entities for corporate actions as well, in which custodians will try to gain more market share.

Nevertheless, exchanges can generate further revenue streams post-MiFID, namely in IT and consulting. However contradictory it may sound, exchanges can sell in-house matching services to banks, and in this sense try to keep control on internalization and the related technology. As banks may not have the in-house IT expertise to become systematic internalizers, exchanges' IT departments may offer their services in the market. Euronext is said to have engaged already in projects with banks to this effect.

Exchanges have also started to establish MTFs to cater to specific niches in the market, such as the small caps markets. Euronext and BME have already done so with Alternext and the Mercado Alternativ Bursatil. They could also consider starting MTFs to facilitate the execution of unwieldy or complex trades that are unfit for entry into electronic order books and which users might prefer to negotiate 'off-market' instead of in an 'upstairs' negotiated deal – thereby coming under less stringent disclosure requirements than those which apply to 'on-exchange' deals. Exchanges could also benefit from the demand for more transparency in OTC markets or the 'exchangization' of certain market segments that were previously essentially OTC. This trend is clearly ongoing in the bond and investment fund markets and gives exchanges a chance to compete where previously there was little opportunity to do so.

Estimating the competitive threat MTFs will pose to exchanges is a difficult exercise at this stage. Much will depend on the response of exchanges to MiFID and their ability to improve their efficiency further in the form of lower fees, better price formation processes and improved infrastructure, as resulted, for example, from the creation of Euronext (Pagano and Padilla 2005). Do these challenges therefore portend a further consolidation amongst exchanges? It will be important in the coming months and years to find the right balance between consolidation and competition in a sector that is already highly concentrated. The four largest European exchanges control 76 per cent of equity turnover and 84 per cent (90 per cent) if the five (six) largest players are considered, upon a total of twenty-two (FESE data, 2007). MTFs may be a useful tool in ensuring that markets do not become too concentrated. MTFs may also enjoy a competitive edge in specific markets or business segments of exchanges, such as the market for new high-growth or high-tech firms, or for the reporting of trading data, as discussed above. Initial data regarding the success of the new trading platform Chi-X indicate that the traditional exchanges will need to be extremely attentive in the post-MiFID era.[5]

Exchanges in the new member states face a particular set of challenges. The large markets – Poland, Czech Republic and Hungary – all had a concentration rule in place. There is little threat for them that local banks will begin siphoning off liquidity by setting themselves up as systematic internalizers. Their capacity to do so is limited by scarce technological resources and by the difficulty in overcoming the first-mover advantages enjoyed by exchanges in a culture where liquidity has always been exchange-driven. The real threat for these exchanges comes from MiFID-induced competition from powerful foreign exchanges and large foreign banks operating out of the City of London or Frankfurt to the more liquid and larger domestic companies. Nevertheless, these exchanges do

[5] Between October 2007 and January 2008, Chi-X managed to get a market share of about 4 per cent of the AEX 25 (Dutch) and 2 per cent in the FTSE 100 (British) and DAX 30 (German). In some blue chip stocks, it realized a market share of 20 per cent in the last quarter of 2007, with a price improvement of about two basic points over the primary market: see www.chi-x.com.

have the advantage that the investor base remains overwhelmingly local; which are essentially, the large and growing pension and investment funds, which still face strict investment limits in foreign securities as a result of currency matching rules, for example. Because liquidity is concentrated in the hands of regional investors, for whom trading costs are lower when routed through the local exchange, the scale of the threat is limited for the time being. However, this may change over time. If it does, and if data vending revenues fall as a result, the main exchanges in the new member states may be forced to consolidate forces with larger exchanges elsewhere in Europe in order to survive.[6]

4.3 Advisory firms and solution providers

Because MiFID's conduct-of-business rules are detailed, buy-side firms may have the impression that MiFID's obligations are essentially geared towards sell-side institutions. This is a mistaken impression. There seems to be a considerable lack of understanding among buy-side firms that MiFID has important implications for the way they, too, conduct their business. A study by EdHec Risk Advisory (2006) suggested that up to 40 per cent of buy-side firms plan to invest no more than €25,000 per year on best-execution arrangements and technologies, suggesting a surprising lack of preparedness among buy-side firms for post-MiFID challenges relating to the search for, and verification of, best execution for their clients.

Like law and advisory firms, business solutions providers are sure to be key winners from MiFID implementation as all market participants seek to cope with a vastly more complex trading landscape. Algorithmic trading is one of those solutions, and as such, it represents one of the ongoing market trends which we identified earlier in this chapter and which are likely to be reinforced or accelerated under MiFID. The expected increase in algorithmic trading will be driven by both demand- and supply-side forces.

On the demand side, pressure on firms to rely more on algorithms post-MiFID comes from the regulatory provisions related to execution obligations. MiFID establishes a requirement that investment firms develop a best-execution policy which is occasionally tested by the investment firm for robustness. In this way, a firm's clients should know *ex-ante*

[6] We are grateful to Slawomir Pycko, Deputy Director for Planning and Business development at the Warsaw Stock Exchange, for valuable insights in this paragraph.

the criteria against which an executed trade will be judged 'best', thereby helping to hold investment firms accountable when the quality of execution is doubtful. For two reasons, algorithmic trading systems are probably the most reliable way for investment firms to ensure they have effective best-execution policy in place. First, they can be programmed to hunt for the best prices across a wide range of execution venues in mere fractions of a second; secondly, the parameters that govern the way the algorithm hunts for a 'best' result and the definition of that 'best' result (e.g., price/cost, speed of execution, market impact, or any linear combination of these or other criteria) are set *ex-ante* by the algorithm developers (and/or traders, depending on how flexible the system is). The smart order-routing systems merely seek to optimize the given algorithm. The fact that an algorithm is based on set, predetermined parameters leads to a clear and transparent presentation of the firm's execution strategy *ex-ante*, so that the firm's clients are duly informed of the criteria used to assess execution venues and route orders. At the same time, consumers can be more confident about execution results, since the algorithm carries out the optimization in a purely mechanical predetermined manner: intelligent systems, unlike real traders, do not face conflicts of interest and merely carry out trades in a disinterested manner as a function of the inputs.

As for the supply-side forces, the vast amount of previously unavailable market data that MiFID generates through more stringent transparency requirements and through the proliferation of execution venues is likely to enhance the development and refinement of algorithmic solutions, whose performance often depends in great part on the volume of high-quality data available. The increase of market data will enable new and next-generation algorithms to be developed, stimulating demand in response to innovation.

Algorithms today do not account for a large percentage of trades in volume terms. A survey of European buy-side firms indicated that they accounted for only 3 per cent of trades, compared to 11 per cent carried out via direct market access (e.g. multi-dealer-to-client platforms, or B2C), 17 per cent via programme trading and 69 per cent in traditional cash transactions (see Cooper 2006). Despite this low figure, the growth rate of algorithmic trading has been brisk, and we predict it will increase significantly in the post-MiFID landscape. A recent survey conducted by IBM even claims that 90 per cent of traders in Europe will lose their jobs to algorithms by 2015, although this figure seems very high to us (see IBM 2006b). Nevertheless, it is a real possibility that as the quality, flexibility and performance of algorithms rise, trading in liquid securities is likely to involve fewer human traders in future.

As greater transparency is introduced into the marketplace and as the speed at which new information is impounded into prices increases, the market impact of block trades has increased. Because of the increasing costs transparency imposes on block trades, eligible counterparties and institutional investors that are trying to offload large positions have been led to seek greater recourse to programme trades, which parcel up blocks into smaller tickets to minimize market impact. It is therefore not surprising that one observes a progressive fall in the size of trading tickets in European equity markets as greater post-trade transparency is introduced into the market.

Finally, in terms of overall market impact, another benefit of smart order execution/routing, whether algorithmic- or programme-based, is that it is likely to enhance both the speed and the quality of price discovery, thereby improving market efficiency.

Apart from buy-side firms, a number of sell-side solutions providers can be expected to gain from MiFID, including data vendors and data consolidators/disseminators, connectivity solutions providers, data management providers, and others who will benefit from the enormous market for market data that is likely to result from MiFID.

5. Outlook

Whether MiFID brings another ten years of growth in Europe's securities markets is of course difficult to predict. But it certainly brings more competition in securities markets and will substantially change the market environment. Trading volumes can be expected to increase further as a result of greater competition between execution venues and enhanced market transparency. As Europe's capital markets become further integrated and the nationality of firms becomes less clear, exchanges will be in more direct competition with each other for the blue chips. In addition, their business model will be challenged on the trade information and settlement side.

The requirements on investment firms to provide best execution and to unbundle their fees for securities transactions should, in addition to other directives adopted under the FSAP, stimulate the confidence of retail investors and increase their participation in securities markets. Transaction fees should decline, and disclosure further improve.

References

Autorité des Marchés Financiers (AMF) 2006. *Consultation on Enforcing Best-execution Principles in MiFID and its Implementing Directive*, July. Paris: AMF.

Cherbonnier, Frédéric and Séverine Vandelanoite 2008. 'The impact on financial market liquidity of the markets in financial instruments directive (MiFID)', *Financial Stability Review*, February, Paris: Banque de France, pp. 75–94. Available at www.banque–france.fr/gb/publications/rsf/rsf_022008.htm.

Clifford Chance 2006. 'Impact of MiFID on research rules', Client Briefing, September. London: Clifford Chance.

Cooper, Tim 2006. 'European firms play by the rules', *FT Mandate*, May.

EdHec Risk Advisory 2006: www.wbresearch.com/tradetechmifideurope/index.html.

Financial Services Authority 2006. *Implementing MiFID for Firms and Markets*, July. London: FSA.

Godeffroy, Jean-Michel 2006. 'Ten frequently asked questions about TARGET2-Securities', speech to the British Bankers Association, London, 20 September.

Gomber, Peter and Claudia Reininger 2006. 'Die Umstezung der MiFID in der deutschen finanzindustrie', Frankfurt University.

IBM Business Consulting Services 2006a. 'A practical guide to preparing for MiFID': www-935.ibm.com/services/uk/bcs/pdf/ibm-mifid-8pp-04–2006-f2lo.pdf.

IBM Global Business Services 2006b. 'Tackling latency – the algorithmic arms race': www-03.ibm.com/industries/financialservices/doc/content/bin/fss_latency_arms_race.pdf.

Infosys 2006. 'Turning RegNMS and MiFID challenges into opportunities', June: www.infosys.com/industries/banking/RegNMS-MiFID.pdf.

JPMorgan 2006. MiFID Report I & II, 'A new wholesale banking landscape'. London: JPMorgan.

KPMG 2006. 'Capturing value from MiFID': www.kpmg-ch/library/pdf/20060503_Capturing_value_from_MiFID.pdf.

Lannoo, Karel and Mattias Levin 2003. *Pan-European Asset Management*, CEPS Task Force Report, April. Brussels: Centre for European Policy Studies.

LECG 2006. 'MiFID implementation. Cost survey of the UK investment industry', October: www.fsa.gov.uk/pubs/international/mifid_cost_survey.pdf.

Pagano, Marco and A. Jorge Padilla 2005. *Efficiency gains from the integration of exchanges: lessons from the Euronext 'naturel experiment'*, Report for Euronext. Paris: Euronext.

van Steenis, Huw, Davide Taliente and John Romeo 2006. 'Outlook for European exchanges and equity trading: Structural shifts in securities trading', in *Handbook of World Stock, Derivative and Commodity Exchanges, 2006*. London: Mondo Visione.

Vhayu 2006. 'Answering the technology challenges of MiFID': www.vhayu.com/pdf/MiFID.pdf.

Wall Street & Technology 2006. 'MiFID rules break the exchange monopoly on trade reporting', 20 October: www.wallstreetandtech.com/showArticle.jhtml?articleID:193400875.

2

Origins and structure of MiFID

1. The ISD and the development of European capital markets

The past decade has seen a sea change in European capital markets. From a predominantly bank-dominated system, the European financial system has become more market-based. According to some indicators, it has even recently surpassed the US in this respect. For example, leading European stock market indexes have become more cyclical than those in the US, and both the issuance of international bonds and the number and total value of IPOs (initial public offerings) in Europe surpassed those in the US in 2005, 2006 and 2007.

The change since 1996, when the Investment Services Directive (93/22/EC) (ISD) came into force, is remarkable. As can be seen from the hexagon in Figure 2.1, bond issuance more than doubled, equity market capitalization tripled and equity market turnover and the total amount of derivatives contracts written increased seven-fold. Figure 2.2 shows that the growth of bank assets was overtaken by the growth in bond assets during several years, which is another sign of the move towards a more market-based system. Although the growth of the IPO market has benefited from the enforcement of the Sarbanes-Oxley Act in the US and from some large-scale privatizations in the EU in 2005, it is a sign that the European regulatory regime is not too burdensome and/or that it manages to cope with diversity.

It is difficult to distinguish the extent to which this phenomenon is the result of regulatory initiatives, as compared to simple market developments. The growth of the European financial markets has occurred against a backdrop of efforts to create a truly integrated market, and has benefited from relatively benign macroeconomic conditions at global level. But it is certain that specific policy initiatives have contributed to the spectacular financial market development in the EU, a fact that has probably not been sufficiently emphasized in the political discourse. Foremost, in our view, there is a clear positive effect of European Economic and Monetary Union (EMU). The introduction of

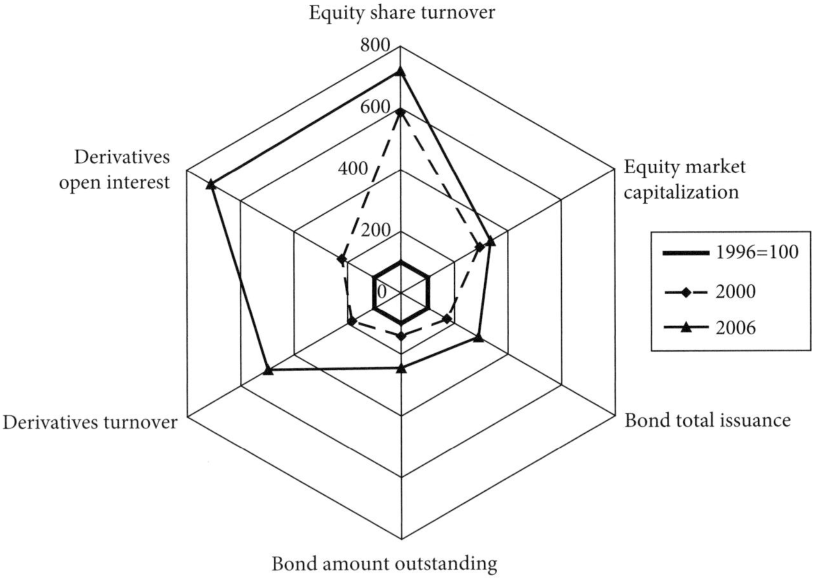

Sources: BIS, OECD, FESE, WFE and derivatives exchanges.

Figure 2.1 EU securities market growth, 1996–2006

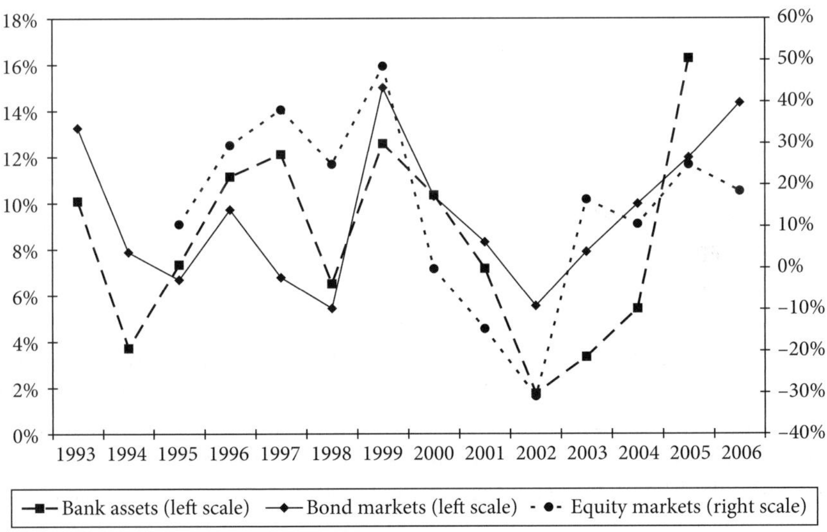

Sources: BIS, OECD, FESE and European Commission.

Figure 2.2 Growth of bank vs. securities markets in the EU

the Euro has created a much bigger, more liquid and stable currency zone, which has created better conditions for issuers and asset managers, and has increased competition amongst intermediaries. A clear indication is the use of the Euro as a currency for international bonds: since 2004, the Euro has overtaken the dollar as the main currency of denomination for international debt issues, and it currently accounts for about 48 per cent of the total value outstanding of international debt securities (as of December 2007).[1] The Financial Services Action Plan (FSAP), launched in 1999, contributed to creating an awareness of the importance of a well-functioning single capital market, and measures adopted under the plan, which are already in force, such as the prospectus directive, have not had a negative impact on European capital markets, contrary to some expectations. The EU Prospectus Directive (2003/71/EC) creates a much more harmonized European regime for issuers on capital markets, and does not exclude other, but 'non-passportable' regimes, such as the Professional Securities Markets (PSM) of the London Stock Exchange or Euro-MTF of the Luxembourg exchange.

Moving more specifically to the effects of the ISD, it is clear that the free provision of trading screens in the EU and the single licence for brokerage services has contributed to the reconfiguration and restructuring of European securities markets. The former allowed the trading activity and liquidity to concentrate on the stock exchange of the home market of a listed corporation, and thus also improve the price formation process. This is apparent from the reduction in the number of foreign listings from firms from other EU countries on EU exchanges. The single licence for brokers increased the competition in securities brokerage services and contributed to the consolidation and scale enlargement in the sector. Many smaller European brokers have been absorbed into larger entities, mostly commercial banks, and not many managed to survive as independent entities. Ironically, the member state which was the most critical of the ISD during the negotiations, the UK, probably benefited the most from these effects.[2] Although conduct-of-business rules were not sufficiently harmonized to allow cross-border provision of services for retail clients, this did not prevent wholesale markets from integrating and investment banks from consolidating their European operations in a few financial centres.

[1] Source: BIS, Securities Statistics, Quarterly Review, March 2008.

[2] It suffices to look at articles in the British business press in the negotiation period of the draft ISD, 1991–92.

Some of these effects had already started well before the ISD came into force. The competition between exchanges started with the creation of SEAQ International, a screen-based quotation system specializing in non-British stocks, by the London Stock Exchange in 1985, and the deregulation or 'Big Bang' of the London market a year later. This allowed London to attract many trades in continental European stocks. Continental European exchanges reacted by improving their auction systems and liberalizing market access and commissions.

The downsides of the ISD, however, were the lack of harmonization of conduct of business rules, and the maintenance of privileged status of the exchanges, alias 'regulated markets', many of which had in the meantime been privatized. This was addressed in the ensuing MiFID.

The review of the ISD happened in the context of (1) the start of EMU and the awareness that the regulatory framework was not ready to cope with these changes and (2) a desire to reform the regulatory and supervisory framework to allow for rapid changes to financial law in 'secondary legislation' and improve cooperation amongst European supervisors. The first element led to the adoption of the FSAP by the Ministers of Finance of the EU in May 1999, the second to the publication of the so-called 'Lamfalussy Approach' in February 2001 and its endorsement by the Stockholm European Council in March 2001. The FSAP was comprised of a set of forty-two legislative and non-legislative measures which the EU wanted to adopt by 2005, in which it largely succeeded. The Lamfalussy Approach provided a new regulatory framework for some of the FSAP measures, whereby the EU adopts principles-based regulations at Level 1, with implementing measures being adopted at Level 2, depending on the facilities provided in framework directives. Closer cooperation amongst supervisors (Level 3) should allow for a more consistent implementation and interpretation of EU law.

2. The ISD review and the origins of MiFID

Initially, there was no consensus about the extent of the ISD review. While there was a broad agreement that the directive should have been amended, there was no consensus how far this review should go. Overall, business was in favour of a limited review of the directive, to clarify certain concepts and abolish the optional monopoly of exchanges. The European Commission, on the basis of two consultative papers, initially hesitated between a radical overhaul, by which the directive would be split into one applicable for exchanges and another for investment firms, and a systematic review, which it chose in the end. In this regard, an important preparatory role was played by the Federation of European Securities Commissions, (FESCO, the precursor of CESR) and their papers on the standards of Alternative Trading Systems (ATSs), the classification of investors and the standards for regulated markets.

The second consultative paper of the European Commission proposed to abolish the concentration provision and allow internalization by broker/dealers subject to key investor protection safeguards. This immediately opened the debate on the core issues of the ISD review, competition and fragmentation versus transparency and liquidity, or the interests of the broker/dealers versus those of the regulated markets. Internalization would thus be allowed only under certain conditions, on the basis of the explicit permission of the client, and the maintenance of key investor safeguards such as 'best execution', client order handling rules, conflict of interest management and transparency obligations. In this sense, the review already signaled that the new directive would be more constraining and complex than the ISD.

The European Commission also proposed a new core ISD passport for ATSs in its second consultative paper, which are defined as multilateral order disclosure and execution mechanisms. This issue attracted much debate around the turn of the century but was a marginal phenomenon in Europe, at least in equity markets. Only 1 per cent of EU equity trading went through ATSs in that period, although they had become the most important trading venues for organized government bond markets. In the view of the European Commission, ATSs will need to follow comparable rules on pre- and post-trade transparency as regulated markets, but for the remaining provisions, it will be introduced as an investment firm regime. The operating conditions are thus less burdensome than for the regulated markets.

The draft Markets in Financial Instruments Directive (MiFID) saw the light in November 2002 after a widely reported last-minute row regarding the addition of an article regarding pre-trade transparency, the so-called 'Prodi amendment' (as it was added at the request of the then President of the European Commission). Although the European Commission staff was not convinced about its need,[3] the final Commission proposals contained an article mandating pre-trade transparency for (systematic)

[3] On pre-trade transparency, the initial Commission proposal stated: 'In view of the marginal benefits, and the likelihood of significant initial investment for regulators and

internalization of 'transactions of a size customarily undertaken by retail investors' (art. 25 in the Commission proposal, became art. 27 in MiFID). This article went on to dominate the ensuing discussion of the MiFID proposal.

In its explanatory memorandum, the European Commission justifies the need for a new directive on the shortcomings of the ISD, which does not establish clear rules within which competition and consolidation of trading infrastructures can take place. These shortcomings are: (1) the insufficient degree of harmonization of the ISD, which does not allow mutual recognition to work; (2) the outdated investor protection requirements of the ISD; (3) the limited scope of the ISD; (4) the new competitive landscape amongst trading platforms; (5) the optional maintenance of the monopoly of the national exchanges (the 'concentration provision') in the ISD: (6) the underdeveloped system for supervisory cooperation; (7) inflexible and outdated provisions, which do not allow for the extensive use of comitology provisions (European Commission 2002b, pp. 6–7). Given these 'extensive shortcomings', and the need to render it more responsive to structural changes, the Commission said it was 'more effective and rational to replace the existing text in its entirety' (European Commission 2002b, p. 7).

Given the size and complexity of the draft directive, its adoption by the European Parliament and Council of Ministers happened fairly smoothly, as the directive was agreed upon less than 18 months after the Commission proposal, in April 2004. Parliament's amendments mostly focused on what was then art. 25 (pre-trade transparency), which, in the words of the Rapporteur Theresa Villiers, MEP, was unacceptable, as it 'unjustifiably tilts the level playing field in favour of regulated markets'. Investors are better served by having a wide range of trading venues, she argued.[4] Exchanges, on the other hand, requested a level playing field for all execution venues/trading platforms, arguing that they had always had the obligation (under the ISD and before) to provide pre-trade transparency in the form of open order books. Parliament's efforts thus focused on making this article more workable and feasible. As far as the

ongoing compliance costs for market participants, and the provision for a package of other measures to support "best execution" and market efficiency, the Commission considers that the disadvantages of a pre-trade transparency rule for off-exchange transactions outweigh the benefits.' See European Commission (2002b), explanatory memorandum to the initial proposal, September, p. 21.

4 Theresa Villiers at the second meeting of the CEPS task force on 'Assessing the Investment Services Directive', 9 December 2002.

position of the industry is concerned, it was interesting to note that their positions were more aligned on nationality than sector grounds, with the large French banks advocating the maintenance of the monopolistic single liquidity pool on the exchange for example.

The implementing measures followed two years later, with the adoption by the European Securities Committee of a Commission regulation and directive. The regulation concerns record-keeping obligations for investment firms, transaction reporting, market transparency, admission of financial instruments to trading and definitions, and is directly applicable in the member states. The directive covers organizational requirements and operating conditions for investment firms and definitions, and – in contrast – is to be implemented by the member states (see table 2.1). In line with the desire to have a truly level playing field, and avoid unnecessary 'gold-plating', the Commission added a tight wording in art. 4 of the implementing directive, which formally requires member states to notify and justify additional national implementing measures.[5]

That the timely implementation by the member states of MiFID would be problematic was already foreshadowed by a formal delay from the implementation dates as foreseen in the directive. Whereas the directive in art. 70 foresaw implementation two years after the publication in the Official Journal of the EU – this would have been 30 April 2006 – an amendment was adopted in April 2006 by the European Parliament and EU Council moving the deadline for implementation to 31 January 2007 and the deadline for application (by firms and markets) to 1 November 2007.[6] The latter deadline applied to the implementing directive and regulation as well.

Notwithstanding this additional delay, almost all member states failed to meet the deadline for transposing the text into national law, 1 February 2007. In June 2007, the European Commission sent warning letters to twenty-two member states for their dereliction – Ireland, Lithuania, Slovakia, Romania and the UK being the exceptions. On the deadline of application of MiFID, 1 November 2007, at least seven member states were not ready (Italy, Spain, The Netherlands, Poland, Czech Republic, Hungary and Finland). As we will show later in this volume, this diversity in preparedness by the member states has important bearings on the competitiveness of firms and ultimately also on local financial centres.

[5] At the time of writing, only two member states had formally notified the European Commission of additional national implementing measures.

[6] Directive 2006/31/EC of the European Parliament and of the Council of 5 April 2006, amending Directive 2004/39/EC on markets in financial instruments, as regards certain deadlines.

Table 2.1 MiFID implementing measures

Measure	Directive	Regulation
Admission of financial instruments to trading		✓
Best execution	✓	
Client assets	✓	
Client order handling	✓	
Conflicts of interest	✓	
Derivative financial instruments		✓
Eligible counterparties	✓	
Inducements	✓	
Information to clients	✓	
Investment advice – definition	✓	
Organizational requirements	✓	
Outsourcing	✓	
Post-trade transparency (regulated firms, MTFs and investment firms)		✓
Pre-trade transparency (regulated markets and MTFs)		✓
Pre-trade transparency (systematic internalizers)		✓
Record-keeping	✓	
Record-keeping: client orders and transactions		✓
Reporting to clients	✓	
Suitability and appropriateness	✓	
Transaction reporting		✓

3. The key elements of the MiFID regime

The MiFID is a very far-reaching piece of legislation, which sets out a comprehensive regulatory regime covering investment services and financial markets in Europe. It contains measures aiming at changing and improving the organization and functioning of investment firms, facilitating cross-border trading and thereby encouraging the integration of EU capital markets. It ensures a high level of investor protection with, *inter alia*, a comprehensive set of rules governing the relationship which investment firms have with their clients.

As highlighted by the European Commission, and already sketched out in the above paragraph, market players needed MiFID because the old Investment Services Directive was out of date and did not function efficiently in several areas. The 'passport' system was not working well enough, because of the large discretional powers left to the host countries. It had to be updated so as to eliminate barriers to cross-border trading and thus inject fresh competition into the European investment services industry which is so vital to the European economy, e.g. in dealing with the financial implications of the so-called pensions time-bomb. As a result, MiFID has increased the scope of product coverage and services, while recognizing new trading platforms and venues. The directive is also establishing a comprehensive regulatory regime surrounding the execution of transactions and the provision of investment services. Integrity, transparency and investors protection are key elements of this new regime, as they are to be enhanced in order to attract new investors to EU capital markets.

The main areas covered by the directive are:

1. **Conduct of business requirements for firms**, e.g. their obligation to divide their clients into different categories ('eligible counterparties', 'professional' and 'retail'); their obligations towards each category of client; their obligation to assess whether the products and services which they provide are 'suitable' or 'appropriate' for their client; and their obligation to secure 'best execution' for their clients (i.e. th best possible result with the emphasis on best price for retail investors).
2. **Organizational requirements for firms and markets**, e.g. compliance, risk management and internal audit functions that operate independently, identification and management of conflicts of interest and limitations on out-sourcing, especially to third countries.
3. **Transaction reporting to relevant competent authorities** of buy and sell transactions in all financial instruments.
4. **Transparency requirements** for the trading of shares (i.e. pre- and post-trade transparency for regulated markets, MTFs and 'systematic internalizers') to ensure a 'level playing field' between exchanges, MTFs and systematic internalizers.

MiFID should improve the choice of investment service providers – who are all required to conform to high conduct of business standards to their clients. This should allow clients to seek out services of the best quality at the lowest price. Firms are subject to greater competition, forcing them to be more responsible vis-à-vis their clients and to offer a better level of service. Notably, consumers enjoy the same level of protection whether they choose a domestic service provider or a foreign one. The draft measures build in a range of tough safeguards for consumers. For example, there will be strict limits on the inducements which banks or financial advisers can receive in respect of the services which they provide to their clients. When executing client orders, firms have to take all reasonable steps to deliver the best possible result ('best execution').

The general idea is that consumers should not be inundated with realms of information which may not be relevant to them and which they may have difficulty in understanding. Instead, the emphasis has been put on the fiduciary duties of firms towards their clients (i.e. their duty always to put their clients' interests first). This will combine a range of measures including a modern and thorough approach to the identification and management of conflicts of interest. Firms are also required, when providing investment services, to collect sufficient information to ensure that the products and services which they provide are 'suitable' or 'appropriate' for their clients.

Clearly, this new investor protection regime – designed to be attractive to investors worldwide – applies to the full extended list of products and services which are now covered by the MiFID, thus ensuring even greater protection for consumers.

3.1 An overview of the main issues addressed by MiFID Level 1

MiFID extends the existing ISD, by establishing EU-wide legislative harmonization for financial services across the thirty member states of the European Economic Area (EEA)[7] and introducing:

1. A **wider range of financial instruments**, including both financial and commodity derivatives. For example, contracts for difference (CFDs) and commodity futures, certain derivatives contracts including commodity, credit, interest rates and even climatic variables and emission allowances are now included.
2. A **wider range of investment services**, including the provision of investment advice.
3. **Alternative trading mechanisms and venues**, Multilateral Trading Facilities (MTFs). In particular, MiFID also eliminates the 'concentration rules' practised in Belgium, France, Italy, Spain, The Netherlands

[7] Norway, Iceland and Liechtenstein are members of the EEA (which includes all EU member states), but are not members of the EU. By operation of the EEA Agreement formed between those states and the EU, legislative measures passed in the EU are automatically adopted by those EEA states; as such the Single European Market incorporates not only the twenty-seven member states of the EU but also those three states.

and the new EU member states, allowing increased opportunity for cross-border trading via other trading facilities. In other words, member states can no longer require investment firms to route orders only to stock exchanges. This means that, in many member states, exchanges will be exposed to competition from multilateral trading facilities (MTFs), i.e. non-exchange trading platforms and 'systematic internalizers', i.e. banks or investment firms which systematically execute client orders internally on their own account (rather than sending them to exchanges). MTFs and 'systematic internalizers' are subject to similar pre- and post-trade transparency requirements as the exchanges. This will ensure a level playing field between the exchanges and their new competitors – and full information on trading activity to the market.[8]

4. **Enhancement of 'passporting'** to provide scope for licensing, with authorization obtained in one country being applicable in other EEA states, without further requirements. 'Passporting' refers to the right of certain types of financial institutions licensed in one member state (its 'home state' or 'country of origin') to provide services and open branches elsewhere in Europe without additional, local regulatory requirements.

3.2 A note on the process for the implementation of MiFID (Lamfalussy process)

MiFID follows the new legislative approach for EU financial market legislation, the so-called 'Lamfalussy process', which distinguishes four levels in lawmaking:

1. **Level 1** is traditional EU decision making, i.e. directives or regulations proposed by the Commission and then co-decided by the European Parliament (EP) and the EU Council of Ministers. These directives or regulations should contain framework principles.
2. **Level 2.** Technical implementing measures to render the Level 1 principles operational, can be adopted, adapted and updated by an EU Committee of Ministry of Finance officials, in the case of securities

[8] MiFID is expected to change the financial market landscape. Cross-border operations within the EU should be easier and there will be competition between regulated exchanges and alternative execution venues, such as investment firms' own electronic trading platforms, throughout the EU. The aim is that pricing will be keener and liquidity deeper and that investor safeguards and compliance requirements will be consistent everywhere.

law the European Securities Committee (ESC), further to a proposal by the European Commission and an opinion of the EP. The Committee of European Securities Regulators (CESR), an independent advisory body made up of representatives of national securities markets supervisors, can advise the Commission on the technical implementing details to be included in Level 2 legislation. This advice is provided in response to specific 'mandates' from the Commission asking for input in particular areas. Level 2 implementing measures do not in any way alter the principles agreed at Level 1; they simply provide the technical details which are necessary to make these principles operational.

3. **Level 3.** In order to facilitate coherent implementation and uniform application of EU legislation by the member states, CESR may adopt non-binding guidelines. CESR can also adopt common standards regarding matters not covered by EU legislation (but these standards have to be compatible with Level 1 and Level 2 legislation).
4. **Level 4.** Enforcement: this refers to monitoring correctness of implementation of EU legislation into national legislation by the Commission and, in case of non-conformity, launching of infringement proceedings which can end before the European Court of Justice.

The Level 1 Directive obliges the European Commission to adopt Level 2 measures in order to ensure uniform application of the Level 1 provisions. In almost all the areas dealt with by the Level 1 Directive, the body of national law is highly diverse. Only through European legislation can national legal systems be sufficiently aligned and uniform application of the Level 1 provisions achieved. Otherwise, the 'passport' will not work; cross-border trading will be sub-optimal; and the wider economic benefits will be weaker.

As far as the choice of legal instruments is concerned, some of the measures were suitable for presentation in a regulation which has direct effect and does not need to be transposed into national law. Others had to be presented in a directive to enable member states, when transposing its provisions, to adjust its requirements to the specificities of their markets and ensure coherence with other areas of national law. The Commission therefore chose to use a combination of a regulation and a directive (the 'Implementing Regulation' and the 'Implementing Directive').[9] In the background note that accompanies

[9] See draft Commission Directive Implementing Directive 2004/39/EC as regards organizational requirements and operating conditions for investment firms, and defined terms for

both implementing measures, the Commission services explain that 'for the majority of envisaged measures, uniform solutions are desirable to avoid "gold-plating" by member states'.[10] The regulation covers those areas where the texts are sufficiently exhaustive to allow direct application in the member states. Where this was technically or legally not πpossible, the Commission proposes a 'principles-based though tightly-worded directive'.[11] The Commission explains that it decided to have a directive for part of the implementing measures in order to 'avoid a "one-size-fits-all" approach by introducing obligations that allow for the calibration of the requirements according to the nature, scale and complexity of the particular investment firm'.[12]

4. The structure of MiFID

The structure of the MiFID is much clearer than in the preceding ISD. It is subdivided into parts dealing with licensing requirements for investment firms, including MTFs, conduct of business rules, licensing and operating requirements for regulated markets (exchanges), and the role of the competent authorities. In the former ISD, articles covering exchanges are mixed up with articles regarding broker dealers. Where a reader may, however, start to lose track is in the degree of detail of the directive, and the interaction between the framework directive's stipulations and the implementing measures. This reflects some of the general problems that have been raised regarding the implementation of the Lamfalussy approach: what is the appropriate level of harmonization? What is technical detail (Level 2) and what are framework principles (Level 1)? And what is left for Level 3, the cooperation between national regulators, and how will this be implemented? A discussion on the basis of MiFID indicates how difficult these ideas are to implement in practice.

Footnote 9 (*cont.*)

the purposes of that Directive (Draft 30.6.06 for Institutional Reference) and draft Commission Regulation Implementing Directive 2004/39/EC as regards record-keeping obligations for investment firms, transaction reporting, market transparency, admission of financial instruments to trading, and defined terms for the purposes of that Directive (Draft 30.6.06 for Institutional Reference). The final text of the above implementing measures was adopted by the Commission (see Commission Regulation (EC) 1287/2006 of 10 August 2006 and Commission Directive 2006/73/EC of 10 August 2006) and subsequently published in the Official Journal L 241/1 on 2.9.06.

10 Background note to the draft Commission Regulation, p. 3.

11 Background note to the draft Commission Directive, p. 4.

12 Background note to the draft Commission Directive, p. 5.

Table 2.2 A comparison of the ISD, the MiFID and its implementing measures

	Number of articles	Articles open to comitology*	Total word count (including recitals and annexes)
ISD I (1993)	32	Few and never implemented	14,381
ISD II (Commission draft, 2002)	67	18	25,556
MiFID Level 1 Directive	73	20	31,451
MiFID Total Level 2	96		39,485
MiFID Implementing Measures Directive (2006/73/EC)	55	Covering 6 articles of level 1 directive	24,424
MiFID Implementing Measures Regulation	41	Covering 13 articles of level 1 directive	15,061
MiFID total	**169**		**70,936**
MiFID = x times the ISD	**5.3**		**4.9**

* An article of the Framework Directive which is open to comitology can lead to the adoption of implementing measures.

What immediately comes to mind when sketching a broad comparison between the ISD and the MiFID is that the MiFID comes across as far more onerous and detailed than its predecessor. While the original ISD had thirty-two articles and no implementing measures, the new MiFID has 169 articles, of which seventy-three comprise the Level 1 Framework Directive and ninety-six are accounted for by the implementing measures (see table 2.2). Not all twenty of the Level 1 Directive's articles, which introduce the possibility to enact implementing legislation, have been addressed in the draft implementing measures released by the Commission. One therefore needs to be mindful that even more implementing measures can be expected to come. At present, however, the implementing measures further double the length of the total MiFID legislation, after the original MiFID Framework Directive was already twice as long as the Investment Services Directive. In other words, combined, the Level 1 and Level 2 MiFID legislation is five times as detailed as the original ISD, if the length of a legislative text is a reasonable gauge of the expanse and depth of a regulatory regime.

It might be misleading to compare the ISD with the MiFID on the basis of the total word count, since the MiFID is broader in scope than the ISD. Investment advice, for example, which was not regulated under the ISD, has now come into the EU regulatory fold under the MiFID regime. The licensing scheme and operating conditions for regulated markets is also much more defined in MiFID than it ever was under the ISD. Likewise, cooperation agreements between competent authorities as regards the transfer of information on the activities of investment firms were not carefully spelled out in the ISD, but are meticulously set out in the MiFID Level 1 and Level 2 texts. That the MiFID is five times as lengthy as the ISD therefore need not necessarily imply that it is more burdensome, since the regulated functions that come under these two sets of legislative texts do not exactly match.

Another caveat about using length as an indicator is that it cannot measure the quality of a regulatory regime. Just because legislation is more detailed does not mean the quality of a regulatory regime need necessarily deteriorate. On the contrary, compliance departments generally prefer more detailed rules, because the more detailed the rules, the greater the legal certainty surrounding a firm's business activities, at least within an EU context. At the same time, it must also be recognized that the more level playing field introduced by MiFID means that large investment firms with operations in several member states no longer need to comply with a panoply of different conduct-of-business rules, thus streamlining corporate legal work and administrative red tape.

Looking at the reasons for this large difference in wordiness between the ISD and MiFID in more detail, the greater burden of regulation surrounding specific regulated functions is to be found specifically in the conduct-of-business rules of MiFID. This result is essentially due to the MiFID's detailed rules, whereas the ISD only set some general principles for conduct of business, which it left up to the member states to design (so long as they were non-discriminatory). This can best be illustrated by a brief overview of the core regulatory concepts of MiFID, client suitability and appropriateness, best execution, conflict of interest provisions, and price transparency in a comparison with what ISD had on the same.

4.1 Client suitability and appropriateness

The MiFID adopts detailed provisions on the exercise of due diligence by investment firms in the recommendation and sale of products and services to non-professional clients. These requirements involve a so-called 'suitability test' and 'appropriateness test', spelled out in arts. 19.4 and 19.5 of the MiFID Framework Directive, respectively. Each of these tests serves a different purpose, responding to the different scope, functions and characteristics of the investment services to which they relate. The 'suitability test' applies only when an investment firm provides investment advice or portfolio management for a client, while the 'appropriateness test' applies to other investment services. Under arts. 36.3 and 36.4 of the Implementing Directive, investment firms must extract the following information from non-professional clients prior to providing a service and/or offering a type of product/transaction (except for execution-only services): source/extent of client income, client assets, including liquid assets, investments and real property, and regular financial commitments (art. 36.3); length of time the client wishes to hold onto investment, risk profile and risk preferences, purposes of investing (art. 36.4); types of service, transaction, financial instrument with which the client is familiar, nature/volume/frequency of previous financial transactions carried out by the client, and the level of education/relevant professional experience of the client (art. 38).

In comparison, all the ISD had to say on the matter is contained in a subpoint of art. 11.1: 'These principles shall ensure that an investment firm ... seeks from its clients information regarding their financial situation, investment experience and objectives as regards the services provided.' This is somewhat elaborated in art. 11.3, which states that the professional nature of the client must be taken into account when executing orders.

4.2 Best execution

Provisions on best execution are part of conduct-of-business rules, and aim to maximize the value of a client's portfolio, in the context of the client's stated investment objectives and constraints. This does not necessarily mean the lowest price of a trade. Unlike the Reg NMS 'trade-through' rule in the US,[13] by which best execution is firmly measured against a clear quantitative indicator, i.e. price, the MiFID takes a more

[13] Regulation National Market System, see Chapter 11.

flexible approach to best execution (art. 21), introducing other factors that could satisfy best execution requirements, such as transaction costs, the speed and likelihood of execution and settlement and other considerations (provided the client specifies non-price criteria as more important than price and identifies them to the broker).

The MiFID provisions on the subject are comprised in three articles (arts. 19(1), 20 (best execution) and 21 (client order handling rules)), all of which have been further elaborated in implementing measures. MiFID art. 20 defines best execution as not only a matter of the price of a trade, but also 'costs, speed, likelihood of execution and settlement, size, nature or any other consideration relevant to the execution of the order'. Investment firms are therefore required to establish and implement order execution policies.

The best execution criteria of the implementing measures are further detailed in two sets of three articles. They further broaden the picture for best execution policy, requiring firms to take into account the characteristics of the client and the nature of his/her order, and the characteristics of the financial instruments and execution venues. The criteria for retail clients seem to be essentially the price and costs. Firms cannot discriminate between execution venues, and are requested to review their execution policy annually.

Provisions on best execution were very vaguely defined in the ISD art. 11, which required that investment firms act 'in the best interest of their clients'. The interpretation of this statutory requirement differed significantly from one member state to another, and the fact that host country authorities could interpret this provision as they saw fit, regardless of the regulatory regime prevailing in neighbouring countries, significantly hampered the cross-border provision of financial services under the ISD. It was one of the reasons why the EU Commission pushed for an overhaul of the directive.

4.3 Conflict of interest

The regulated function which has changed the most under MiFID as compared to the ISD is the duty of investment firms to ensure that they are taking all possible measures to mitigate conflicts of interest, and when they are unavoidable, promptly to inform their clients of this potential. MiFID art. 18.1 requires investment firms to take 'all reasonable steps' to identify conflicts of interest and to 'maintain and operate effective organizational and administrative arrangements' (art. 13.3) with a view to mitigating them. MiFID art. 18.3 mandates the Commission to adopt implementing measures to 'define the steps that investment firms might reasonably be expected to take to identify, prevent, manage and/or disclose conflicts of interest'.

Under the MiFID Implementing Directive (art. 22), investment firms are expected to implement a comprehensive or holistic conflicts of interest policy covering all business lines. Disclosure is not a substitute for aggressively resolving conflicts of interest. In fact, client notification is a last resort meant to act as a final safeguard only after an investment firm, having taken 'all reasonable steps' to suppress conflicts of interest with a 'reasonable degree of confidence', finds that the organizational and administrative arrangements it has undertaken under its general conflicts of interest policy are insufficient. These steps include measures such as the severance of direct remuneration linkages between functions, giving rise to conflicts of interest and separate supervision of these functions.

Again, the ISD had only basic principles on the subject. Among the general conduct of business rules in art. 11, the ISD required an investment firm to 'try to avoid conflicts of interest, and when they cannot be avoided, ensure that its clients are fairly treated'. In addition, art. 10 required firms to have general procedures in place to safeguard a client's interest.

4.4 Price transparency

The primordial difference between the MiFID and the ISD is that, under the new regime, investment firms and banks are allowed to create a market for shares by trading on own account, or acting as 'internalizers'. The ISD allowed member states to maintain the monopoly of exchanges or regulated market. The MiFID abolishes this 'concentration provision', but requests banks that want to trade against their own book and are doing so on a 'systematic' (i.e. organized and frequent) basis to publish quotes for shares that are admitted to trading on a regulated market and for which generally a liquid market exists (pre-trade transparency). The implementing regulation defines the scope for the concept of liquid market of shares. Once they choose to undertake business activities that would classify them as a 'systematic internalizer', banks/firms need to act almost as exchanges: they need to execute the transactions at the quoted prices (or even better), and disclose this information to a regulated market or MTF as close to real time as possible (maximum delay of three minutes, with an exception clause for unwinding large positions, i.e. large tickets – Implementing Regulation art. 27) – or to find another way of making this public – in order to maximize the effectiveness of the price formation mechanism.

5. Conclusion

Although the ISD was only about ten years old when the discussions on a new regime started, the deep transformation of European capital markets, to which the predecessor of MiFID contributed, probably justified a review. The outcome is a complex but comprehensive piece of legislation, which combines a new classification of trade execution venues with tight regulation of investment services providers. In addition, the directive is the first piece of EU financial services regulation that makes ample use of the possibilities created by the 'Lamfalussy approach', by which much room is left for implementing or secondary legislation, of which the European Commission has made ample use.

Whether MiFID will continue the process set into motion by the ISD, and further deepen Europe's capital markets, is at the time of writing difficult to say. It has certainly created the ingredients for a more competitive market on the side of the suppliers of securities market services, while given investors much higher levels of protection. The effects this will have on Europe's capital markets are discussed in the next chapter.

References

European Commission 2002a. Revision of Investment Services Directive (93/22/EEC), Second Consultation, March.

European Commission 2002b. Proposal for a Directive of the European Parliament and of the Council on Investment Services and Regulated Markets, and Amending Council Directives 85/611/EEC, Council Directive 93/6/EEC and European Parliament and Council Directive 2000/12/EC, COM(2002) 625 final of 19.11.2002.

Levin, Mattias 2003. *Competition, Fragmentation and Transparency, Assessing the ISD Review*, CEPS Task Force Report, April. Brussels: Centre for European Policy Studies.

3

Client suitability and appropriateness under MiFID

1. Introduction

MiFID's stated objective is 'to further integrate the European financial markets, thus creating a real level playing field for all European stakeholders. In order to reach this objective, we need to guarantee an appropriate level of transparency and information as well as investor protection against the complexity of the market.'[1] To this end, MiFID introduces two new key concepts in European law, i.e. client suitability and appropriateness assessments. Together with the best execution requirement, they form the core building blocks of the new conduct-of-business rules of MiFID.

A broad conduct of business framework was in place in the ISD, also introducing elements of suitability and appropriateness at a very high level. However, similarly to best execution, its definition was vague and its enforcement was left to the country where the service was provided. The ISD requested firms to act in the best interest of their clients and to seek information about their 'financial situation, investment experience and objectives' (art. 11.1). The ambiguous wording led to a variety of rules, creating hindrances to an effective single market in securities trading for both professional and retail investors.

Under the MiFID regime, investment firms have to comply with an entirely new set of obligations, requiring them to re-map and re-classify new and already existing clients into three main categories. These are 'eligible counterparties', 'professional clients' and 'retail clients'. The severity of conduct of business rules is graduated and predicated upon a client's classification, retail clients being afforded the highest level of protection. On such a basis, investment firms have to assess the 'suitability' and 'appropriateness' of the products/services rendered to their customers.

[1] P. Bérès, Chair of the Economic and Monetary Affairs Committee, European Parliament, European Commission's Public Hearing on Non-Equities Markets Transparency, 11 September 2007.

The appropriateness assessment aims to determine whether clients of investment firms have the necessary knowledge, experience and understanding to invest in complex financial instruments and to understand the associated risks, while suitability is an obligation to consider a client's broader investment objectives, risk profiles and understanding of financial instruments when providing investment advice. They represent an elaboration of the general obligation to act fairly, honestly and professionally – previously defined under the general umbrella of the 'fiduciary duty' – and in accordance with the best interests of the client.

This chapter begins with a discussion of the new client classification hierarchy under MiFID, as it forms the basis of the new but complex 'know-your-customer' regime, which is discussed in the second section. The chapter ends with some considerations of the operational implications of the new regime.

2. MiFID clients' classification

The client classification regime is the starting point of conduct-of-business rules under MiFID, defining firms' specific business obligations with respect to each client category. MiFID distinguishes between three types of clients: retail, professional and eligible counterparty (ECP). As spelled out in art. 19 of the Framework Directive and art. 28 of the Level 2 Directive:

- Retail clients are afforded the highest level of protection.
- Professional clients have sufficient experience, knowledge and expertise to make their own decisions and to assess properly the risks incurred. The general conduct of business rules of the directive are applicable, but in a less onerous way.
- Eligible counterparties (ECP) are investment firms, credit institutions, insurance companies, UCITS and their management companies, other regulated financial institutions and, in certain cases, other undertakings. They are not subject to certain conduct-of-business provisions of the directive.

Annex II of MiFID establishes which clients can be considered professional clients *de facto*. These clients – known as *per se professionals* – include investment firms, credit institutions, institutional investors, broker/dealers, large undertakings and public bodies. Retail clients form a residual – but nevertheless large and diversified – category. They are defined as clients who are not professionals by default. In other words, any client not listed in Annex II of MiFID is considered a retail client.

Eligible counterparties are investment firms, UCITS managers, insurance companies, pension funds managers and possibly other authorized financial institutions (art. 24.1). They need to have their legal status as eligible counterparty explicitly authorized. But, as with best execution, they can choose to opt into the suitability and appropriateness regime either on a general basis or on a trade-by-trade basis (art. 24.2). When ECPs opt in the suitability and appropriateness regime, they are considered as professionals by default or, if expressly requested, as retail customers (art. 50, Level 2 Directive). The same rules apply to professional clients (MiFID Annex II.1.4). Clients may fall into different categories according to different products or services.

Investment firms have a duty to tell their clients which category they have been classified in (art. 28, Level 2 Directive). Customers should also be informed of the levels of protection attached to their category. Once classified in one category, clients are allowed to change their classification, if meeting certain criteria and complying with a particular procedure. A retail investor, for example – who feels they have sufficient knowledge and experience to cope with lower levels of protection – may ask to become a professional investor (MiFID Annex II.2.1). Equally, a professional investor who prefers a higher level of protection may ask to become a retail investor. MiFID requires investment firms to take reasonable steps to ensure that retail clients requesting professional client treatment meet 'qualitative' and 'quantitative' criteria. The qualitative criterion obliges the firm to undertake 'an adequate assessment of the expertise, experience and knowledge of the client' in order to ensure 'in light of the nature of transactions or services envisaged, that the client is capable of making his own investment decisions and understanding the risks involved'.[2]

In assessing the client's experience and knowledge, the client must satisfy at least *two* of the following quantitative criteria:

- the client has carried out transactions, in significant size, on the relevant market at an average frequency of ten per quarter over the previous four quarters;
- the size of the client's financial instrument portfolio, defined as including cash deposits and financial instruments, exceeds €500,000;

[2] MiFID Annex II.2.1.

- the client works or has worked in the financial sector for at least one year in a professional position which requires knowledge of the transactions or services envisaged.

Retail investors must be adequately informed of the lower levels of protection associated with professional client status. Moreover, they must explicitly state that they are aware of the consequences of waiving retail client protection.

MiFID clarifies that a distinction should be made in the way the rules are applied to retail clients and to professional clients. Most of the specific rules established in Chapter III of the Implementing Directive apply to retail clients, since professionals should have the expertise and resources necessary to protect their own interests in the market. However, the fact that they are not covered by most of the implementing measures does not reduce or in any way modify the protection afforded to professional investors by the principles set out in the Framework Directive.

The eligible counterparty category renders the classification even more cumbersome. Eligible counterparties are all professional investors but not all professional investors are automatically eligible counterparties. MiFID art. 24(2) sets out a list of *per se eligible counterparties,* i.e. those entities which are automatically recognized as eligible counterparties. MiFID also gives member states the option to recognize as eligible counterparties entities other than the *per se eligible counterparties* defined in art. 24(2) if those entities so request. The Implementing Directive (art. 50) specifies the requirements that such entities need to meet.

3. The suitability and appropriateness tests

Two types of client assessments may apply when investment firms provide products and/or services to their clients in the new 'know your customer' regime, the suitability and appropriateness tests. The suitability test applies to investment advisory services, whereas the appropriateness test to non-advised services. Both tests are contained in arts 35–37 of ch. III, Section 3 of the Implementing Directive, based upon MiFID art. 19.

3.1 The suitability assessment

When providing advisory services or managing a client's portfolio, investment firms need to assess whether the advice provided or the product bought in the portfolio is 'suitable' to the client's expertise, risk profile and financial situation. Investment firms must carry out the suitability test when offering a service or transaction entailing an element of recommendation such as investment advice or discretionary portfolio management (i.e. to purchase, hold or sell any securities or make any other investment decisions).[3] According to MiFID, in such situations the investment firm has to obtain 'the necessary information regarding the client's or potential client's knowledge and experience in the investment field relevant to the specific type of product or service, his financial situation and his investment objectives so as to enable the firm to recommend the client or potential client the investment services and financial instruments that are suitable for him'.[4]

In the case of the provision of investment advisory services (which is upgraded to a core investment service that can be passported under MiFID whenever it involves a personal recommendation) or discretionary portfolio management, each investment firm has to assess the suitability of any investment advice or suggested financial transaction prior to the information being given to its clients (see box 3.1 and explanatory table).

The suitability duty is owed not only to retail clients, but also to professional clients, even though, in the case of the latter, the duty is much less onerous. In fact, the practical effect of the entire test is limited by the Level 2 Directive, which allows firms to assume that a professional client has the necessary experience and knowledge, i.e. the firm only needs to consider the client's financial situation and investment objectives. In addition, when a firm is providing investment advice to a professional client (other than one that has opted up from retail status) it can also assume that the client is financially able to bear any financial investment risks consistent with his investment objectives (art. 35.2, Implementing Directive; see box 3.1).

3.2 The appropriateness assessment

When providing execution-only services and reception and transmission of orders, investment firms must assess whether the order is 'appropriate'

[3] The key element of 'personal recommendation' under the MiFID implementing rules is that the recommendation must be *personal.* In order for a recommendation to be personal, it must be presented to the client as being suitable or based on a consideration of the personal circumstances of the client. The recommendation must include an express or implied recommendation to deal in a designated investment.

[4] MiFID art. 19(4).

Box 3.1

Suitability test, Level 2 Directive 2006/73/EC, art. 35:

1. Member States shall ensure that investment firms obtain from clients or potential clients such information as is necessary for the firm to understand the essential facts about the client and to have a reasonable basis for believing, giving due consideration to the nature and extent of the service provided, that the specific transaction to be recommended, or entered into in the course of providing a portfolio management service, satisfies the following criteria:

(a) it meets the investment objectives of the client in question;

(b) it is such that the client is able financially to bear any related investment risks consistent with his investment objectives;

(c) it is such that the client has the necessary experience and knowledge in order to understand the risks involved in the transaction or in the management of his portfolio.

2. Where an investment firm provides an investment service to a professional client it shall be entitled to assume that, in relation to the products, transactions and services for which it is so classified, the client has the necessary level of experience and knowledge for the purposes of paragraph 1(c).

Where that investment service consists in the provision of investment advice to a professional client (…), the investment firm shall be entitled to assume for the purposes of paragraph 1(b) that the client is able financially to bear any related investment risks consistent with the investment objectives of that client.

3. The information regarding the financial situation of the client or potential client shall include, where relevant, information on the source and extent of his regular income, his assets, including liquid assets, investments and real property, and his regular financial commitments.

4. The information regarding the investment objectives of the client or potential client shall include, where relevant, information on the length of time for which the client wishes to hold the investment, his preferences regarding risk taking, his risk profile, and the purposes of the investment.

5. Where, when providing the investment service of investment advice or portfolio management, an investment firm does not obtain the information required under Article 19(4) of Directive 2004/39/EC, the firm shall not recommend investment services or financial instruments to the client or potential client.

to the client's expertise, risk profile and financial situation. This new requirement introduced by MiFID impacts non-discretionary portfolio management and other non-advised services. The appropriateness assessment applies in a risk-based manner, so it affects non-advised transactions for retail clients involving what MiFID regards as 'complex' products (for example complex structured products and derivatives, such as options, CFDs and warrants).[5]

Where it applies, investment firms shall 'ask the client or potential client to provide information regarding his knowledge and experience in the investment field relevant to the specific type of product or service offered or demanded so as to enable the investment firm to assess whether the investment service or product envisaged is appropriate for the client'.[6] In the event of the firm considering the product or service inappropriate, the investment firm shall warn the client.

The amount of information investment firms need from clients to conduct the appropriateness assessment as well as the extent of disclosure depends on the complexity and risk of the transaction at hand. That is, the more complex and risky the product, the higher the required information flows from and to the client. For example, transactions involving plain vanilla stock options require less exchange of information than transactions of leveraged OTC derivatives. Likewise, the sale of European blue chip stocks necessitates lower information and disclosure than the sale of equities in small-cap Japanese entities because the latter transaction entails a higher degree of risks (e.g. foreign exchange risk and liquidity risk).

Taking into account the nature of the client and of the service being offered as well as the complexity and risk of the product, the information necessary to assess clients' or potential clients' knowledge and experience in the investment field, implies the following: (a) the types of service, transaction and financial instrument with which the client is familiar; (b) the nature, volume, and frequency of the client's transactions in

[5] An instrument is to be considered 'non-complex' if it: (1) is (a) a listed equity security; (b) a money market instrument; (c) a bond; (d) a securitized debt instrument that does not embed a derivative; (e) UCITS; (f) any other instrument that is not a derivative, is not a compound product (i.e. a financial instrument that combines two different financial instruments, or one financial instrument and an investment service); (2) has frequent opportunities to dispose of, redeem, or otherwise be realized at prices that are publicly available to markets participants; (3) does not involve any actual or potential liability for the client that exceeds the cost of acquiring the investment; (4) has comprehensive information on its characteristics publicly available and likely to be readily understood, see art. 38, Implementing Directive 2006/73/EC.

[6] MiFID art. 19(5).

financial instruments and the period over which they have been carried out; (c) the level of education, and profession or relevant former profession of the client or potential client.[7] Where clients have had a long-standing relationship with the investment firm, the amount of new information required to test appropriateness may be minimal. This fact highlights the flexible approach investment firms may adopt when deciding the amount of information necessary to judge clients.

In practice, the application of the appropriateness assessment is limited in a number of respects. Article 36 of the Level 2 Directive allows firms to assume that professional clients have the necessary experience and knowledge to understand the risks involved. Moreover, art. 19(6) permits investment firms to skip the appropriateness test for execution-only services to retail clients when a number of conditions are met: (i) the service relates to shares admitted to trading on a regulated market, bonds or other forms of securitized debt, UCITS and other non-complex financial instruments; (ii) the service is provided at the initiative of the client; (iii) the client has been warned that it will not have the benefit of any suitability assessment by the firm; and (iv) the firm complies with its obligations under MiFID regarding conflicts of interest. The exemption has some advantages: it allows clients to receive faster and cheaper services. However, it should not result in unjustifiably increased risks for the client, which is exactly what the above conditions are trying to avoid.

In the context of appropriateness assessment, the Level 2 Directive specifies various criteria for non-complex instruments.[8] These provide, *inter alia*, that all financial instruments not mentioned in MiFID art. 19(6) are considered complex, resulting in the inclusion of all derivatives in the appropriateness assessment. In a post-MiFID scenario, the cost of execution-only derivatives business may well outweigh the existing or potential revenues. This is, in particular, the case for investment firms offering online transactions in derivatives as these must request, assess

[7] Implementing Directive 2006/73/EC, art. 37. The level of education and the profession or former profession of the client could help the firm to establish that the client's level of knowledge is appropriate for complex products such as derivatives and structured products. For example, individuals having a finance-related background or qualifications are more likely to understand the risks in complex products than individuals who do not have such a background. By the same token, firms should consider whether a client is illiterate or has some incapacity preventing a complete understanding – for example, when documentation is in a language that is not the client's first language.

[8] Implementing Directive 2006/73/EC, art. 38.

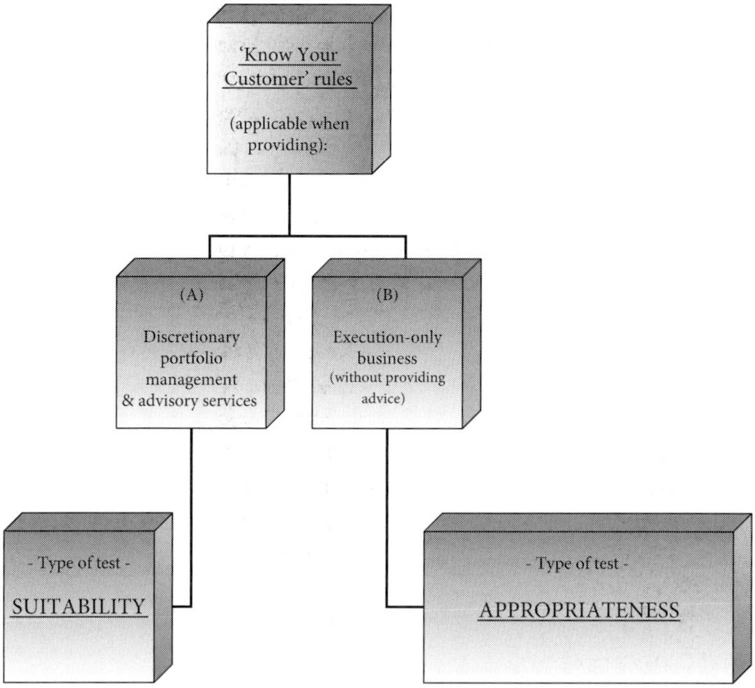

Figure 3.1 – Suitability and appropriateness scope under MiFID's 'know your customer' rules

and store extensive information about each client. These investments firms must also ensure that clients receive appropriate risk warnings. Finally, firms must keep record of all information, including risk warnings – a non-insignificant 'detail' which can be rather costly.

4. The business implications of implementing the new rules

Implementing the new client suitability and appropriateness rules raises conceptual, operational and strategic questions for firms. How do both tests interact? What are the operational implications in terms of data management and privacy? How can the huge implementation costs be translated into strategic advantages for firms?

'Suitability' and 'appropriateness' generate certain *conceptual* difficulties. Although investment firms can supply 'inappropriate' products or services as long as the client is given sufficient notice and warnings as in MiFID art. 19(5), they cannot provide 'unsuitable' products or

Explanatory table

Type of test	Type of service	Information required	Disclosure to clients	Exemptions
Suitability	Discretionary portfolio management and provision of investment advice	Client's knowledge and experience with regard to: (a) the types of service, transaction and financial instrument with which the client is familiar; (b) the nature, volume, and frequency of the client's transactions in financial instruments and the period over which they have been carried out; (c) the level of education, and profession or relevant former profession of the client or potential client.	Periodic statements on the financial instruments in the portfolio, their valuation, performance, dividend or interest income obtained, fees, etc.	– The assessment is more comprehensive for retail clients, including whether the client is able to financially bear the investment risks. – When servicing professional clients and eligible counterparties, the client's knowledge and experience can be assumed, making the entire test less onerous. – The ability to bear financial risks can be assumed for professional clients and eligible counterparties.
Appropriateness	Non-advisory services, this is execution-only business (i.e. receiving and transmitting orders)		Confirmation of order; trading information, such as venue, instrument, price, fee, etc. . . .	– Does not apply to professional clients. – Does not apply for listed shares; money market instruments; bonds; securitized debt (no derivatives); UCITS; non-complex financial instruments, *provided that*: ○ the service is provided at the initiative of the client or potential client, ○ the client receives a proper risk warning, and ○ the investment firm complies with the requirements relating to conflicts of interest.

services. Put differently, while 'appropriateness' cannot stop banks from executing their clients' orders, 'suitability' can prevent investment products to be proposed or securities being added to clients' portfolio.

The suitability test raises the question from which moment onwards selling a financial product becomes 'advice'. When has the initiative been taking by the bank and when by the client for a given investment? The advice may be suitable for the client today, but not necessarily tomorrow. A given investment product may be suitable for a client today, but not necessarily tomorrow.

The appropriateness test applies to complex products, but what is complex cannot be easily defined, and MiFID does not provide guidance. Some products which are defined as non-complex, such as some UCITS, may be more complex or risky than for those where the appropriateness rule applies. The 2002 amendments to the 1985 UCITS Directive allowed the use of derivative instruments and hedge fund techniques in UCITS funds, but maintained quantitative restrictions for equity funds. Hence it allowed more complexity in standard UCITS products, but, on the other hand, maintained the false belief that quantitative asset allocation restrictions are a good means of investor protection.[9]

On the *operational* side, abiding by the new suitability and appropriateness rules requires distributors of investment products to increase their capacity to store and access information. The mechanisms employed to retrieve that information have to be integrated in a firm's information systems for client sales purposes, but also be available to clients, regulators or internal compliance officers. Consequently, having document management systems ready to provide immediate and secure information is important. In addition, the mechanism of record keeping will need to be more resilient than in the past, as MiFID provisions place much emphasis on the client servicing and reporting aspects. Much of the content of the data should be managed at the account opening stage where appropriateness and suitability tests can be built into the business processes. The data will also need to be updated continuously, as something which was suitable for a client in the past may no longer be suitable in the future.

As far as existing clients are concerned, investment firms have to undergo a quite time-consuming and costly reclassification process. They need to verify whether products and services currently provided are suitable and/or appropriate for existing clients; what kind of investments can

[9] See Casey and Lannoo (2008) for a more elaborate discussion of this subject.

Box 3.2

Client suitability and appropriateness checklist:

1. When providing advisory services and/or portfolio management, have you confirmed that the suitability obligation applies to the transactions under consideration?
2. Have you confirmed that the appropriateness obligation applies to the transactions under consideration?
3. Have you established a process for assessing suitability?
4. Have you established a process for assessing appropriateness?
5. Do you have a mechanism in place to keep the information updated regularly?
6. Do you have a mechanism in place for reviewing suitability in the event of a material change?
7. Do you have a mechanism in place for reviewing appropriateness policies and procedures in the event of a material change?
8. Have you included a clear and prominent warning in your policy that any product or service may not be appropriate for a client?
9. Do you have systems in place for recording client details and any relevant correspondence with clients?
10. Do you have record keeping mechanisms in place which adequately record the manner in which suitability and appropriateness have been assessed for each client?

Source: JPMorgan

be recommended to clients given their knowledge and experience are sufficient. They also have to keep track of clients who fail to provide necessary information.

The extension of client data retention may open up new unexpected risks where the custody of client data will need to be more secure. The handling and processing of new clients' data needs to be tightly monitored, while allowing bank branch managers easy access. Litigation may arise if the privacy of the data is violated. On the other hand, the ability to manage and use the data could also allow banks to better target their customers with their product range. Proper calibration of client files in line with a firm's product supply should result in a competitive advantage over less organized competitors.

Whether the implementation of these rules will be more burdensome for large globally operating wealth managers than for small private banks or investment advisors remains to be seen. Whereas application of suitability and appropriateness requirements is standard practice and part of the franchise of small players, large groups may benefit from better resources and stronger logistical and IT planning. The one-off implementation cost may thus be higher for large groups, but once the system is well in place, the long-term benefits may be higher for them as well.

For both groups, the remaining challenge will be to continuously train front-office staff about the different products a bank is selling, whether products which are developed in-house or products for which it is purely a distributor.

5. Conclusion

The new 'know-your-customer' rules are the most burdensome part of the MiFID Directive. They introduce new concepts in EU law, which are not necessarily always clearcut. An investment may be appropriate for a client, although it may be unsuitable. Complex financial products may in some cases be more appropriate for a client, or less riskly, than non-complex ones. Some have therefore argued that the rules may reduce financial innovation, insofar as firms may be wary of providing anything but the most basic financial products or because retail clients would shun complex products. However, the 2008 financial crisis has evidenced the need for tight client suitability and appropriateness rules. Whether the rules will effectively work will depend on proper implementation by member states and tight enforcement by supervisory authorities.

References

Casey, Jean-Pierre and Karel Lannoo 2006. The MiFID *Implementing Measures: Excessive detail or level playing field*, ECMI Policy Brief No. 1, May.

—2008. *Pouring Old Wine into New Skins? UCITS and Asset Management in the EU after MiFID*, Report of a CEPS-ECMI Task Force, April.

Clifford, Chance 2007. MiFID Connect Guidelines on Suitability and Appropriateness.

Sykes, Andrew 2007. 'MiFID for Asset Managers', conference speech.

Wright, Gary 2008. 'Where MiFID and SEPA collide', BISS Research.

4

Best execution[1]

The requirement to seek the most favourable execution reasonably available for securities transactions is one of the core concepts of the new conduct of business regime of the MiFID Directive. Under MiFID, the EU has put in place a framework under which best execution is regulated in a harmonized framework. In conjunction with the abolition of the monopoly of exchanges, it provides the basic structure for competition among trading platforms and execution venues. Investment firms are requested to execute a trade on the basis of the best possible result for their clients. Its practical implementation holds many conceptual and practical challenges, however.

In this chapter, we argue that best execution originated from the common contract law's concept of fiduciary duty in light of the agency relation between brokers and their clients. Provided that brokers hold superior information and have conflicting interests with respect to their clients, regulators mandated best execution to ensure investor protection. However, because of high monitoring and measuring costs, best execution must stress process and market competition over a strict quantitative enforcement. Thus best execution mutates from a pure investor protection objective to both an investor protection and a market efficiency objective. In effect, MiFID follows exactly this approach: by allowing flexible best execution policies and encouraging trading venues' competition, MiFID aims at achieving investor protection and market efficiency without cumbersome and unenforceable regulation.

A broad fiduciary duty concept already existed in EU law, but its definition was vague and its enforcement was left to the host country. The ambiguous wording led to a patchwork of rules, creating serious hindrances to an effective single market in securities trading for both professional and retail investors. A better defined best execution concept already existed in the US, which provided inspiration for EU policy-makers,

[1] This chapter was prepared in cooperation with Piero Cinquegrana.

although MiFID's design of best execution differs importantly from its US counterpart.

In the first part of this chapter, we discuss the origins and economics of the best execution concept, the problems related to implementation and enforcement of a best execution policy, and the pre-MiFID framework. The second part discusses the best execution concept as defined in the MiFID Directive and its practical application in current EU legislation.

1. The origins of the concept of best execution

The interaction between the broker and the investor is characterized by an agency relation. The Restatement of Agency 3d[2] (2006) claims that 'an agent has a fiduciary duty to act loyally for the principal's benefit in all matters connected with the agency relationship' (§8.01). Best execution in securities regulation and the fiduciary duty are linked through the duty of care, whereby the agent has the duty to deliver the best possible performance (Easterbrook and Fischel 1991, p. 433). Hence, best execution is grounded in the common contract law's concept of fiduciary duty. The relationship between the broker and the investor is based on trust, confidence and responsibility. In light of the impossibility to envision all the potential situations arising from a mutual relation and the difficulty in monitoring the agent's actions, the fiduciary duty ensures that the broker will act in the investor's best interest (ibid., p. 426). In effect, Coase (1960) demonstrated how contracts such as the fiduciary duty may help solving coordination issues originating from considerable transaction costs and scarce information in the bargaining process between parties. Based on these premises, regulators have felt the need to mandate best execution.

The US Securities and Exchange Commission (SEC) first mentioned implicitly best execution in a litigation case against a broker. The broker had received a stock sell order but failed to execute it promptly in order to profit personally and misrepresented the delay to his customer as not dependent upon his will. When claiming that brokers with respect to their clients' sell orders have a 'fiduciary duty . . . to sell the stock at the highest possible price', the SEC was the first supervisory authority formally to enshrine best execution in securities regulation (SEC 1962). In 1971 the establishment in the US of the National Association of Securities

[2] Restatements are collections of legal principles published by the American Law Institute. Despite not being primary legal sources, US courts widely cite and accept them. The Restatement of Agency concerns the principles surrounding agency relationships.

Dealers Automated Quotations (NASDAQ) – the world's first electronic quotation system for financial products – increased the competition among trading venues, making it possible for brokers to get quotes outside traditional stock exchanges. This event renewed the significance of best execution, whereby, ideally, brokers seek best execution on competing venues offering the lowest possible transaction costs. The definition of best execution in the US, however, remained vague, and the legal uncertainty surrounding the issue hindered the effective enforcement of this obligation in courts (Macey and O'Hara 1997).

The introduction in the London Stock Exchange (LSE) in 1986 of the Stock Exchange Automated Quotation System (SEAQ) coincided with the drafting of the first best execution rule in the UK. The LSE defined best execution as the best possible bid-ask spread on the SEAQ (Board and Wells 2001, p. 350). Given the limited competition in the UK equity market, however, best execution was not a primary concern of supervisory authorities. Only in the late 1990s and early 2000s, did technological changes and increased competition among venues lead the Securities and Futures Authority – a predecessor of the FSA – to take a close interest in best execution.

Since its inception, best execution has been framed as instrumental in achieving *investor protection* – one of the three pillars of securities regulation.[3] Because of its origins in contract law and in the fiduciary duty, best execution was seen as protecting the investor in his agency relationship with the broker. However, the shift from a focus on best execution as best price to best execution as an overall reduction of transaction costs led to expanding its objectives. Not only does best execution contribute to achieving investor protection, but it also has positive externalities on market efficiency, insofar as transaction costs are reduced – a point stressed below.

2. The economics of best execution

The legalistic vision of best execution has increasingly come under attack. Since the analysis of Garbade and Silber (1982), economists have utilized the principal–agent paradigm and the concept of costly information to argue that not only is best execution a legal fiction, but it *may* also lead to suboptimal market efficiency. On the one hand, since the broker/investor

[3] The International Organization of Securities Commissions (IOSCO) recognizes that the three main objectives of securities regulation are: investor protection; market efficiency and transparency; and financial stability (IOSCO 2003, p. 5).

is characterized by an agency relation, the broker will have no incentive to pursue his client's best interest. On the other hand, if interpreted literally, the SEC position on best execution mandates to obtain the best possible price, regardless of cost (Smidt 1982, p. 520). This ignores the fact that the search for best execution is a costly process that consumes real resources. Because of the costly nature of information, the principal may be happy with the agent's performance whether or not it is his 'best execution'. Put differently, 'the agent's second "best execution" may be better than the principal's best' (ibid.).

Harris (1996) and Macey and O'Hara (1997) are also sceptical of the need to regulate best execution. Assuming perfectly competitive markets, Harris argues that the inability of retail investors to monitor best execution will lead brokerage firms to accept poor quality execution and use order flow inducements to lower their commission fees, which are highly visible (Harris 1996, p. 5). Moreover, he contends that there is a trade-off between the price and level of brokerage services and execution quality because the total transaction costs are constant in perfect competition, regardless of how best execution is regulated (Harris 1996, p. 4). Macey and O'Hara (1997) emphasize the fuzziness of the legal concept of best execution and point to the correspondingly arduous enforcement process. Furthermore, the authors illustrate how best execution may increase market fragmentation because orders are routed to different venues in search of the best price, reducing overall market liquidity and efficiency. In the context of MiFID, other authors have underlined the fallacies in the concept of best execution. For example, Giraud and D'Hondt (2006) accuse MiFID's best execution obligation of being too prescriptive for principles-based regulation but too vague to be effectively enforced.

Why is best execution such a disparaged concept? Are economists right in criticizing the fiduciary duty as the wrong tool for obtaining best execution? To respond to these questions, the rationale and definition of best execution needs to be analyzed. The rationale behind best execution lies in transaction cost theory and the principal–agent relation.

Transaction costs are the costs of operating an economic exchange (trade), and helping to explain why these occur (Coase 1937). Logically, it follows that the lower (higher) transaction costs are relative to the value of the trade, the more (less) likely it will be for the trade to take place. Thus, best execution serves the worthy objective of encouraging trading and market participation by lowering the costs of transacting. This reasoning was also used by the SEC in Reg NMS.

The other reason to pursue best execution is the principal–agent conflict (Ross 1973; Mitnick 1973). The broker has no interest in engaging in costly research efforts to find the best possible price for its customer because the principal has no cost-effective way to monitor his agent's performance. Because of conflicting self-interests and information asymmetries, the broker will route its customers' orders to its preferred venues with a suboptimal amount of research, either because it receives inducements from dealers or because it deems the venue to be the most liquid. The legal mandate to make the research effort is created to counteract this misalignment of incentives. In short, while the concept poses a number of theoretical economic problems, the 'duty' of best execution seeks to reduce transaction costs and to overcome the principal–agent dilemma.

3. Measuring best execution

The definition, measurement and implementation of best execution are subjective concepts, which have not given rise to any kind of general consensus, as they will often depend on the circumstances relating to a particular trade. Best execution means different things to different market participants and stakeholders. Although some retail investors – especially in the high net worth market – may sometimes value anonymity and the quality of personalized services they receive more than the pure commercial terms they are offered, best execution and best price most often coincide in terms of the ranking of various execution factors. For professional investors, other factors – such as speed and reliability of execution, timing, market impact, and settlement probability – may count as much as price. Moreover, the definition of best execution varies with the instruments being considered, as well as with the market structures in which they are traded.

In the case of large-cap equities, for instance, shares can be easily exchanged on highly liquid centralized markets, where information is readily available and monitoring, if not simple, is at least possible. The transparency and ease of access to market data due to centralized trading on-exchange mean that the definition and measurement of best price, market impact and liquidity are far less contested than in the case of the fragmented OTC markets. In the case of the latter, the concept of best execution is more ambiguous: the need for anonymity, counterparty risk, the ability to trade in sizeable lots, and liquidity will often be more important factors to consider than price alone (see SIFMA 2008), yet they are by definition more difficult to quantify, not to mention that, unlike in equity markets, there is no consolidated price tape in OTC markets.[4] This renders the verification of execution quality more challenging.

Another reason why the concept of best execution as applied to shares does not easily translate to fixed-income and structured products is that they are traded far less frequently than most shares. This means that the concept of best execution as best price does not always sit well in the fixed income space, not least because market participants are prepared to pay a premium to obtain liquidity in fundamentally illiquid instruments, and because certain fixed-income and structured products have a limited set of market makers, who can hold considerable market power in these instruments. It is therefore clear that the meaning of best execution changes according to the principal involved, the instrument traded, and the markets in which the instrument trades.

To understand why this is the case, let us turn to the question of how to gauge transaction costs. When applied to securities trading, transaction costs can be divided into explicit and implicit costs. Explicit costs refer to brokerage and exchange fees, taxes or stamp duties. Because of their simplicity and transparency, explicit costs are likely to be a pivotal factor for retail investors when making investment or trading decisions. On the other hand, the research effort needed to evaluate implicit costs, including bid-ask spreads, market impact and opportunity costs, deters the average consumer from including them in their computations.

The *bid-ask spread* is the difference of the price available for an immediate sale (bid) and an immediate purchase (ask). The *market impact* refers to the exhaustion of the best spread because of the large size of the transaction. In other words, the sheer size of the trading consumes the liquidity and the spread must increase to encourage more offers on that particular price. *Opportunity costs* relate to the costs arising from the market moving against the trade between the time of the placement of the order and its actual execution (Edhec-Risk Advisory 2007). Implicit costs are determined by factors such as speed of execution, timing, trading strategy and size. Therefore, these elements must be taken into account when formulating a best execution policy, as sophisticated clients also factor implicit costs into their execution strategies.

Despite the predictions of economic theory that the proliferation of trading venues would have a negative impact on the quality of

[4] There are specific differences in fixed-income and structured markets in the EU and the US. However, for the purpose of this chapter, a general discussion of the characteristics of these markets is sufficient. For a more detailed analysis of bond markets, see Casey (2006).

execution, empirical evidence has pointed to the contrary. In effect, due to technological advancements and increasing competition across trading venues and brokers, transaction costs have decreased substantially in the past decade. In one recent study, Munck (2005) calculates that explicit costs have fallen 28 per cent while implicit costs have dropped 11 per cent over 1997–2004 on average across the most important European stock exchanges. This fact has important implications for market liquidity. Lower transaction costs encourage market participation, thereby facilitating the exchange of securities rapidly, with minimal loss of value and at the expected price. Hence, best execution has not led to excessive fragmentation as economists had forecast, because transparency has ensured interconnectivity of trading venues. In effect, the easy accessibility of competing quotes facilitates arbitration, reducing spreads of the same security across venues. To conclude, not only does the reduction of transaction costs in securities trading enhance individual welfare and help to achieve investor protection, but it also has positive externalities in terms of overall market efficiency insofar as capital is directed to the most productive investment opportunities (Iseli, Wagner and Weber 2007; FSA 2002).

4. Regulation of best execution pre-MiFID

Although not formally enshrined in US securities regulation until the promulgation of the Reg NMS of 2005,[5] the duty of best execution had been incorporated in self-regulating organization (SRO) rules and had been enforced by judicial review and SEC decisions (NASD 2001). However, the enforcement of best execution in the US stressed mainly *process* and *disclosure*, given the lack of clear definition and measurability standards of what constitutes best execution (Macey and O'Hara 1997, p. 190). With the advent of Reg NMS, the SEC has embraced a much more rule-based approach to best execution, whereby the concept mostly coincides with best price. This compromise allows US regulation to get rid of the ambiguities inherent in the definition of best execution, facilitating enforcement decisions by the SEC and perhaps reducing litigation.[6]

In Europe, the 1993 Investment Service Directive (ISD) provided some basic principles for a best execution framework in the context of conduct of business rules. Article 11 states that:

[5] Reg NMS is an important piece of SEC regulation promulgated in 2005 aimed at modernizing US capital markets. To find out more about Reg NMS, see ch. 11.

[6] See ch. 11 for a more elaborate discussion of this subject.

> Member States shall draw up rules of conduct which investment firms shall observe at all times . . . These principles shall ensure that an investment firm:
> – acts honestly and fairly in conducting its business activities in the best interests of its clients and the integrity of the market,
> – acts with due skill, care and diligence, in the best interests of its clients and the integrity of the market . . .

The observance of the implementation and compliance with these rules was left with the member state in which the service is provided; this is the host country in the case of cross-border provision of services. In addition, art. 11 allowed taking into account the professional nature of the investor in the execution of client orders.

However, the unclear phrasing of best execution in the ISD directive led to differing interpretations across Europe and raised concerns about a level playing field. In a recent survey of best execution rules pre-MiFID, Iseli, Wagner and Weber (2007) found that eight out of fifteen countries surveyed had a rather general definition of best execution; four focused on price alone; and three remaining countries included both price and execution time. The UK rule was the most detailed, and it was predominantly focused on price. The firm had to execute any order at a price no less favourable than the best price available for the customer, unless it would be in the customer's best interest not to do so (FSA 2001). The development of best execution rules in the UK was related to increased competition across execution venues.

The unlevel playing field of securities trading in Europe was one of the main reasons for undertaking a systematic review of the ISD (see Chapter 2). The European Parliament in 2001 exposed the flaws in art. 11 of the ISD with the Kauppi Report (European Parliament 2001). The ISD regime failed adequately to differentiate between professional and retail investors, which have diverging expectations on execution. The differing interpretation of art. 11 and the resulting judicial insecurity mainly stemmed from its ambiguous wording (ibid., p. 33).

5. The MiFID rules

The new rules of MiFID state what is considered best execution in an EU context, who shall apply it, to whom it applies, which orders are covered, and what procedures need to be respected. The core rule is set out in art. 21 of the Framework Directive, but this should be read in conjunction with arts. 19 and 22, and with arts. 44–46 of the Level 2 Directive.

According to MiFID art. 21, member states shall require that investment firms take all reasonable steps to obtain, when executing orders, the best possible result for their clients taking into account price, costs, speed, likelihood of execution and settlement, size, nature or any other consideration relevant to the execution of the order. To this end, investment firms shall establish and implement an order execution policy explaining how, for their client orders, they will obtain the best possible result. This policy shall include, in respect of each class of instruments, information on the different venues where the investment firm executes its client orders and the factors affecting the choice of execution venue. This policy shall be evaluated on a regular basis.

Because MiFID defines a concept of best execution in broad strokes without being prescriptive, it offers a great degree of flexibility to investment firms to develop their own best execution policies in line with their business models and corporate strategies. If the rules appear onerous, it is only because, in a post-MiFID world, the burden of proof falls upon firms to document they are complying with the best execution policy they have presented. Thus, while firms are required to take 'all reasonable steps' to obtain the 'best possible outcome' for clients based on a series of factors, the respective weightings of those factors and the implementation of the execution strategy are left up to the firm. To further increase MiFID's flexibility, these factors can be negotiated with the client, depending on the client's categorization and status.

In line with its principles-based philosophy, MiFID establishes different definitions for 'best possible outcome' according to the client's categorization as a retail or professional investor. This differentiation aims at reflecting different clients' needs when implementing execution decisions.

For retail clients, 'best possible' means the most favourable result in terms of price for instrument, net of the explicit costs associated with the execution. The combination of best price and lowest transaction costs is called the 'total consideration' of the trade.[7] This means that if, all else being equal, venue A offers an instrument for €100 and the costs of executing on that venue (e.g. exchange fees, settlement fees, etc.) amount to €5 (making the total consideration equal to €105), while another venue B offers the same instrument for €102, with costs of execution equal to €2, the investment firm should execute the client's order on venue B, since the total consideration of €104 delivers a better result for the retail

[7] See art. 44 of the Implementing Commission Directive 2006/73/EC.

client.[8] Note that, for retail clients, the standard industry practice is for the 'total consideration' to factor only explicit costs of execution (implicit costs such as market impact and opportunity cost are therefore neglected).

On the other hand, for professional clients other factors – such as the speed of execution, market impact, the probability of execution and settlement – may be even more important than price in determining an execution strategy. For example, a large pension fund engaged in a major portfolio rebalancing may be very sensitive to the market impact of offloading a large block of securities. Therefore, it would prefer to pay a premium for the trade to be executed in stages 'off-market' rather than obtaining the best price per tranche but seeing the market move against his position. Moreover, types of retail investors such as day-traders may have execution preferences that more closely resemble those of institutions. For example, if they believe they have superior information, day-traders may want their transactions to be executed as fast as possible. These instances highlight the various trade-offs that must be considered as an integral part of an execution strategy. Recognizing the need for flexibility, art. 44 of the Implementing Directive sets general criteria to determine the factors' relative importance when executing an order:

(a) characteristics of the client, whether retail or professional;
(b) nature of the client order;
(c) characteristics of financial instruments that are the subject of that order;
(d) characteristics of the execution venue on which orders can be routed.

This very flexible approach must be contrasted with its counterpart in the US, the best execution rule under Reg NMS, where delivering the best price available is the overriding objective. The reduction of best execution to best price in Reg NMS is driven by two interrelated concerns. The first bears upon the imperative of achieving a single securities market across the US by minimizing arbitrage opportunities in the same security across trading venues. The second pertains to best execution's legal certainty: anything that is not quantifiable is not easily enforceable. In effect, in its relatively long legal history, the concept of best execution had proved to be difficult to enforce in US courts (Macey and O'Hara 1997). Indeed, the

[8] This example has been provided by the European Commission (see *Frequently Asked Questions on MiFID: Draft implementing 'level 2' measures*, available at http://europa.eu/rapid/pressReleasesAction.do?reference=MEMO/06/57&format=HTML&aged=1&language=EN&guiLanguage=fr).

Table 4.1 Factors affecting best execution[9]

Costs	Costs can be both explicit and implicit. Explicit costs could include transaction costs (for example, settlement costs) and the costs of accessing particular execution venues (for example, costs of the necessary software/hardware to link to an execution venue). Implicit costs result from how a trade is executed (for example, immediately or patiently, in a block, aggregated with other trades, or in segments at different execution venues). A trade may appear more expensive in terms of explicit costs but may be less expensive when implicit costs are considered. For example, a broker that works a large order patiently, preserving the client's confidentiality, may achieve the lowest total costs (and the best net price).
Size	The best price in a market usually represents an opportunity to trade in a particular size (that is, number of relevant securities, contracts, units or the like), which may not match the size that the client wishes to trade. Where the client wishes to execute a larger size, if part of the order is executed at the indicated size, the price for subsequent executions may become less favourable (that is, the market may move). On the other hand, if the client wishes to execute a smaller size, the same price may not be available. In the context of selecting execution venues in an execution policy, size can refer to order sizes that an execution venue typically accepts.
Speed	Obviously, prices change over time. The frequency with which they do so varies with different instruments, market conditions and execution venues. If a firm considers that the cost of an adverse market movement is likely to be great, speed of execution may be very important. For large orders and orders for less liquid instruments, under certain market conditions, other considerations may outweigh speed.
Likelihood of execution	The best price may be illusory if the execution venue in question is unlikely to complete the order. In the context of selecting execution venues for an execution policy, the depth of trading opportunities at an execution venue – and thus, the likelihood that the execution venue will be able to complete the client order – may be relevant.
Likelihood of settlement	Best price also can be illusory if the execution venue offering that price cannot settle according to the customer's instructions.

[9] As specified by the UK FSA in its Discussion Paper DP06/3, *Implementing MiFID's best execution requirements* (May 2006). See, in particular, pp. 15–17.

Table 4.1 (*cont.*)

Nature of the order	The particular characteristics of an order, such as buy, sell, limit order, facilitation order, programme trade, stock loans, are always relevant to how it is executed. So any order constraint may be an important aspect of arrangements to obtain the best possible result. In the context of selecting execution venues for an execution policy, a firm that needs to execute these types of orders may consider whether and how well an execution venue performs.

main drawback of MiFID's flexible approach to best execution may reside in its limited enforceability.

In a 2006 discussion paper on best execution, the FSA clarified how the different factors affecting best execution can be interpreted. This overview is reproduced in table 4.1.

The best execution policy of a bank or investment firm must specify the relevant importance of the different factors in best execution. The detailed elaboration of the execution policy is the core provision of the best execution obligation under MiFID, which must follow the general criteria the directive sets. In this sense, MiFID concerns as much the process as the outcome. The means by which an investment firm aims to achieve best execution for its clients are as important as the outcome. Investment firms need to provide appropriate information about their best execution policy to their clients. In that way, clients can determine the quality of execution they are receiving, and clients as well as regulators can question the process the firm followed. In case client orders are internalized, investment firms need to obtain prior express consent in the form of a general agreement or on a transaction-by-transaction basis. A regular assessment of the firm's best execution policy must take place, and – when appropriate – an update should be implemented. Clients must be provided with the necessary information about the transaction, and be able to check whether the transaction was executed according to the firm's policy.

An investment firm does not need to provide best execution to 'eligible counterparties' such as investment firms, UCITS managers, insurance companies, pension funds managers and other authorized financial institutions (art. 24.1). If the national regulator permits, an investment firm can also treat major non-financial corporations as eligible counterparties. However, eligible counterparties can choose to opt in the best execution regime, either on a general basis or on a trade-by-trade basis (art. 24.2). Since institutional investors such as large asset managers act on behalf of an underlying beneficiary (often retail clients), they may feel obliged to ask for conduct of business protections in order to comply with their general fiduciary duty. Indeed, this has largely turned out to be the case in the post-MiFID world.

Some have argued that the broad definition of best execution in MiFID could lead to litigation, setting the standard for a more limited application of the best execution criteria in the future. Because MiFID's best execution relies on process as much as outcomes, fears about litigation may be overplayed. To the extent that a firm is able to demonstrate that it followed the process it set out in its execution policy, it faces a lesser degree of risk. Moreover, by allowing flexibility in devising a best execution policy that suits the agent, MiFID increases the likelihood that investment firms will abide by their own standards.

6. Application of MiFID's best execution requirements to non-equity instruments: fixed income and structured products

MiFID's duty of best execution covers all financial instruments, except spot foreign exchange. However, given the differences in market structures and in the nature of financial instruments, it may be difficult to identify and apply a uniform standard of best execution across the board. Therefore, best execution obligations need to be applied in a manner that takes into account the different circumstances associated with the execution of orders related to particular types of financial instruments.[10]

For equity securities, detailed pre- and post-trade transparency requirements apply because the securities are mostly traded on a central order book of an exchange. On the other hand, fixed income securities, certificates and structured notes, derivative financial instruments (other than exchange-traded futures and options) and forward foreign exchange contracts are mostly traded over-the-counter (OTC), that is in bilateral, self-regulated transactions.[11] The fragmented nature of trading in OTC transactions means that transparency requirements do not fit neatly with these types of instruments. Best execution is a concept that is best suited to an environment where economies of scale naturally lead trading to cluster on a centralized trading venue, such as a consolidated limit order book.

[10] As stated in recital 70 of the Commission Implementing Directive.

[11] The International Swaps and Derivatives Association (ISDA) provides guidelines and standardization for OTC contracts as well as arbitration protocols.

This model does not extend easily to the *fixed income* universe. Unlike the equity space where a company issues a single share class (or maybe a handful, if preference shares are considered), the issuance of debt securities does not benefit from economies of scale due to the vast number of debt instruments a single issuer can emit in various forms. Hence most of these securities will be much less liquid than shares. Naturally, the question of how best execution applies for such instruments arises. This issue should not be overemphasized, however. Best execution under MiFID is based on more than price alone; it takes a broad set of criteria into account, and must be laid down in a detailed execution policy of the bank. Yet the fact that no price transparency requirements apply and no centralized order books exist leaves users in the dark in verifying best execution.

Structured products present another interesting challenge, as their creation is the result of intense proprietary development techniques and heavy intellectual capital input. Because only developers are equipped to understand and price the structure of complex financial instruments, issuers often act as the sole liquidity point. This means they can effectively create a captive secondary market by virtue of the product's nature. In effect, if investors wish to redeem their investment prior to maturity, they must accept the price issuers' offer without the possibility of getting quotes from other trading venues.

Undoubtedly, if product manufacturers were forced by regulation to prise open the hood of their product to reveal the engine, so to speak (which would be a necessary condition for other market makers to price the product accurately), other firms could easily replicate the characteristics of a structure. Yet these proprietary characteristics are what give a structured product its competitive edge in the market. Forcing greater transparency in the secondary market (and even the primary market) for structured products would provide manufacturers with little incentive to invest in the people and technologies needed to develop leading-edge products that offer solutions to their clients' investment needs. From the point of view of investment strategy, this would be particularly damaging, as structured products have emerged as an asset class of their own right. They also give investment managers a unique ability to fine-tune their clients' portfolios to suit their investment needs by acting as a 'tactical overlay' to a modelled investment strategy, either for hedging purposes or to give the flexibility to underweight or overweight certain asset classes, sectors, and geographies in a portfolio.

Certain structured products are called 'vanilla', which means they are relatively straightforward, easy to replicate, and common in the marketplace. These products ought to be subject to best execution rules as such, since they are sufficiently standardized for multiple market makers to offer quotes rivalling those posted by the issuer, thereby creating competition in secondary market dealing. Moreover, 'vanilla' products do not involve the same degree of intellectual capital and technological inputs, which weakens the argument that they ought to enjoy a limited monopoly – much as in pharmaceutical patents – for the developer to recoup the sunk costs of their development.

While the concept of best execution does not associate with any particular market transaction, the characteristics of structured products call into question its applicability to this class of instruments. The fact that the manufacturers of a structured product have the ability to create a captive secondary market for their product means that they must apply some formalized policy of 'fair pricing' in the absence of competition in the secondary market. Likewise, on competitive trades where a product developer runs an auction to select a single counterparty from a panel of market makers to act as liquidity provider, best practice would dictate that the selection of counterparty should be sensitive to the secondary market pricing that counterparty can commit to.

Further to MiFID art. 65.1, the European Commission presented a report to the European Parliament on the issue of price transparency in non-equity markets in April 2008, and concluded that there is no need to extend pre- and post-trade transparency requirements at Community level to non-equity securities (see also Chapter 9). However, the report highlighted one concern: the access by retail investors to bond market prices. For the time being, the Commission indicated, this issue could be dealt with through self-regulatory measures. Industry federations, such as ICMA and SIFMA, have taken initiatives in this regard, which will be monitored by regulators. In particular, SIFMA (2008) published best execution guidelines for fixed-income securities, although it does not clearly indicate what best execution effectively is in fixed income transactions and how the guidelines will be monitored. Going forward, the success of the self-regulatory model will depend entirely on the ability of the industry to develop an effective solution to evidence and monitor the quality of execution in the non-equity space.

7. Implementing and monitoring a best execution strategy

Best execution is the basic concept underpinning the open architecture philosophy of MiFID. Whereas in the past, banks could internalize trades at least in certain jurisdictions, they now have to adapt to new requirements. Their systems must ensure that transactions are executed under the best possible conditions, following their best execution policy. Banks may have to outsource trade execution to third party providers, in case these can perform execution more efficiently than in-house entities. This should bring more competition in trade execution, leading to sizable benefits in terms of investor protection and market efficiency.

However, the practical implementation of best execution requirements raises administrative, technological and competitive challenges. IT systems need modernization to implement new best execution policies, and the updates must be reviewed on an ongoing basis in order to verify the technological infrastructure allows for the best possible result. A study estimated the one-off costs of the IT adaptations to be on the order of €100 million for large banks (JP Morgan 2006, see Chapter 1). These challenges are not limited to the development of a best execution strategy alone. They also extend to the documentation and monitoring of best execution. Importantly, investment firms have to analyse the performance of their best execution policy and adapt it in case it does not deliver the desired outcomes. They will have to keep records justifying their execution methodologies and decisions for five years. Thus, not only is the active monitoring of the execution quality paramount to the success of an individual firm's execution strategy, but it is also critical to the correct implementation of MiFID's principles-based approach to best execution.

There are several components in developing a sound execution monitoring framework. Connectivity comes at a price, yet it will be a central facet to any successful execution architecture post-MiFID. In the early days, it is very unlikely that liquidity will flow off the major exchanges such as LSE and Euronext. However, over time, if exchanges do not pay attention to changes in the competitive landscape by reducing fees and scaling up their service levels (e.g. reduced latency to facilitate fast-paced algorithmic trading programmes), in all likelihood they will lose market share. Brokers and buy-side firms have to closely monitor the evolution of liquidity flows across trading venues if their execution models are to remain competitive. The landscape may change rapidly once new multilateral trading facilities (MTFs) have established themselves as competitive actors. Initial evidence suggests that new MTFs such as Chi-X and Turquoise have been successful in capturing relatively large market shares in short periods of time. Antiquated software architectures, which have implicitly assumed that the major exchanges will remain the dominant liquidity pools by hard-coding them into their systems, will have to be upgraded or replaced at considerable expense to enable flexibility and connectivity to the leading execution venues as liquidity migrates over time.

Further, access to good quality data will be vital, not only to keep up to date on where the liquidity in the marketplace is flowing, but also to sustain a robust programme of post-trade analytics. It is only by regularly analysing execution data and by presenting execution metrics that a firm will be seen as having established a credible execution policy. Thus, the ability of investment firms to develop a coherent and robust methodology to monitor the quality of execution they are receiving is just as important to their execution strategy as the selection of execution venues.

In order to meet the requirements of MiFID's best execution obligation, firms may have to forego certain sources of income and adapt their operational structure. Vertically integrated investment firms may have to outsource certain parts of their business, which can no longer be executed competitively in-house. This will benefit third party services providers, be it new trading venues, IT consultants or solution providers. MiFID will thus have a long-lasting impact on the structure of Europe's financial markets.

While the best execution obligation is often portrayed as a costly administrative burden, it would be a mistake to overlook the strategic and marketing opportunity it presents for nimble firms with foresight. Precisely because MiFID amounts to a principles-based regime, the execution strategies firms implement are likely to be diverse – across EU member states and within them. The ability of broker-dealers and alternative trading systems to siphon liquidity off the main exchanges and the heavy investment necessary in software, connectivity protocols, and talent to support a leading-edge execution platform present innovative firms with great strategic opportunities. This strategic opportunity extends equally to buy-side firms, whether they have the capability to feed client orders directly into the order books of trading venues via direct market access (DMA) protocols or whether they invest in developing a sophisticated order handling strategy, tailored to clients' preferences and to the instruments being dealt, using a network of market-facing firms which are recognized as specialists in the said instruments.

Buy-side firms (i.e. firms such as pension funds and asset managers) in addition to brokers will have to remain attuned to changes in the execution landscape, as they are bound by a duty to monitor the quality of execution they are achieving for the beneficiary owners underlying pooled funds. In addition, buy-side firms should have a commercial imperative to deliver best execution. Irrespective of the regulatory obligation best execution imposes, quantitative finance has demonstrated that the reduction of transaction costs is an often overlooked way to generate alpha (or out-performance over a benchmark). Fund managers who do not internalize explicit as well as implicit costs in their execution decisions will see the ability of their fund to outperform a benchmark suffer. Managers of passive funds following index-tracking strategies are likely to see wider tracking errors if they do not manage transaction costs carefully.

While the introduction of MiFID did not and will not have the explosive overnight effect on execution models that the 1986 'Big-Bang'[12] had on the London financial centre, it is likely that, over time, its effects on market structures will be just as significant. Prior to the implementation of MiFID, particularly in the UK, the overriding theme was generalized concern on the negative competitive impact MiFID would have by increasing firms' cost bases. While the costs are evident to all, the opportunities are more difficult to detect. Those market participants who can anticipate the new competitive threats they face post-MiFID, as well as identify and capitalize on the opportunities the new landscape presents, will emerge as the clear winners of the regime shift.

References

Board, John and Stephen Wells 2001. 'Liquidity and best execution in the UK: A comparison of SETS and Tradepoint', *Journal of Asset Management* 1(4): 344–65.

Coase, Ronald H. 1937. 'The nature of the firm', *Economica* 16(4): 386–405.

1960. 'The problem of social cost', *Journal of Law and Economics* 3(1): 1–44.

Easterbrook, Frank H. and Daniel R. Fischel 1991. *The Economic Structure of Corporate Law*. Boston, MA: Harvard University Press.

Edhec-Risk Advisory 2007. 'Transaction Cost Analysis in Europe: Current and Best Practices', European Survey, January.

[12] The 'Big-Bang' is a term used to describe the fundamental changes to the execution landscape in the UK following significant reforms by the Thatcher government. Trading volumes skyrocketed within a very short period of the combination of de-regulatory and pro-competitive reforms such as the abolition of fixed-commission charges and the shift from open-outcry trading to electronic trading platforms.

European Commission 2008, *Report on non-equity markets transparency pursuant to art. 65(1) of Directive 2004/39/EC.*

European Parliament 2001. A5-0105/2001, *Report on the Commission communication on the application of conduct of business rules under article 11 of the Investment Services Directive (93/22/EEC) (COM(2000) 722–C5–0068/2001–2001/ 2038(COS)),* Committee on Economic and Monetary Affairs, 23 March.

Financial Service Authority 2001. 'Best Execution', Discussion Paper, April.

2002. 'Best Execution', Consultation Paper 154, October.

Garbade, Kenneth D. and William L. Silber 1981. 'Best execution in securities markets: an application of signaling and agency theory', Papers and Proceeding of the Fortieth Annual Meeting of the American Finance Association, Washington DC, 28–30 December, 1981, *Journal of Finance* 37(2): 493–504.

Giraud, Jean-René and Catherine D'Hondt 2006. *MiFID: Convergence Towards a Unified European Capital Markets Industry.* London: Risk Books.

Harris, Lawrence 1996. 'The economics of best execution', paper presented at New York Stock Exchange Conference on the Search for the Best Price, New York, 15 March.

International Organization of Securities Commission 2003. 'Objectives and principles of securities regulation', May.

Iseli, Thomas, Alexander F. Wagner and Rolf H. Weber 2007. 'Legal and economic aspects of best execution in the context of the Markets in Financial Instruments Directive', *Law and Financial Markets Review* July: 31–43.

JP Morgan 2006. MiFID Report I & II. A new wholesale banking law.

Macey, Jonathan R. and Maureen O'Hara 1997. 'The law and economics of best execution', *Journal of Financial Intermediation* 3(6): 188–223.

MiFID Connect 2007. *Guidelines on the application of the best execution requirements under the FSA rules implementing MiFID in the UK,* January.

Mitnick, Barry M. 1973. 'Fiduciary rationality and public policy: The theory of agency and some consequences', paper presented at the 1973 Annual Meeting of the American Political Science Association, New Orleans, Louisiana, September.

Moloney, Niamh 2002. *EC Securities Regulation.* Oxford: Oxford University Press.

Munck, Nikolaj Hesselholt 2005. 'When share transactions went high-tech', OMX Exchanges Focus Series No. 105, December.

NASD 2001. 'NASD Notice to Members 02-11', April.

The Restatement (Third) of Agency 2006.

Ross, Stephen A. 1973. 'The economic theory of agency: the principal's problem', *American Economic Review* 62(2): 134–9.

Securities and Exchange Commission (1962) 'INVESTMENT SERVICE CO.' Release No. 6884, 1962 SEC LEXIS 577; 41 S.E.C. 188 (15 August).

SIFMA 2008. 'Best execution guidelines for fixed-income securities', Asset Management Group, White Paper, January.

Smidt, S. 1982. 'Best execution in securities markets: an application of signaling and agency theory: discussion', Papers and Proceeding of the Fortieth Annual Meeting of the American Finance Association, Washington DC, 28–30 December 1981, *Journal of Finance* 37(2): 519–21.

5

Financial market data and MiFID[1]

The opening up of the market for equity market data, as foreseen in the MiFID, raises the question of whether data will be sufficiently consolidated and of high enough quality, or whether the information will become too fragmented, thereby hindering price transparency and the implementation of best execution policies. This chapter outlines the market for financial market data, the provisions of MiFID and the implementing measures regarding financial data and data consolidation. It also looks at the approaches taken by Committee of European Securities Regulators, the FSA and the US authorities. It concludes that markets should be capable of adapting and that additional licensing requirements, such as those proposed by the FSA, are in fact premature and might act as a barrier to the single market. Nor does it find that a US-style monopoly consolidator would be needed.

1. Introduction

One aspect of the MiFID that is rarely discussed is its impact on the financial market data business. MiFID not only abolishes the concentration rule for trading of equity securities, but also for market data generated from these trades. Whereas today market data on equity transactions is primarily controlled by the exchanges, MiFID leaves open how and by whom this information will be consolidated in the future. It says only that it should be done on a reasonable commercial basis, and as close to real time as possible. This raises the question of whether the market will provide sufficiently consolidated market data by itself or whether the data will become too fragmented, perhaps requiring an initiative by the authorities to create a single consolidated tape along the lines of the US

[1] This chapter is based on a paper that was first presented at the conference on MiFID Implementation 2007, which took place in Brussels on 8–9 March 2007. An earlier version was published in the *Journal of Securities Operations and Custody*, (2008) 1(2).

National Market System (NMS) model devised by the Securities and Exchange Commission (SEC).

Data consolidation is an essential prerequisite for the emergence of a true single market in equity trading, because it ensures that: (1) the law of one price holds across trading venues (i.e. the same security is traded at the same price) which is a precondition for market efficiency; (2) market participants have equal access to price discovery, so that there is a level playing field as regards access to market information; (3) best execution can more readily be verified. Given that business decisions are driven by private returns rather than by considerations of public good, it remains to be seen whether the industry will be able to come up with credible solutions to overcome coordination failures in achieving consolidation within an acceptable time frame, without regulatory intervention. Yet what is the optimal role for the regulator to play to this end, and what precisely is the scope and degree of desirable regulatory intervention in the field of data consolidation? These questions remain unanswered.

2. The financial market data business

The demand for market data is dominated by a few global data providers such as Bloomberg, Thomson Financial and Reuters (the latter two are in the process of merging their operations), and a multitude of specialist providers, amongst which are the exchanges for equity and derivatives data and other trading platforms and trade associations. But the market is extremely competitive – this is reflected in the relatively low valuation of the incumbents – and is undergoing rapid change as a result of technological progress and regulatory developments. In addition to the IT companies, ratings agencies and financial media which are striving for a higher share of the data vending business, firms such as Google have also indicated their interest in providing financial information for free. The core competitive strength of these firms is their ability to amalgamate financial information from different venues as rapidly and accurately as possible and to disseminate it to a wide range of subscribers simultaneously.

The large data vendors generate revenues of about €2 billion each from data vending. Reuters generated income of about €2.5 billion from data vending, of which about 55 per cent comes from Europe. Thomson Financial generated €1.6 billion from data vending, predominantly in the US. Bloomberg, which is not listed but incorporated as a partnership (LP), provides no financial data about itself at all on its website, which is

Table 5.1 Revenues of the three largest data vendors versus three largest European stock exchanges' information divisions

€ million	**2004**	**2005**	**2006**
Big Three data vendors			
Reuters Group plc	3,431	3,534	3,753
Bloomberg	n.a.	n.a.	n.a.
Thomson Financial	1,397	1,510	1,605
Big Three stock exchange information divisions			
Deutsche Börse	122	130	148
Euronext	87	94	112
LSE	128	147	156

Source: Annual reports. Data for LSE are for book year closed on 31 March 2007.

surprising for a firm that lives by selling financial information about others.

By comparison, the total revenue from data vending reported by the six largest EU exchanges was €546 million (2006), which is 12.5 per cent of their total revenues. The most important are the Deutsche Börse and the London Stock Exchange, with about €150 million revenues each. Over time, this source of revenue has stayed *grosso modo* within the same proportions for exchanges, but has moved according to market activity. The overall ratio, however, varies widely with some exchanges being much more dependent on trade data revenues than others (see table 5.2). In the US, (equity) market data revenues totalled $434 million (2004), 90 per cent of which was shared by the - self-regulatory organizations (SROs), which are connected to the exchanges.[2]

Investment banks have not stayed on the sidelines either, and see a possibility in MiFID to 'internalize' market data revenues, rather than pay others for data which they generate themselves. In September 2006, a consortium of nine investment banks launched the Project Boat, a venue for trade-data reporting. The nine investment banks behind the project are ABN Amro, Citigroup, Credit Suisse, Deutsche Bank, Goldman Sachs, HSBC, Merrill Lynch, Morgan Stanley and UBS, which have about a 50 per

[2] SEC Release No. 34-51808, File No. S7-10-04, p. 238.

Table 5.2 Stock exchange revenues from trading relative to revenues from information sales

Ratio	1999	2000	2001	2002	2003	2004	2005	2006
LSE	0.56	0.74	0.75	0.97	1.04	1.16	1.24	1.54
Euronext	3.37	3.88	2.20	5.22	5.35	5.89	5.86	6.27
Deutsche Börse	4.48	5.31	4.66	4.46	5.10	5.12	5.19	5.49
Borsa Italiana					2.13	1.63	1.89	2.47
OMX				4.98	3.98	3.25	2.22	2.19
BME					6.43	6.38	6.77	6.22

Source: Annual reports. Data for LSE are for book year closed on 31 March 2007.

cent market share in equity trading in Europe.[3] Under existing rules, intermediaries must report equity trades made off-exchange to a recognized trading venue, i.e. the main regulated market in every member state. Under Project Boat, exploiting the opportunities created by MiFID, banks consolidate equity trade data information pre- and post-trade themselves, pre-trade to coordinate prices for shares which they offer in systematic internalization, and post-trade to commercialise their trade information.[4]

3. The MiFID regime and its implementation

The concentration rule of the Investment Services Directive (ISD) not only gave the exchanges control over the market in trading of equity securities, but also over the market in trade data. With its abolition under MiFID, and the expected multiplication of trading venues, several questions arise. On the regulatory side, the issue is to what extent market data will remain sufficiently consolidated to allow the price discovery process to function efficiently. On the market structure side, the question is how the markets will adapt: how are banks going to react, to what extent will the data vending activities of exchanges be affected, what will the big data vendors do, and what opportunities arise in markets where price transparency does not yet apply.

3 The information about Project Boat is based upon a presentation by Will Meldrum of Markit at a conference on MiFID in Brussels, 8–9 March 2007. In January 2008, Markit confirmed it acquired Project Boat from the consortium of nine investment banks which set it up.

4 Data indicate that Boat was one of the early winners of MiFID, acquiring a market share of 16 per cent in European equity market data: see www.reuters.com/mifid.

MiFID requires regulated markets (art. 45), multilateral trading facilities (MTFs) (art. 30) and systematic internalizers (art. 28) 'to make public the price, volume and time of the transactions' 'as close to real time as possible' and 'on a reasonable commercial basis'. For internalizers, the directive adds that this should also be 'in a manner which is easily accessible to other market participants' (art. 28.1). The same requirements apply *grosso modo* for pre-trade information for regulated markets (art. 44), multilateral trading facilities (MTFs) (art. 29) and systematic internalizers (art. 27), with the obligation 'to make public current bid and offer prices and the depth of the trading interest at these prices', which can be waived for large transactions. This only applies to equity transactions for the time being, as there is no mandatory pre- and post-trade transparency for other financial instruments. In addition, recital 34 of MiFID recommends that: 'Member States remove any obstacles which may prevent the consolidation at European level of the relevant information and its publication.'

A core issue in MiFID is thus that market data can be commercialized. MiFID recognizes the proprietary nature of market data, which can lead to a fairly profound alteration in the structure we have in place today.[5] Investment firms can publish trade information (art. 27.7 for pre-trade and art. 28.3 for post-trade) through three avenues: through exchanges or MTFs; through third-party distributors (data vendors); or through 'proprietary arrangements'. Articles 44.1 and 45.1 specify that the services of exchanges can be used: 'Regulated markets may give access, on reasonable commercial terms and on a non-discriminatory basis, to the arrangements they employ for making public the information to investment firms.' Precise conditions were left to the implementing measures.

MiFID's implementing regulation regime (Commission Regulation 2006/73/EC) on the publishing of pre- and post-trade information regarding equity transactions is essentially identical, irrespective of the trading venue. These harmonized trade publication requirements were introduced to ensure that orders being routed through a particular trading venue enjoy the same level of transparency (at least in terms of price) as those being routed to other venues. Article 27 requires the post-trade transparency along six information points: trading day; trading time; instrument identification; unit price; quantity and quantity

[5] The EU took a similar approach for the dissemination of price-sensitive information with the Transparency Directive (2004/109/EC), where it abolished national monopolies, and introduced a series of minimum criteria.

notation; and venue.[6] Article 29 sets a maximum of three minutes for the publication of post-trade information, with publication delays applying for large transactions,[7] and art. 30. states that pre- and post-trade information can be judged to be publicly available if it is available through an exchange, an MTF, the facilities of a third party, or proprietary arrangements. The criteria for making this information public are set in art. 32, which determines that:

- the procedures must be in place to check that the information published is reliable and monitored continuously for errors;
- consolidation of data with similar data from other sources must be facilitated;
- information must be available to the public on a non-discriminatory basis at a reasonable cost.

Transparency measures aimed at overcoming market fragmentation rely on an efficient market data infrastructure spanning trading venues, and interlinking them in real time through regular, accurate, complete and simultaneous information flows. With the MiFID, European regulators decided that, by dismantling the concentration rule, the benefits of a competitive information market outweighed the potential risks. Nevertheless, they hedged the risk of market fragmentation damaging those benefits by introducing a strict pre- and post-trade transparency regime for equity transactions, also for internalizers.

The means through which post-trade information should be published, how widely post-trade information should be disseminated, and to whom it should be accessible were left undefined. These are questions which the directive leaves unanswered, with the result that the optimal degree of regulatory intervention in the field of trade data transparency will be a difficult equilibrium to find. That a discussion has arisen around a particular transparency issue – the required degree of market data consolidation – is therefore not in the least surprising.

Further to a consultation of market participants, CESR came to the conclusion, for the time being at least, that no binding measures were needed to ensure data quality, consolidation and dissemination, but that

[6] Table 1 of Annex I of the Regulation.

[7] A maximum delay of up until the end of the second trading day following the day on which the trade was executed applies. The European Commission has taken a relative, not absolute, view of trade size when considering deferred publication. In order to qualify for deferred publication, what matters more than ticket size is the ratio of the ticket size to the average daily turnover in that share.

a series of guidelines and recommendations would suffice (CESR, 2007). They comprise data quality, publication arrangements, availability of transparency information, and publication standards. To facilitate data consolidation, CESR proposed that investment firms that internalize trades or trade OTC use only one primary publication channel. In addition, CESR considered it useful for data consolidators to 'flag a trade' of which they are the primary publication channel. This should allow data consolidators to distinguish between primary and secondary publication and limit the risk of duplication.

As regards the time limit for the availability of trade information, the CESR guidelines restate the maximum three minutes of the implementing regulation, but that as a rule it should go much faster. Inadequate technology cannot be used as an argument 'for publication close to three minutes on a frequent basis'. In addition, CESR states that the supply of pre- and post-trade information cannot be made conditional on the purchase of other services (guideline 9). Other guidelines concern the need for an ongoing process of verification by data providers, contingency procedures and the use of industry standards.[8]

The UK's Financial Services Authority (FSA) took a diametrically opposed route to CESR, and proposed binding rules for data providers in order to ensure data quality and to counter fragmentation. The FSA claims that the expected growth of off-exchange trading will increase the probability of data fragmentation. This will 'reduce market transparency, hinder price discovery and undermine equity market efficiency', which will make it harder for firms to check best execution. Data should continue to be monitored effectively, also under MiFID, and the FSA argues that it cannot afford to take the risk of waiting to see if market forces will deliver a solution: 'acting to consolidate after fragmentation has occurred would be more costly' (FSA 2006, pp. 103–4).

Consequently, the FSA introduced minimum standards for data consolidators, which it terms Trade Data Monitors (TDMs), which came into force with MiFID in November 2007 (FSA 2007, pp. 59–63). Before authorizing a TDM, the FSA will make a series of assessments covering security of information, data integrity, timely dissemination, systems and resources, and contingency planning. A TDM must make trade

[8] An MoU was signed between the two dominant players in the messaging business: Swift, which has a quasi-monopoly over back-office post-trade reporting with the ISO 15022 and 20022 standard, and FIX, which is the dominant player in the pre-trade space with its latest Fix 4.4.

information available on a reasonable non-discriminatory commercial basis, in a manner which is easily accessible to other market participants. TDMs would be responsible for monitoring in real time the trades reported to them for errors, and for contacting the reporting firm for correcting the trade information. The FSA says it does not intend to limit the number of TDMs, and that they could also be non-UK based entities.

The FSA was not, therefore, prepared to wait for the outcome of a report, requested of the Commission under art. 65.4 of MiFID one year after the entry into force of the directive, i.e. in October 2008, 'on the state of the removal of the obstacles which may prevent the consolidation at the European level of the information that trading venues are required to publish'. Although it judged the risk too high to wait, it is in fact another example of gold-plating, in addition to the four that were formally communicated by the FSA to the European Commission further to art. 4 of the 2006 MiFID implementing directive (FSA 2007), but in this case, it was for a matter covered by the Implementing Regulation, which is directly applicable in national law, and does not need to be implemented. It could also be seen as a way to protect the data services of the London Stock Exchange, which is already doing what TDMs are expected to do under the new regime. The question can be raised how TDMs will apply to foreign firms, such as non-UK exchanges, which are selling data on the UK market. Will non-UK consolidators also need to have an FSA licence? How will the UK FSA monitor compliance of consolidators established outside the UK? These questions are discussed in the next section.

4. Will a market-led approach to data consolidation work?

A comparison with the debt markets does not immediately offer any reassurance that a market-led approach to post-trade data consolidation will work.[9] Debt markets, which mostly take place OTC and are decentralized over a multitude of trading venues, are hardly a good example of a transparent market, despite initiatives underway to increase their level of transparency. Retail investors lack good data on bond markets, and no or limited consolidated data sources exist to verify best execution, which will be required under MiFID.[10] The FSA, which argues that it is too risky to

[9] For a more detailed discussion of this issue, see Chapter 9.

[10] The International Capital Markets Association (ICMA) launched www.BondMarketPrices.com in December 2007 to provide retail investors with direct access to an extensive range of pricing information on bonds. It offers visitors that day's traded and quoted pricing information at the end of each day.

wait for equity market data to fragment and to affect price formation and market efficiency, may thus have a point when it is proposing to set criteria for TDMs.

However, price transparency now essentially concerns equity markets, and they remain fundamentally different from debt markets. Transactions in the latter still take place predominantly OTC, are characterized by a multitude of instruments and maturities, and only a fraction of the debt securities outstanding are traded regularly. Equity securities are much more homogeneous, they are traded much more frequently, and there are only about 890 highly liquid European shares (according to CESR's MiFID database, i.e. shares on which trading may be internalized by European banks following the rules set in MiFID art. 27).

In this sense, it could be argued that the FSA initiative is premature and even poses risks to pan-European consolidation. It is likely that the markets will adapt to the new environment, for a variety of reasons:

1. As exchanges are expected to remain the main source of liquidity and price formation after MiFID, they will also be the primary source of the trade data.
2. There are competitors to the data aggregation activities of exchanges in the market, which have the necessary structure and processes in place, and the incentives to react.
3. MiFID creates the possibility for new providers to enter the market.

Most studies so far agree that exchanges will remain the main source of liquidity after MiFID (see, e.g., JPMorgan 2006). This means that their trade data will also remain qualitatively the best, at least for some time to come, and that, therefore, exchanges can be expected to continue to benefit from network effects. The revenues derived from these services will, however, most likely decline. Exchanges will need to be more active to sell their services and buy data from internalizers, whereas in the past they used to get this for free. And there will be more competitors active in the data market to take a slice of this market. On the other hand, as trading volumes are expected to grow with MiFID as a result of increased competition and lower transaction costs, so will the market-for-market data. In addition, because of the conduct of business and best execution rules, banks will need to check trades more regularly and maintain records, thereby reinforcing demand again.

Apart from the exchanges, data vendors and other firms can also be expected to react to the opening up of the market for equity market data. Reuters and Bloomberg will certainly not sit aside, as the data can be commercialized and because this has been their core business for many years. Other firms too, which are active in IT or consulting, may see this as an opportunity to develop new products and enter the market for data. Banks themselves may see this as an interesting opportunity to make money from market data – a market which can be expected to grow with MiFID. The announcement of Project Boat fits with this supposition.

In addition, it is not as though data were of top quality pre-MiFID. In markets not applying the concentration rule, trades executed off-market were not necessarily reported or incorporated rapidly in the on-market statistics. The extensive use of off-exchange trading in the German inter-dealer and institutional market means that many trades went unreported. In the UK, off-exchange trading was mostly reported through the London Stock Exchange, but non-domestic trades will surface, which today account for 8 per cent of overall trade volume.[11] Hence MiFID, by formally mandating disclosure and allowing commercialization, could improve the quantity and quality of market data.

But there are certainly drawbacks and risks to a market-led approach, the most important of them being data quality and the lack of technical standardization. As trades diverge over a multitude of venues, trade data quality may diminish, making the best execution requirement, which applies across markets, more difficult to ensure. Will exchanges and data aggregators be capable of consolidating this information at a high level? As data become proprietary, exchanges may no longer be interested in paying to aggregate the data from third parties. In addition, there is the question of the public availability of market data. These are issues that are probably best left to the European Commission to address in its 2008 review. However, setting unilateral national standards, as the FSA proposes to do, constitutes an obstacle to European consolidation.[12] Although the FSA says its standards are optional, it is difficult to see how a data provider would not be bound by these rules, or how a bank could use a non-licensed data provider to monitor best execution.

[11] *Securities Industry News*, 27 January 2007.

[12] If other national regulators decide to follow the FSA example by imposing national standards, it seems inevitable that MiFID's intention of achieving pan-European data consolidation will be made more difficult, if not impossible. It could also be argued that the FSA initiative goes against the EU E-commerce Directive (98/48/EC), which outlawed national authorization schemes for information society services.

5. Market data consolidation under the US NMS rule

The EU's approach differs radically from what is in place in the US, and what is being modified in the context of the Regulation National Market System (Reg NMS). The US requires mandatory consolidation of market data in a mutualized entity, and has a complex formula-based system in place to allocate the revenues to the nine self-regulatory organizations (SROs) that feed the data into the plan and set the pricing.

The provisions, adopted under rules 601 and 603 of Regulation NMS, as well as joint industry plans, are designed to promote the wide availability of market data. They should strengthen the existing market data system, which provides investors in the US equity markets with real-time access to the best quotations and most recent trades in the thousands of NMS stocks throughout the trading day. For each stock, quotations and trades are continuously collected from many different trading centres and then disseminated to the public in a consolidated stream of data. As a result, investors of all types have access to a reliable source of information for the best prices in NMS stocks. When the US Congress mandated the creation of the NMS in 1975, it noted that the systems for disseminating consolidated market data would 'form the heart of the national market system'.[13]

A single consolidator model for the dissemination of market data remains, however, very controversial. As with other networks, it exposes the problems that a single entity can cause.[14] For a European reader, not only does it appear to be alien to the US system, it also means that competition is removed in data markets, which may negatively impact on the quality of the data and increase prices. In addition, all sources of data must be accessed and all data bought, meaning that users retain less freedom to get trade data that is best tailored to their needs. This means higher data fees for the end user, since the distributor/vendor must subscribe to all data sources. Furthermore, the complex pricing system leads to gaming ('tape shredding') and distortion, since the SROs have no incentive to lower their pricing.[15]

In consultations in the US with market participants regarding a proposal to overhaul the existing consolidation, several market commentators argued for a competing consolidators model, where pricing and consolidation specifications are determined by market forces. Several

[13] SEC, Release No. 34-51808, File No. S7-1l1-04, p. 30

[14] It is interesting to note that in the area of securities settlement the US also has a single entity, whereas the EU has competing entities.

[15] For a detailed discussion on this question, see Mehta (2006).

commentators, for example, were convinced that the level of the fees was too high. Following the recommendations of an ad-hoc committee, the SEC considered that the single consolidator model was to be preferred, as it benefits investors, particularly retail, to help them to assess quotes when they place an order and to evaluate the best execution of their orders.[16] Changes to that model would thus compromise the integrity and reliability of the consolidated data stream, according to the SEC.

6. Conclusion

The opening up of the market for equity market data is part of the MiFID revolution, but the impact on the market structure is difficult to forecast. It can be expected that exchanges will fight to defend their position, but they will certainly lose revenues from data vending, and may be forced to consolidate this activity with other operators. Many other groups are, however, preparing to enter into that market or to increase their market share, which should give comfort to regulators. In addition, the competitive effects of MiFID could improve data quality and availability.

The European Commission and CESR will have to closely monitor market developments and data quality in the months following the entry into force of MiFID. The maintenance of a single consolidator model in the US is a useful reminder that the most developed capital market in the world chose a radically different model from the EU. The UK's FSA, with its regime for Trade Data Monitors (TDMs), opted for a model of regulated competition, although this raises serious questions from a single market perspective, as it is in fact another example of national gold-plating – or silver-plating in this case (since it is optional) – but it is still difficult to see how a data provider would not be bound by these rules.

Another item to watch is data pricing. How prices will move is difficult to predict, but competition and the arrival of newcomers should keep them in line. Pricing will need to be watched in particular in relation to smaller players, as they will need similar access to data as their larger competitors to guarantee best execution, but may not have the same market power. Competition authorities will thus have to watch carefully how markets will adapt.

16 The Seligman Committee (or Market's Data Advisory Committee) was instituted by the SEC in 2001 to advise on the market data structure in the US. Interesting to note is that although a majority of members of the Committee apparently favoured a competing consolidators approach, the Committee did not formally propose it.

References

CESR 2007. *Publication and Consolidation of MiFID Market Transparency Data*, February: www.amf-france.org/documents/general/8069_1.pdf.

Financial Services Authority 2006. 'Implementing MiFID for firms and markets', CP 06/14, July. London: FSA.

Financial Services Authority 2007. 'Implementing MiFID', PSO7/2. London: FSA.

JPMorgan 2006. MiFID Report I & II. *A new wholesale banking landscape*. London: JPMorgan.

Mehta, Nina 2006. 'Reg NMS to drive tighter markets', *Traders Magazine*, November: www.tradersmagazine.com.

Wall Street & Technology 2006. 'MiFID rules break the exchange monopoly and trade reporting', October: www.wallstreetandtech.com/showArticle.jhtml?articleID=193400875.

6

Managing conflicts of interest: from ISD to MiFID

1. Conflicts of interest at the heart of financial services

Conflicts of interest are endemic to the provision of financial services in a free-market capitalist system. On the one hand, the senior management of the bank are held accountable to shareholders to maximize profits yet, on the other hand, the core of the activities banks undertake in retail client segments involves acting in a fiduciary capacity: whether the nature of the service provided is custodial (safekeeping of client assets), advisory (recommending a course of action to a client) or discretionary (being empowered by the client to act on their behalf), there is a breach of trust, and possibly of contract, if the bank and its staff do not act in a way that is aligned to clients' best interests. At a high level, these two fundamental objectives of a bank – maximizing corporate profits and acting in the best interests of clients – are, if not irreconcilable, at least difficult to align.

In the long run, one would expect that acting in the best interests of clients would be intimately tied to the ability of a bank to remain profitable. As game theory predicts, because traditional banking is a business activity which generally involves relationship-building and continuous service, as opposed to one-off contact with consumers, a bank or investment firm which is not seen by actual or potential clients to be treating them fairly or effectively managing its conflicts of interest is essentially doomed to fail as its clients leave with their assets for another institution. Presumably then, a self-regulatory solution to any potential conflict of interest would be effective, as a bank would be keen to align its interests with those of its clients.

The reality is more complex. Market imperfections can lead to a breakdown of the natural alignment of interests that prevails in perfectly competitive markets with perfect information. The financial services industry is characterized by a high degree of market imperfections including information asymmetry, agency costs and switching costs (Llewellyn 2005).

Asymmetric information describes situations where a product provider naturally knows much more about the financial product, having modelled it, developed it, stress-tested it, and knowing what the competing product set is and how it performs, than retail investors, who may not get hold of this information or understand it prior to entering into a contractual agreement. As a result, retail clients do not know as well as their adviser whether they are being sold a suitable investment. Another dimension of asymmetric information arise from the very nature of financial products, which is that it is only after the contractual agreement has been entered into, and only once the product has been 'consumed', that retail investors will know whether or not the product delivered what it promised (Llewllyn 2005).

The principal–agent problem arises when an agent is paid to carry out specific services on behalf of a client, within pre-agreed parameters defined by a contractual agreement. In imperfect markets, such relationships present particular challenges for the alignment of incentives between agent and principal, not least because, apart from the information asymmetries present, there are monitoring costs and the consumer does not purchase financial services frequently – thus having little with which to compare their experience. Therefore, it may be unclear what exactly is the value the agent is delivering to the principal, versus the amount that is charged for the service. Conflicts of interest arising in financial services also differ from those arising from principal–agent relationships in other professions, because, unlike other professions, financial advisers are bound by contracts only, and not by some kind of ethical norm – 'structural features' of the profession, such as a 'Hippocratic oath', as Boatright (2003) argues. Discretionary portfolio management is a good example of where agency risk arises in financial services, although the MiFID obligation to pre-agree a benchmark helps mitigate some of the agency risk by holding portfolio managers more accountable than they were before.

Finally, financial services are characterized by high search and switching costs. It takes time, effort and money to find new service providers. One of the built-in protections principals have in a competitive market is the ability to switch agents when they are unhappy with the service they receive. This protection is obviously less effective when retail investors are not sophisticated enough to compare the quality of service or product between different providers, or where switching costs are high, as they are in financial services compared with many other service industries.

The pressure for listed financial institutions to generate profit growth increased as a result of the financial liberalization carried out in advanced economies over the past three decades. Consequently, a more commercial mindset became embedded in the market for retail investments. Sales targets and minimum margin targets across various product offerings became widespread, leading to a sales mentality being adopted in financial institutions in some countries, as opposed to a genuine commitment to a fiduciary obligation accompanying the provision of financial advice. The UK Financial Services Authority (FSA) has even gone so far as to describe the market for retail investment products as 'broken', highlighting what it perceives to be a wide range of market failures (FSA 2007). The size and complexity of global financial institutions has also grown significantly since the 1980s, culminating in the reversal of the Glass-Steagall Act of 1933 by the Graham-Leech-Blailey Act of 1997. The long-held separation between investment and commercial banking imposed by the SEC presented significant new challenges for the management of conflicts of interest.

In light of these market imperfections, it becomes evident there is a need for financial regulation to be implemented in order to protect retail investors' interests. With respect to conflicts of interest, MiFID attempts to address such market imperfections in a more comprehensive manner than any previous European legislation relating to financial services.

The purpose of this chapter is several-fold: to give a brief summary of the evolution of European law on conflicts of interest with regard to the provision of investment services, to highlight the key differences between the conflict of interest provisions of the ISD and MiFID; to explain when a conflict must be managed by an investment firm, because it presents a 'material risk' of damaging client interests; to explain how to identify which type of control is most appropriate for managing certain kinds of conflict of interest; to define the process around the identification, management and disclosure of conflicts; and to list typical activities investment firms undertake, which are particularly susceptible to certain types of (potential) conflict(s) of interest.

2. Evolution of European law on conflicts of interest management in finance

Prior to the ISD, the regulation of conflicts of interest in the European financial services sector was very much a national competence. That is, few rules in this domain had been codified into European law – largely a reflection of the institutional nature of cross-border capital flows within the EEA, and the relatively unregulated nature of that business, where large institutional players were expected to look after their best interests. In addition, the cross-border provision of retail financial services was very limited pre-ISD. There was consequently no perceived need to develop a European retail investor protection regime, which also sought to harmonize regulation around the management of conflicts of interest.

Interestingly, regulatory regimes around conflicts of interest in financial services were largely undeveloped even at national level at the time. They were not prescriptive and did not impose much in the way of formal requirements on financial institutions, other than to develop an ill-defined obligation for regulated firms to 'act in clients' interests', in recognition of the fiduciary duties investment firms assume when acting as agent on behalf of a client.

With the ISD, the EU made its first attempt at developing a pan-European code of practice on conflicts of interest in relation to securities markets. Yet this attempt cannot in any way be considered to have been very serious. While the ISD recognized the 'danger of conflicts of interest',[1] even requiring this threat to investor protection to be explicitly addressed in the report on the ISD review, which the Commission was asked to submit to the Council of Ministers not later than December 1998, it did little to tackle this danger head-on. For example, arts. 10 and 11 ISD, both of which address conflicts of interest as the antecedents of respectively MiFID's organizational and conduct of business requirements, left enormous discretion to national regulatory authorities to develop conflicts of interest regimes as they saw fit.

In addition to the absence of a clear set of European rules defining proper conflicts of interest management, the ISD also provided for an explicit carve-out from the principle of home country control in this sphere: '. . . where a branch is set up the organisational arrangements may not conflict with the rules of conduct laid down by the host Member State to cover conflicts of interest'.[2] The effect of this carve-out was that a firm's internal governance model could not be leveraged across its European branches under the ISD 'passport'. Financial services providers therefore had to tailor their conflict management practices to local requirements, curtailing their ability to operate under a single internal governance platform, such as a standardized compliance policy framework. In the early years of the ISD this mattered little, since national regimes in this area were not very developed. Yet as member states had begun to put into

[1] Found in the preamble of Council Directive 93/22/EEC of 10 May 1993.
[2] Investment Services Directive, art. 10.

place more defined rules around conflicts of interest management at national level in the later years of the ISD, when the early stages of discussions on an ISD 2 (MiFID) had begun, the costs of the carve-out became more obvious.

Between the time of the ISD's and MiFID's respective implementations, certain developments had led to the elaboration of more defined regulatory requirements around conflicts of interest. These developments were a mixture of the necessity to respond to evolutions and events in the marketplace, such as major corporate scandals arising from conflicts of interest (described below), and the outcome of an influential school of thought known as the 'new institutional economics', which gained prominence during the 1990s with its focus on transparency, governance, process and institutional quality as key factors contributing to economic growth.[3] Outputs of the academic literature generated from proponents of this school yielded important insights into how institutional and corporate structures can lead to misaligned incentive structures.

Market events in the late 1990s underscored the need for more aggressive and robust regulation around conflicts of interest management, leading to the only serious attempt at European level to address conflicts of interest in the financial services sector prior to MiFID, in the form of the Market Abuse Directive (MAD).[4] MAD's provisions on conflicts of interest followed in the wake of corporate scandals that arose during the tech bubble of the 1990s, especially in the US; they were the reflection of a growing concern by European regulators that the existing policy framework was insufficient to tackle what could potentially develop into a significant problem. The FSA was particularly concerned, citing its lack of conviction: 'that there is sufficient understanding or acceptance in the market of the standards of conduct necessary [to deliver effective conflict management], or that investment banks' internal systems and controls are robust or consistent enough'.[5]

Because the MAD requirements on managing conflicts of interest arose largely as a targeted regulatory response to specific market failures that had been identified in the US, the scope of their application was limited, focusing mainly on investment research and activities relating to underwriting, such as the allocation of shares in Initial Public Offerings. Research analysts were seen to be inappropriately influenced by investment banking activities, something which regulators felt was happening

[3] See e.g. Brousseau and Glachant (2008).
[4] Market Abuse Directive 2003/6/EC.
[5] FSA (2003b, p. 2).

largely behind the scenes and required more transparency. The preferred policy tool to address this market failure and bring these hidden arrangements and interests into the light was to force disclosures by those producing or distributing research, so as to empower clients, users and stakeholders to make their own assessments of the potential for conflicted activity to damage their interests.

While MAD's framework for addressing these conflicts of interest did centre mostly around disclosure obligations, it nevertheless introduced elements prescribing more proactive conflicts of interest management. Though limited in scope, these elements provided an important stepping-stone towards the more comprehensive conflicts of interest regime MiFID would usher in. Under MAD, the areas which required better defined and more robust internal management controls, as opposed to reliance on disclosures alone, concentrated almost entirely on the activities of research and underwriting. On the research side, specific focus was given to: 'the supervision of a firm's analysts by the investment banking and sales and trading divisions of a firm; the involvement of analysts in marketing activities, such as pitching for investment banking mandates; their remuneration structures; and their susceptibility to pressure from subject companies'.[6] 'On the underwriting side, specific focus was given to discouraging the practices of 'spinning' and 'laddering'.[7]

Combined, these two pillars of the MAD conflicts regime – disclosure obligations together with a duty to proactively manage a limited set of conflicts – went significantly beyond the ISD's approach, which did little more than impose an ill-defined general fiduciary obligation in the area of conflicts management.

Although the FSA was one of the few European regulators which had enshrined general principles around the management of conflicts of interest as a pillar of its regulatory architecture prior to the introduction of MiFID (even independently of MAD), the requirements laid out in MiFID have since formalized the conflicts governance regime to a significantly greater extent than it was before, either at national or at the EU level. On the European continent, the formalization of regulatory norms around conflicts of interest management is relatively newer than in the UK. It is therefore likely that the various approaches taken by EEA securities regulators in transposing MiFID's conflicts sections into

6 FSA (2003b, p. 7).

7 The practice of brokerage houses exchanging IPO shares with top executives for reciprocating business from their companies (Investopedia definition).

national law may well be quite different, necessitating some work by CESR to ensure supervisory convergence in this area.

On the other hand, it can safely be assumed that the absence of investment research – which was the main focus of the conflicts of interest provisions of MAD – from the list of priority areas for the European Commission's ongoing review of MAD under the Lamfalussy process[8] – is, if nothing else, at least an implicit recognition that the MAD regime on conflicts of interest, combined with MiFID's, is considered to be at a minimum reasonably effective in achieving its objectives – at least for the time being.

The contrast between the ISD's and MiFID's wording on conflicts of interest is telling. It was symptomatic of the EU's intent to tackle them head-on, as it overhauled its conduct of business regime against the backdrop of new economic realities which presented their corresponding regulatory challenges. In the decade that elapsed between the implementation of the ISD and the birth of MiFID, global capital markets evolved rapidly along all dimensions: breadth, depth and scope. Financial deregulation, together with heightened international competition and a revolution in telecommunications, all of which had begun in earnest during the 1980s but accelerated during the 1990s, was rapidly changing the nature of financial services. In order to survive in the new landscape, banks and investment firms had to adapt to the new reality of the frenetic pace of global competition, necessitating new organizational structures which put a premium on agility and flexibility.

These new organizational structures were not without their risks. Banks increasingly turned to capital markets, as opposed to deposits, for funding to grow their balance sheets aggressively, buoyed by their strong credit ratings, leading to a massive over-leveraging of the financial sector. The rapid pace of financial innovation allowed little time to analyse properly the risks inherent to new products and entirely new asset classes. Incentive structures within and between firms were designed to maximize short-term profits and skewed, often to the detriment of firms' clients, market stability and shareholders. Consolidation in the sector led to the creation of financial behemoths that were considered 'too big to fail', amplifying systemic risk and moral hazard in the financial system.

While the ISD did little more than pay lip service to conflicts of interest management, a MiFID-style approach to conflicts in 1993 could have

[8] The promotion of inflated pre-IPO prices for the sake of obtaining a greater allotment of the offering (Investopedia definition).

been seen by market participants as a public recognition by European regulators that universal banking was a dangerous and unstable model for the banking industry. Politically, this could hardly have been a desirable message to convey at a time when Anglo-American financial institutions were establishing global dominance, and the universal banking model still remained stigmatized in the US since the Glass-Steagall Act of 1933 – at least until its reversal in 1997 by the Graham-Leech-Blailey Act. On the other hand, risk-taking by European universal banks only began to increase markedly once the pressures from competing with American investment banks led to a relaxation of traditionally strict risk controls, and to venturing into traditionally less familiar territory, such as the securitization market.

As banks remained the predominant vehicle for the distribution of financial services (accepting deposits, providing financial advice, manufacturing and selling investment products) to retail clients in Europe, their involvement in increasingly risky investment banking activities, and the potential for conflicts of interest to damage client interests, began to emerge more clearly, prompting corrective regulatory action. MiFID recital 29 is an explicit recognition that the more vigorous involvement of banks in capital markets, especially in continental Europe, could lead to more potential conflicts of interest: 'The expanding range of activities that many investment firms undertake simultaneously has increased potential for conflicts of interest between those different activities and the interests of their clients.'

3. Differences between MiFID and the ISD on conflicts

Unlike in the ISD, conflicts of interest do not fall under MiFID's conduct of business rules, but rather under the heading of organizational requirements. As a consequence, national regulators cannot invoke MiFID art. 31(7), which maintains a carve-out from home-country control for regulated activities carried out by locally authorized branches – yet the carve-out is limited to conduct of business rules and does not cover organisational requirements. In other words, under MiFID, host countries do not have discretion to impose their national regime on conflicts of interest on branches of foreign banks. Thus, large banks and investment firms providing services via branches in other EEA countries will be able to operate a uniform governance model – based on their home country regulators' implementation of MiFID – across all thirty EEA member states, covering the areas of conflicts of interest management, risk management (including operational risk derived from outsourcing functions), business continuity management, records management and asset safekeeping. Firms which leverage the uniform governance model MiFID affords could achieve economies of scale in infrastructure areas such as compliance and risk functions by operating under a single set of policies and procedures, thereby increasing operational efficiency.

Though the difference may appear subtle, the wording of MiFID art. 13(3) actually stands in stark contrast to ISD arts. 10 and 11, which it replaces (in part). While ISD art. 10 requires investment firms to '. . . be structured and organized in such a way as to minimize the risk of clients' interests being prejudiced by conflicts of interest', and Art. 11 ISD requires that firms 'try to avoid conflicts of interests and, when they cannot be avoided, ensure that clients are fairly treated', the mere fact of 'minimizing' or 'trying' is not considered sufficient under MiFID. Rather, firms are required 'to maintain and operate effective organizational and administrative arrangements with a view to taking all reasonable steps designed to prevent conflicts of interest from adversely affecting the interests of its clients'. The difference is not only one of degree, i.e. 'trying to avoid conflicts of interest' versus taking 'all reasonable steps'. It is also that MiFID properly spells out the main types of conflicts investment firms face, the types of situations giving rise to those conflicts, and it lays out the steps it expects firms to take to manage conflicts of interest. Nothing comparable appears in the ISD about the way firms must be structured and organized to minimize conflicts, or indeed how firms must avoid conflicts.

One could, therefore, argue that because of the lack of harmonizing principles giving effect to the provisions in ISD arts. 10 and 11, the ISD conflicts regime amounted less to a principles-based attempt at EU-wide harmonization than to a total devolvement of conflicts of interest regulation to national regulators. MiFID changed this, and ushered in a departure from existing rules in five important respects:

3.1 Scope

MiFID extended its provisions on conflicts management to cover transactions with all clients irrespective of their client categorization, including eligible counterparties. This is interesting, since it imposes a regulatory requirement to manage conflicts even in the institutional market. Prior to MiFID, where there were explicit rules around conflicts of interest management, they typically did not extend to professional investors, institutional players and wholesale markets.

3.2 Requirement to manage conflicts

The standard regulatory treatment of conflicts of interest pre-MiFID relied heavily on disclosures to clients. Under MiFID, disclosure alone is no longer considered a sufficient instrument for managing conflicts. Firms will have to proactively identify and manage conflicts, including potential conflicts, with different controls. Firms may only disclose the conflict to clients, if they have taken all reasonable steps to manage it first, and even so, they must obtain client consent prior to proceeding with the conflicted activity.

3.3 Inducements

MiFID imposes a general ban on inducements, unless they satisfy strict criteria, including a 'value-added' test, by which the firm must be able to demonstrate that accepting the inducement 'enhances the quality of the service' for its clients. This is a strong position, since they even extend to intra-group payments, and inducements are a pillar of product/service provider–distributor relationships in financial services. The ISD had made no mention of inducements.

3.4 Formal conflicts policy

There is a new requirement under MiFID for investment firms to maintain and regularly update an internal conflicts of interest policy, which sets out appropriately suited controls around the main conflicts of interest the firm faces. A summary of that policy must be circulated to all clients upon request.

3.5 Record-keeping

MiFID imposes a new requirement for firms to keep a record of material conflicts identified and the measures taken to manage them. The purpose of this rule is clearly to create an audit trail, which the regulator will be able to assess at any time in order to get an understanding of the quality of a firm's conflicts management and its management culture more generally. Maintaining proper documentation around conflicts of interest will be especially important in a post-MiFID, where the burden of proof is reversed and now sits squarely on the shoulders of firms.

4. Identifying conflicts of interest

4.1 The theory: an anatomy of conflicts

Conflicted activities hardly ever arise of their own right, but rather emerge in an environment that is conducive to them. A serious conflicts of interest management programme will therefore seek to understand how such an environment comes about, and identify mitigating factors, which can be implemented to minimize the risk of client detriment that might result from conflicted activity.

Proper management of conflicts under MiFID will therefore require an analysis of the various stages of the lifecycle of conflicts of interest. Broadly, this lifecycle can be thought of as comprising three distinct elements: root cause, proximate source and specific conflict (see figure 6.1). Working backwards from a situation where a specific conflict of interest has arisen, one can identify the type of activity which has given rise to the conflict (the proximate source), as well as the root cause at the origin of the conflict. One or more core 'ingredients' lie at the heart of every conflict of interest, either breeding them directly, or indirectly contributing to their development. These can be called the 'root causes'.

Figure 6.1 Identifying the root cause

The common denominator between all root causes of conflicts of interest is almost always a misaligned incentive structure. Misaligned incentive structures occur when the firm or its staff have an incentive – monetary or otherwise – to act in a way that is not aligned with their clients' best interest. Effective conflicts management will therefore almost always require that incentive structures are designed in such a way that they align the interests of the firm and its staff with those of its clients.

For this reason, identifying and removing the root causes from which all conflicts of interest originate constitutes an essential building block in the development of a sound governance model. In addition, such an approach is essential to comply with MiFID, since conflicts must be prevented and managed in the first instance under the Directive's rules, before resorting to disclosure. Table 6.1 below sets out the four main root causes underlying most conflicts of interest.

Table 6.1: The various root causes of conflicts of interest

Root causes	Description
Inappropriate influence	The firm and/or staff have an economic incentive to act in a manner that is not aligned to clients' best interests, whether this incentive is given by the firm, third parties, or some clients who seek favourable treatment
Misuse of private information	Access to private information flows can give staff an incentive to act on that sensitive information in a manner that is not aligned to clients' best interests
Failure to segregate duties appropriately	Carrying out simultaneous or sequential activities, for example, a single individual sitting on various committees, having multiple reporting lines or being involved in various tasks which may require independence, can incentivize an individual to consider the interests of clients or stakeholders who are not directly impacted by the activity, possibly to the detriment of clients who are serviced through that activity.
Divided loyalties	Situations of divided loyalty are those where a member of staff or the firm has an incentive to consider their own interests over those of clients, or to consider the interests of one client over another, or to consider the interests of parties not immediately concerned by the service (e.g. shareholders or clients who are not subscribed to such a service) when delivering such a service to a client. For example, operating a collective investment fund is an activity where acting in the best interests of both subscribers and redeemers is a delicate balance to strike.

Source: Authors

As can be seen from figure 6.2, poorly designed incentive structures can lead to the root causes of conflicts of interest spreading like a cancer throughout the various activities of the firm. It highlights the importance of attacking conflicts of interest at their source, before they can spread and jeopardize the firm's ability or the ability of the firm's staff to act in a manner that is consistently in the interests of its clients.

To take the example of the root cause called 'inappropriate influence', there are various channels by which it can lead to directly conflicted activity. At an initial stage, inappropriate influence can be exercised via one of three means: (1) third parties exercising inappropriate influence on the firm or its staff to act in a certain manner; (2) the private interests of the firm's staff influencing those staff members to act in a manner (divided loyalties), which may be detrimental to clients' interests; and (3) pressure from top management encouraging staff to act in a certain manner, whether indirectly via softer-toned communications aimed at encouraging more sales, or directly by factoring in product-specific sales targets into remuneration structures. For example, where the advisers/salesforce of a financial services firm receive differentiated product commission credits for sales of various kinds of financial instruments, they may well be incentivized to advise/sell more of those for which they obtain higher credits. Such a scenario immediately induces the risk of a conflict of interest, since the sales advice may be biased as a result of the asymmetric remuneration structure, jeopardizing the compliance with the MiFID suitability obligations.

Likewise, there are cases where external parties, such as intermediaries and product or service providers, may seek to influence an investment firm and try to align the incentives between the product/service providers, as opposed to aligning the incentives between the firm owning the client relationship and the client who is being serviced. A classic case is product providers paying retrocessions to distributors in the form of recurrent payments such as trail commission, which is a percentage of the annual management charge levied on the product (Chapter 7). By moving forward with its proposals on the Retail Distribution Review,[9] the FSA has implicitly concluded that MiFID's combination of conflicts of interest, suitability and inducements rules is not sufficient to safeguard retail clients' interests against an established industry structure which the FSA believes can lead to biased investment advice that is detrimental to consumers' interests.

[9] See FSA (2008).

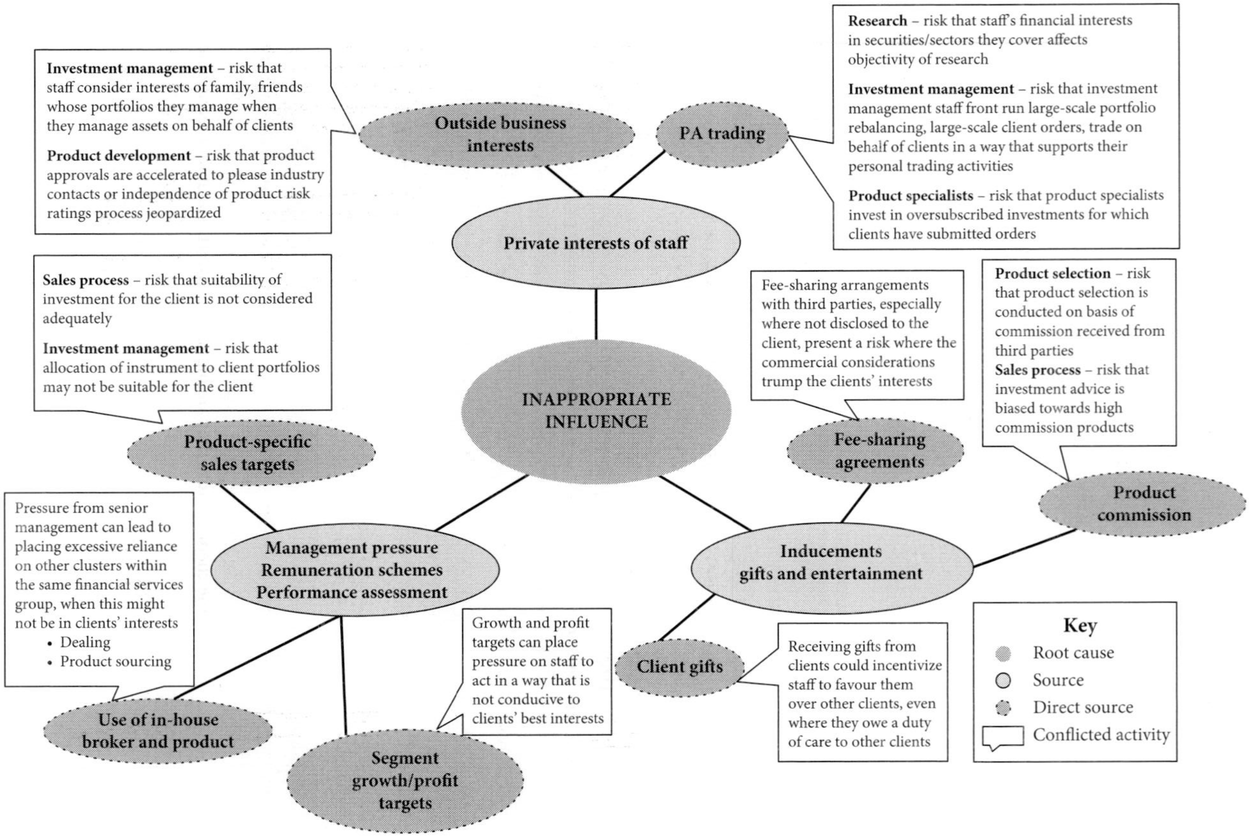

Figure 6.2 Anatomy of conflicts of interest

Table 6.2: The practice: identifying conflicts in an investment firm

Business activity	Main types of conflict	Types of controls
Valuation	• Exercising pricing discretion where creating a secondary market in warehoused illiquid instruments	• Middle office – no front office involvement, unless with compliance and legal input; third party valuation; validation by depositary
	• Setting NAV of fund while acting as operator of the fund and taking management and/or performance fees on the fund's AuM	• Independent verification of process to move from mark-to-market to mark-to-model and back again • Independent verification of mark-to-model valuations and valuation methodology • Auditor sign-off (but auditor may himself be conflicted)
	• Pricing of structured products by the product originator/ manufacturer, where distribution costs are embedded in the cost of the product	• Improve transparency and unbundle the costs of manufacturing the product as opposed to distributing it; make the valuation methodology publicly available or have it vetted by an independent third party
Investment advice	• Advising in-house products over cheaper or outperforming third party products	• Set remuneration structure such that credits advisors receive for product sales are equalised across in-house and third-party products
	• Advising a client to purchase an investment product when client is better served paying off personal debt	• Charge a simple per-hour fee for financial advice
	• Advising unsuitable products to the client because they are higher margin	• Robust sales process that embeds MiFID suitability requirements
	• Advising a client to turn over his portfolio more often than would be in his best interest, in order to collect more revenues from product up-front charges	• Regular checks of contents of client portfolios by legal, compliance, investment specialists and front office managers, to monitor suitability

Table 6.2: (*cont.*)

Business activity	Main types of conflict	Types of controls
Discretionary portfolio management	• Allocating in-house products to client portfolios to collect management fees on the product as well as on portfolio (double-dipping)	• Waiving product charges on in-house products when they are being allocated to client portfolios on a discretionary basis
	• Churning the portfolio to generate broker's fees (where brokers pay for order flow)	• Setting a formal portfolio re-balancing process driven by research views and governed by an investment committee
	• Simulating portfolio out-performance by selecting irrelevant or inappropriate portfolio benchmarks	• Selection of portfolio benchmarks and calculation of portfolio performance is validated by an independent function
Product development	• Wrapping third party products in in-house investment structures to collect more fees from clients with little value added	• Documented justification of value-added provided by wrapping third party product in in-house structure (e.g. tax treatment; use of a nominee)
Product selection and distribution	• Selection of third party products on the basis of inducements received from the product provider, such as trail commission on mutual funds	• Implementing proper sequencing in the process flow from market research to product/manager research, to selection of third party products, to negotiation of commercial terms of distribution
	• Re-negotiating commercial terms of distribution to increase commission levels taken from product provider after clients are already invested in those products	• Setting an upper limit on level of product commission accepted • Re-disclosing any material increase in product commission to clients who have holdings in those products

Table 6.2: (*cont.*)

Business activity	Main types of conflict	Types of controls
Research	• Research views being influenced by need to offload assets from the firm's balance sheet • Research views being influenced by investment banking activity undertaken for inducements from issuers	• Chinese walls separating research function from investment banking activities, as per relevant Market Abuse Directive and MiFID requirements
	• Publishing research to investment management and in-house portfolio/fund management teams prior to dissemination to clients	• Releasing research simultaneously via electronic means to external and internal clients
	• Research being used as a vehicle to support a product launch or product push to clients	• Preventing research pieces from making specific references to third-party or in-house investment products which the firm is promoting
Stock lending	• Lending client assets to finance risky activities or investments with maturity mismatching	• Receiving authorization from clients to lend their assets according to pre-determined, risk-bound activities which are disclosed to the client ex-ante
Allocations	• Discriminating between clients who are signed up to the same service, when allocating limited investment opportunities (IPOs, closed-ended funds) or managing over-subscriptions	• Implementation of a pro-rata allocation process for clients who are signed up to and pay for the same service; pro-rata allocations across discretionary and non-discretionary investment management mandates, where possible
Outsourcing	• Selection of outsourcing partners on basis of cost reduction alone as opposed to service quality delivered	• Regular review of performance of outsourcing partners along several dimensions, measured by quantifiable performance metrics (i.e. KPIs)

Table 6.2: (*cont.*)

Business activity	Main types of conflict	Types of controls
Underwriting	• Stuffing discretionary (institutional) portfolios with IPOs or other securities underwritten	• Validation of instruments in which discretionary portfolios can invest via an investment committee that is independent of investment banking activities
Trading	• Late trading, i.e. allowing investors to place after-hour orders for a security or fund at that same day's closing price • Market timing	• Imposing and sticking to the strict rule that orders which are submitted after a certain time will not be dealt at that day's NAV but at the next dealing day • Especially in the case of mutual funds, which calculate NAVs only once daily, at the close of the dealing day when the NAV is struck, investors should not be allowed to trade in and out during the course of the day

Source: Authors

5. Managing conflicts of interest

MiFID's regime on managing conflicts of interest places more obligations on firms to prevent situations where conflicts occur, that is, to take a very proactive approach to embedding a governance culture where conflicts of interest are always considered in decision-making processes rather than curing. These new governance obligations will impose considerably higher administrative requirements on infrastructure areas in investment firms, as MiFID specifies the need for firms to implement concrete organizational requirements and rigorous procedures to be put into place around the identification, management and disclosure of conflicts of interest. This is particularly true as proper conflicts management can be labour-intensive and require the frequent collection and reviewing of management information (MI).

If, however, it is inevitable that conflicts arise, MiFID places a heavy onus on firms to prevent them from harming the interests of clients. Disclosure should rarely, if ever, be used, and regulators will no longer stand for firms' taking a lazy approach to conflicts management. There is even an explicit recognition in the text of MiFID to this effect: 'While disclosure of specific conflicts of interest is required by Article 18(2) . . ., an over-reliance on disclosure without adequate consideration as to how conflicts may appropriately be managed is not permitted.' Some firms have even adopted the stance that, where they cannot effectively manage a conflict, they should consider abandoning the practice.

In order to ascertain whether a particular conflict must be managed, three questions should be asked (see figure 6.3)

- Does the conflict arise in the course of carrying out a regulated or ancillary activity?
- Does the conflict arise in the course of providing a service to a client?
- Does the conflict present a material risk of damage to client interests?

If the answers to these questions is positive, the conflict must be managed. MiFID places particular emphasis on portfolio management, research, investment research and advice, proprietary trading and corporate finance business, including underwriting or selling in an offering of securities and advising on mergers and acquisitions, as activities around which particular care must be exercised in managing conflicts.

Importantly, the requirement to maintain a record of all the conflicts of interest that have been identified by the firm should not be confused with the need to implement and continually refine measures to contain them. In other words, the MiFID requirements will not be satisfied by publishing a conflicts of interest policy alone and keeping a log of conflicts.

Only in situations where it becomes clear the firm is not in a position to manage its conflicts effectively:

- Is the conflict being managed effectively?
- Is it clear to clients that they are unable rely on the firm to act in their best interest?

Certain types of conflict of interest are intractable, and may therefore need to be disclosed to clients in general terms and conditions and/or in service-specific terms or product literature. These tend to be client versus client conflicts of interest, which is a type of conflict specifically mentioned in recital 24 of MiFID's Implementing Directive as one which must be managed. For example, it is a common occurrence in large investment firms that discretionary portfolio managers will be in a position immediately to reallocate portfolios on the back of the publication of

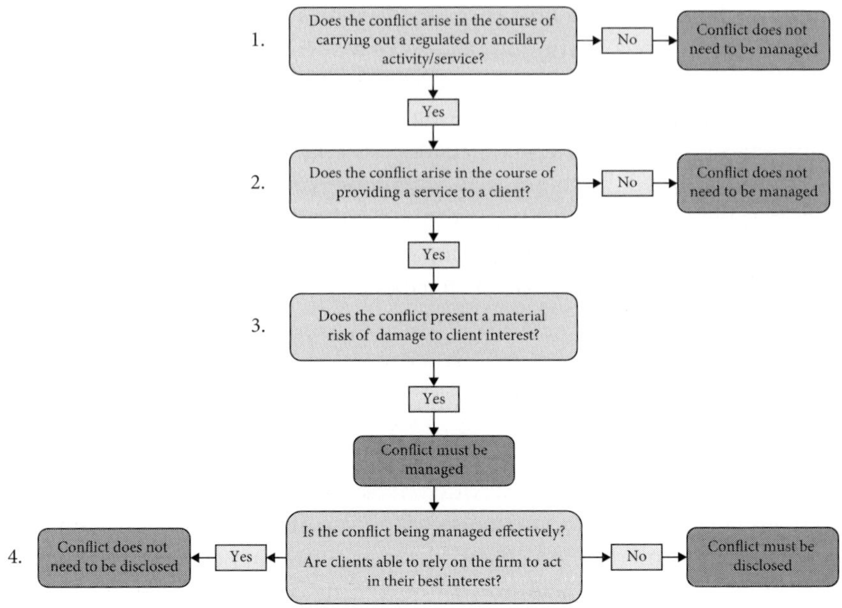

Source: MiFID Connect (2007)

Figure 6.3 When to manage conflicts of interest

a research note, giving the impression that discretionary managed clients have an opportunity to act upon the research prior to clients who have signed up to advisory investment management mandates; yet it is simply a reflection of the different levels of service provided and the nature of those services.

6. Maintaining effective procedures and controls

The adoption of a formal conflicts policy alone will not improve conflicts of interest management in any significant manner. Written internal policies and procedures cannot safeguard the interests of clients if those policies and procedures are not implemented, policed, enforced and occasionally reviewed. Regulators have also indicated that when conducting supervisory visits post-MiFID, they will look less to the firm's policies and procedures to verify that regulatory policy has been properly embedded in the firm, than they will to how those policies and procedures are actually adhered to in particular situations on a day-to-day basis. This is a fundamental shift in tact on the part of the supervisors of large financial groups in the UK.

If designed properly, the conflicts register MiFID firms are required to maintain can serve a dual purpose. It can increase awareness among staff of the root causes of conflicts, the various situations or activities that can give rise to conflicts of interest, and the potential material risk to client interests that various conflicts can give rise to. At the same time, the register is also a record of the steps senior management have taken to instil throughout the firm a culture of conflicts awareness, prevention and management. It will enable senior management and compliance departments to assess periodically whether the controls and procedures that have been put into place result in effective conflicts management and proper disclosure to clients when necessary.

Operationalizing the conflicts register is vital in getting staff to 'live and breathe' conflicts of interest management and must therefore be seen as a 'live' document, meaning that each business within a firm should exercise ownership of its own register via its 'conflicts champion', who assumes ultimate responsibility for the maintenance of the register for the whole of the relevant business line. The conflicts champion should be either the COO of a business line, or an appropriately senior delegate, in order to ensure that conflicts of interest identification and management has the visibility and accountability it needs to comply with MiFID and be effective.

Fundamentally, a successful conflicts of interest management programme can be thought of as consisting of five key steps:

1. Removing misaligned incentives and addressing the root cause of the conflict of interest.
2. Ensuring that appropriate controls are in place around situations or activities that lie at the source of potential conflicts of interest.
3. Identifying and resolving any practices that present a material risk to client interests.
4. Disclosing to clients any situation where the firm is not comfortable that the controls around a conflict are sufficient to manage it without notifying the client of its existence.
5. Periodically checking the robustness of controls around conflicts of interest to ensure no business practices result in a material detriment to client interests.

Whenever new types of (potential) conflicts are identified, controls introduced, existing controls revised, or a decision to disclose a conflict to a client is made, the conflicts register should be updated. Conflicts champions should develop a workable process to achieve this in their business lines as they see fit. For MI purposes, the conflicts champions may want to develop a way to record the number of times various teams in their business report conflicts, with breakdowns by activity conducted and teams, so as to know where problem areas lie, where there is room for improvement, etc.

The firm must ensure that the arrangements it puts into place to identify and handle conflicts of interest remain effective and are adequately monitored on an ongoing basis. To this effect, periodic reviews should be carried out by firms' compliance or business control units in order to:

- Ensure that conflicts are being identified by the business on an ongoing basis.
- Review whether the existing arrangements to prevent and manage conflicts are sufficiently robust.
- Suggest the creation of new instruments for managing conflicts of interest if needed.
- Identify which business lines/activities are the most susceptible to conflicts and attempt to determine why.
- Create a forum to discuss firm-wide initiatives where conflicts implications arise, for example, firm-wide, high-profile product launches or joint ventures.

Results of such reviews should be presented to senior management committees on a regular basis, so that the committee in question can decide on any appropriate actions in terms of bolstering existing controls, where they are deemed to be insufficient to manage conflicts properly.

References

Boatright, John 2003. 'Conflict of interest in financial services: a contractual risk-management analysis', The Hastings Center, Garrison, NY, 10 April; Tenth Annual Meeting Promoting Business Ethics, St. John's University.

Brousseau, Eric and Jean-Michel Glachant (eds.) 2008. *New Institutional Economics*, Cambridge: Cambridge University Press.

European Council 2003. Directive 2003/6/EC of the European Parliament and of the Council of 28 January 2003 on insider dealing and market manipulation (market abuse).

European Council 1993. Directive 93/22/EEC of 10 May 1993 on investment services in the securities field.

FSA 2003a. 'Conflicts of Interest: Investment Research and Issues of Securities', Consultation Paper 171.

2003b. Consultation Paper 171 Newsletter.

2008. 'Retail Distribution Review – Including feedback on DP07/1 and the Interim Report', FS 08/6.

Llewellyn, David 1999. 'The economic rationale for financial regulation', Occasional Paper Series No. 1, April. London: FSA.

MiFID Connect 2007. 'Information Memorandum on the Application of the Conflicts of Interest Requirements under the FSA Rules Implementing MiFID and the CRD in the UK'.

7

The MiFID approach to inducements – imperfect tools for a worthy policy objective

1. Introduction

This chapter looks at the MiFID rules on inducements. It argues that while the policy objectives underpinning the rules are valid and necessary, the instruments regulators have chosen for achieving those objectives are in need of fine-tuning, and especially clarification, if the objectives are to be met without inflicting collateral damage on the European fund industry.

2. Implementing the MiFID inducements rules

2.1 Regulating distribution models: the pros and the cons

The MiFID requirements on inducements, particularly around disclosure, represent a controversial and bold attempt to shed more light on the mechanics of the distribution channels through which savings products make their way from the product factory into client portfolios.

Broadly, there are three distribution channels through which savings products enter client portfolios: advised sales, unadvised sales (execution-only), and allocation of product to discretionary managed funds. The mix of product – whether homespun or sourced from a third party – that is channelled to client portfolios will depend on an investment firm's distribution architecture. These models range from a 'closed-shop', where a firm only distributes its own product, to a 'guided architecture' where the firm sources product from a select panel of providers, to a 'whole of market' proposition (also known as 'open architecture').

In the HNW client space, closed-shop models are a relict of the past. Set against the backdrop of the increasing competition in financial services that has accompanied the dismantling of national regulatory barriers to trade at the European level, investment firms are gradually shifting from pushing product to developing a product set that offers innovative solutions to clients and responds to a client 'pull'. They are increasingly doing so in the retail space as well. A necessary consequence of this shift has been to expand the product offering beyond those sourced in-house only. Where a gap has been identified in its own product offering, or where a third-party product displays a materially superior performance, an investment firm will recognize the commercial imperative of sourcing product from third parties in this more competitive landscape.

Though an expanded product offering could only be thought to improve consumer welfare, greater recourse to open or guided distribution models by investment firms also brings with it new challenges for the fair treatment of consumers. These challenges have attracted regulatory scrutiny. From a regulatory perspective, the two fundamental issues are ensuring that the selection of products to be put 'on the shelf' of distributors, and the subsequent advice given, are not biased as a result of product commission.

Open architecture models of distribution present their own challenges for regulators; from an industrial organization perspective, the reality of an open architecture distribution framework is for product providers to give an economic incentive to distributors to distribute their products. In the absence of such an incentive, it would be commercially unviable for a profit-driven firm to market the products of any third party: there is no other mechanism by which a free market economy can operate, if it is not by incentives.

While regulators hail the benefits of open architecture models of distribution, they also recognize that they present certain risks for the end customer. For example, it is commonplace among regulatory bodies and consumer advocacy groups to view product commission in a negative light. This logic is driven by a fear that product commission incentivizes distributors to act in a manner that is not aligned to their clients' best interest. High levels of product commission can pose three types of risk of client detriment.

First, there is the risk that higher commission rates offered by fund providers will bias the selection of products for access to a firm's distribution platform (biased product selection). If product commission is considered an important factor in the selection of third-party products, there is a risk that the quality of the products selected is mediocre, as distributors place more emphasis on revenues earned from distributing a product, rather than considering the product on its own merits. Top-performing managers do not need to pay high distribution commission, as there is a natural pull for their product from distributors. This leaves startup managers with little or no track record who seek seed capital for a new fund, or mediocre managers who need to increase fund sales, as typical examples of managers who pay higher rates of distribution commission.

Second, there is a risk that high commission paid by a provider will encourage the firm's management to incentivize sales staff to sell as much of the fund as they can (possibly in breach of suitability requirements), in order to maximize revenue for the firm, as opposed to selling better performing or more suitable products. In some cases, it may be in the client's best interest not to sell any product at all.

Third, there is the risk that firms with large distribution networks can exercise considerable leverage over fund management groups to negotiate excessively favourable terms in distribution agreements, to the client's detriment. For example, smaller fund groups or new fund houses may be prepared to sacrifice revenues in an initial phase in order to gain the publicity and legitimacy that accompanies access to the distribution platforms of large and reputable firms. These situations can lead to cases where the distributor is rebated such a large amount of the annual management charge that the fund manager no longer has an economic incentive to service the fund properly. This is clearly not in the best interest of the distributor's clients.

In the regulator's view, these risks were sufficiently grave to warrant a response in the form of legislation, hence the MiFID rules on inducements, which cover all of these types of arrangement. This is not to say that a return to the closed-shop model is in customers' interests.

2.2 Policy objectives of inducements rules

There appear to be three key policy objectives regulators are driving at through the MiFID inducements rules:

1. Removing the potential bias in product selection and investment advice, which could result from the commission product providers pay to distributors.
2. Empowering the consumer to challenge the price they are paying for financial advice, by revealing the cost of that advice.
3. Fostering greater transparency in the market for distribution of investment products to enhance competition.

Transparency around distribution agreements empowers consumers because they become aware of the incentives which might drive the product or investment recommendations advisers make, and because having an idea of the level of remuneration received by the distributor enables the consumer to challenge the fees they are charged. As a consequence, the consumer is better positioned to make an assessment of whether the advice received may be biased as a result of commission. The consumer might also be able to negotiate lower fees as a result.

In the absence of price transparency, competitive markets cannot blossom. Transparency should lower distribution costs, thereby making the market more competitive, to the benefit of consumers. Greater transparency in remuneration agreements between product providers and distributors is likely to put downward pressure on the total cost of a product for a client by squeezing distribution margins, which often account for a large percentage of the TER of funds on the European continent. In the UK, packaged products[1] have been subject to commission disclosure rules for a number of years. On the other hand, on the Continent, the commercial terms of distribution agreements have, until recently, remained largely opaque.

All the policy objectives mentioned above are valid in and of themselves. The imperative driving them is obvious: in a world where 'open architecture' models of distribution are accelerating, regulators want customers to get a look into the black box of third-party product selection to make their own decision about whether the product selection process is objective. They also want customers to understand that financial advice does not come free of charge, and is often subsidized by commission paid by product providers. Whether the policy requirements have been formulated in such a way that the above objectives are met and do not lead to unintended consequences is an entirely different matter.

2.3 Lamfalussy Level 3 work on inducements

CESR issued its consultation paper on the application of the MiFID art. 26 provisions on inducements in December 2006. This paper met with such vehement protests from the industry that CESR had to issue a second consultation on the same subject four months later. Even so, some of the main industry concerns with the first consultation paper remained unresolved after the second version was issued. These protests revolved around two points of controversy in particular.

[1] Investment funds, life assurance products, personal and stakeholder pensions.

First, the meaning of the word 'inducement'. A number of firms, especially from the Anglo-Saxon world, argued that the word 'inducement' had a clear connotation of a payment structure deliberately designed to incite a behavioural outcome on the part of the distributor, i.e. one that gave rise to unambiguous conflicts of interest detrimental to the client. In other words, the industry argument was that standard commercial agreements between product providers and distributors did not amount to 'inducements' and therefore would not be caught under MiFID's inducements provisions. CESR clarified, however, that the MiFID rules on inducements were meant to cover any agreement with a third party in relation to a MiFID service provided to a client.

The second point of controversy revolved around CESR's interpretation that art. 26 implied a price quantum being attached to the tests a firm had to apply to assess whether or not an inducement was acceptable under MiFID. CESR stated in its December 2006 Consultation Paper (CESR 2006) that: 'a commission which gives disproportionate benefit to the firm relative to the value of the service provided to the client is likely to impair the firm's compliance with its duty to act in the best interests of the client.' Nowhere does art. 26 mention a price quantum, nor does it specify a condition that the relative value of a commission has to be balanced in favour of the client or, at the minimum, not skewed disproportionately in favour of the firm.

CESR's interpretation elicited nothing less than a firestorm of protest from the industry, which argued that it had not only proposed unworkable interpretations, but that it had overstepped the bounds of its mandate by reading into MiFID provisions that many stakeholders and observers claimed were not to be found in the text. In other words, CESR was accused of legislating, whereas under EU law it has no ability to do so. The industry also argued that by taking a position that the benefits of inducements had to be roughly equally shared between distributors and clients, CESR's interpretation of a 'proportionality test' basically amounted to price regulation.

The debate did not completely die down during the second round of consultation, where CESR laid out recommendations to its members on implementing a common understanding of the MiFID inducements rules. Particularly contentious was recommendation 4, in which CESR outlined the 'factors that an investment firm should consider in determining whether an arrangement may be deemed to be designed to enhance the quality of the service provided to the client and not impair the duty of the firm to act in the best interest of the client'.

Recommendation 4b lists as one of these factors 'the expected benefit to the client, including the nature and extent of that benefit, and any expected benefit to the investment firm'.[2]

It seemed to many observers and industry groups that CESR had not completely moved away from implementing some kind of 'proportionality test', based on the relative benefits commission arrangements brought to clients and their advisers. Concerns remained that recommendation 4(b) was a way to reintroduce the proportionality test through the back door. The choice of wording, which indicated that firms would have to assess 'the nature and *extent of that benefit*' (emphasis added) might have been read by some CESR members as firms' having to come up with a *quantitative metric* that measures the extent of the benefit accruing to clients. It is an easy jump from measuring the extent of the benefit accruing to clients to regulators' holding up those benefits against the benefits accruing to the firm, and subsequently making a comparison of scale – and that means reversion to the hotly contested proportionality test and price regulation.

Such a requirement would be impracticable. For example, if a firm were to receive a 50 basis points (bps) per annum trail commission for including a third-party fund in its proposition to a client, would that fund need to outperform its class of funds by more than 50 bps to justify the commission received? CESR's initial interpretation might have led to such an exercise on a wide scale. Regulators have often complained that a market failure approach to legislation, which requires regulators to quantify the benefits of legislation and compare them to costs, is often a far more difficult and subjective exercise than quantifying the costs it might impose on firms.[3] The same argument was made by firms which were concerned about having to quantitatively demonstrate that on balance, inducements were beneficial to clients. Thus, the industry argued that recommendation 4(b), if left unrevised by CESR after the second consultation (not their preference), should be looked at as a judgement call for firms to make, based on the principle of treating their customers fairly.

During the consultation process in the early spring of 2007, CESR changed its approach regarding the application of the art. 26(b)(ii) requirement for firms to demonstrate that they were 'enhancing the quality of the service' for a client. Notably, two important clarifications were made by CESR during the consultation process.

[2] CESR (2007b), p. 11.

[3] By the FSA's own admission, 'it is in the nature of regulation that costs are relatively easier to define and quantify for firms while benefits can be harder to pin down'. FSA (2006), p. 5.

First, CESR moved away from imposing a positive requirement on firms to demonstrate that they were effectively 'enhancing the quality of the service', i.e., placing the burden of proof squarely on investment firms, to defining the term negatively. This interpretation was powerful, in that it substantively reversed the position taken by the EU Commission initially. Whereas the way the legislative text was crafted took as a starting position that all inducements were banned, unless firms were able to demonstrate that they 'enhanced the quality of the service' for the client, the practical outcome of CESR's interpretation was that *all* inducements were *de facto* considered to 'enhance the quality of the service to the client,' so long as they did not prevent a firm from acting in the best interests of its clients. In other words, the scope of what was permissible was considerably widened as a natural consequence of CESR's revised interpretation.

A common form of product commission in the funds business is 'trail commission' – commercial agreements where a product provider rebates to the distributor (usually on a quarterly basis) part of the fees (annual management charge) they levy for managing the fund. There was considerable concern among the industry during the national transposition exercises that 'trail commission' would have to be phased out post-MiFID, on the basis that it would not satisfy the inducements test to 'enhance the quality of the service' to the client.

Because of the reasons cited above, these fears have, to a certain extent, since been allayed. The European Commission has taken an unofficial position that trail commission will not be banned under MiFID, so long as the art. 26 criteria are satisfied.[4] CESR, for its part, has more officially recognized trail commission as acceptable in principle, so long as distributors are in a position to demonstrate that, by taking these payments, they are 'enhancing the quality of the service' for the client, as well as disclosing the amount and nature of these payments to the client prior to the service being delivered.

By coming out with these interpretations, CESR and the Commission reassured the fund industry that a fundamental redesign of the distribution architecture was not what MiFID was driving towards. It is worth noting that trail commission represents a major source of revenue for

[4] The position is deemed unofficial because the European Commission's online FAQ on MiFID, while having a certain legitimacy as guidance given by the EU executive, cannot be deemed legally binding, since the European Court of Justice has the ultimate (and sole) power to interpret EU legislation.

firms with large distribution networks. Rebates to the distributor of 50 per cent of annual management charge (AMC) are common, and higher rates, sometimes reaching 80 per cent, are not uncommon. Since annual management charges on long-only equity funds are typically around 1 to 1.5 per cent of assets under management (per annum), this means that trail commission revenues may range from 50 bps to 120 bps for each currency unit of invested funds. If a firm manages several billion pounds of assets under management, the potential revenues it can earn from trail commission are obvious. There is therefore a clear commercial imperative for distributors to maintain the status quo.

CESR made another important concession to the industry in interpreting the art. 26 tests as being conducted 'at the level of the service' provided to the client (as opposed to each individual transaction effected). This interpretation allows for some flexibility in operationalizing the inducements rule, in that it seems to allow for a utilitarian logic to be applied when assessing whether an inducement is generally beneficial for the client. In other words, this interpretation means that an inducement can be considered to 'enhance the quality of the service', even if a particular commission arrangement was not beneficial to an individual client, so long as the majority of the clients who signed up to that service clearly benefit from the existence of the inducement.

2.4 How firms can justify accepting trail commission post-MiFID

In a post-MiFID world, as part of the exercise to make inducements MiFID-compliant (see Annex I), distributors will have to justify why they accept product commission from third parties, and how it is in their clients' best interests to do so. Several arguments can be put forward to this effect.

First, it could be argued that trail commission, far from being a mechanism for product providers to influence unduly the advice given by advisers, can be an important tool in aligning the interests of the client and the distributor. This alignment arises because trail commission provides an ongoing incentive for the distributor to look after the best interests of its clients and to continue delivering adequate post-sales service, for example, by conducting ongoing due diligence on the product provider.

The standard initial service charge (ISC) for clients purchasing retail funds directly with a fund management group will vary typically between 3 per cent and 5.5 per cent. This is to cover the set-up and dealing costs incurred by the fund management group and the payment of initial commission fees to an introducer/adviser, which are typically 3 per cent of the initial subscription. This arrangement is standard for any independent financial adviser (IFA) and individual discounts may be applied by sacrificing commission to reduce the ISC payable by the client. This discount may be offered to maintain competitiveness (versus other IFAs) or as an incentive for the client for the placement of a bulk or large deal.

Second, if distributors did not accept trail commission from third-party providers then, in all likelihood, the initial sales charge to clients would increase significantly in order to cover the costs of maintaining the same quality of service. For example, for some equity funds, where the initial service charge (ISC) can be up to 5 per cent of invested capital (meaning only 95 per cent is invested), turning off trail commission would lead to up-front fees of close to 9 per cent of invested capital (assuming the investment would be held over five years and trail commission is 75 bps per annum). It is highly unlikely an investor would want to pay such a sum up-front. The higher charges would reflect the fact that commission from product providers essentially subsidizes the provision of financial advice free of charge to clients.

Commission also covers other costs essential to the provision of investment services, such as the production of marketing material, which clients would otherwise have to pay in its absence. These costs should not be underestimated. Printing professionally a single copy of a brochure for a fund may cost up to £10. Clients are likely to object to being charged for such expenses, yet they nevertheless constitute an essential component of the services they receive. It would be both incorrect and misleading to suggest that the abolition of commission and fee-sharing agreements would necessarily lower the costs of a service for clients. On the contrary, the discussion above demonstrates that the opposite is more likely. It highlights the difficulties associated with the cultural shift that would necessarily accompany any prohibition of commission arrangements: clients would be charged for elements of a service that are essential to its provision, but which they historically have not paid due to the existence of commission arrangements.

Third, there is little cause for concern around inducements, so long as the receipt of distribution commission is coupled with a robust conflicts of interest governance regime, in tandem with a framework to ensure that the products being advised are suitable for clients. Since taking trail from third party product providers can be a source of potential conflicts of interest, distributors must put into place various measures to manage them effectively. These could include:

1. Segregating teams negotiating distribution agreements from those involved in investment management decisions.
2. Ensuring that proper sequencing is followed, such that research analysts select the managers/funds they think display the greatest potential to deliver risk-adjusted outperformance and only subsequently, commercial teams negotiate the distribution agreement.
3. Not accepting certain forms of remuneration from product providers (e.g. bonus over-rides, asymmetrically tiered commission).
4. Monitoring that advisers are rigorously applying suitability tests when recommending financial products to clients.
5. Ensuring that advisers do not have a view on the amount of commission the firm takes for third-party products.
6. Ensuring that the remuneration of advisers is not linked to the commission the firm earns from certain products.

Box 7.1 Arguments for excepting trail commission

1. **Access to investment products** – Offering access to leading specialized fund managers and product providers is beneficial to clients by expanding their range of investment opportunities. In many cases, clients would not be able to access top-performing managers and strategies on a stand-alone basis in exchange for offering third-party providers. By facilitating this access, distributors are clearly enhancing the quality of the service to their clients. It is logical that they should be remunerated for this by accepting and retaining (at least part of) the commission payments offered by these product providers.
2. **Ongoing due diligence on the investment** – Conducting ongoing due diligence on the fund managers is a post-sales service which is beneficial to the client, since it gives him some degree of protection, especially in an advised relationship. In order to cover the costs of providing such an ongoing service, including ongoing monitoring of manager performance and the risks the manager is undertaking – which will involve maintaining close contact with the manager – the distributor must either charge clients directly or cover those costs through the receipt of commission.
3. **Ongoing research on the market** – Conducting extensive research on the universe of available funds is an essential part of any

research/advisory offering, since recommendations to divest from certain investments must be accompanied by ongoing research on the wider universe of funds, which might act as a suitable replacement for one where a manager is underperforming, or whose operational risk procedures are not up to par, or whatever the reason for the distributor's analysts to issue unfavourable recommendations. As in point 2, this is a service which is provided at a cost to the firm.

4. **Providing ongoing advice** – Providing ongoing advice to clients on products incurs costs, including the costs of ensuring that advisers remain trained and competent in respect of certain investments. Front-office staff are also supported by various infrastructure areas, for example, receiving ongoing compliance support to ensure advice is given according to regulatory requirements.
5. **Lowering the initial service charge** – Often, in exchange for accepting product commission, firms will negotiate lower initial service charges (the fee they charge up-front for advice and the costs associated with providing clients with the services listed in points 1–4 of this box). The initial service charge for long-only equity funds can reach up to 5 or even 6 per cent of the invested amount, meaning only 95–94 per cent is invested. Offering clients this access on favourable terms (i.e., subscriptions and redemptions at NAV) because of the size of a distribution network is a clear example of an enhancement of the quality of the service clients receive.

3. Points of uncertainty around MiFID's inducements rules

There are several important points of uncertainty revolving around the MiFID inducements provisions which, if unresolved, are likely to lead to a fragmented and uncompetitive market for the distribution of MiFID financial instruments.[5]

[5] Insurance products were carved out of MiFID as a result of a political compromise, leaving insurance products such as unit-linked life insurance, which have similar properties to units in collective investment schemes, at a distinct advantage in terms of the transparency distributors need to provide to clients with respect to the terms of the arrangements they have with product providers. This carve-out is unsustainable in the long term.

3.1 Whether tiered commission arrangements are allowed

CESR has been very cautious not to pronounce itself on the types of commission structure, which it would deem to be acceptable post-MiFID. Indeed, it has deliberately not given further guidance, for fear that: (1) such guidance could not cater for all circumstances and situations; (2) it would not pass relevant cost-benefit analyses; (3) 'the work would become out of date and incomplete very quickly'; and (4) that it would be a 'formidable task to set out to perform'.[6]

Though one might understand why CESR was reticent to go further in defining examples of acceptable inducements under MiFID – it was especially afraid of having its hands tied, and of an industry backlash[7] – the same reticence to give a proper definition does not allow firms to anticipate or gauge the expectations of regulators with respect to the structure distribution arrangements can assume. Regulators themselves may have differing interpretations of what forms of fee-sharing agreements or commission are allowable under MiFID, possibly leading to an uneven playing field at European level.[8]

A fairly common form of remuneration paid by product providers to distributors in the financial services industry is tiered commission. Tiered commission refers to arrangements where distributors receive step increases in the level of commission, wherever sales exceed predetermined thresholds. Although CESR has explicitly recognized that tiered commission arrangements are not automatically banned under MiFID, neither has it established that tiered commission structures will always be acceptable.[9] Regulators seem to understand that there are clear commercial reasons for tiered arrangements.[10] At the same time, it is

6 CESR (2006), p. 12.

7 CESR's hands would have been tied because, if it had produced an exhaustive list of what constituted acceptable models of distribution or intermediation, it would have been bound by it. As for its fear of an industry backlash, producing a discreet list of acceptable inducements (beyond mere examples) would have opened it to accusations from market participants that it was prescribing distribution models.

8 See point 4 of this section for a more detailed discussion on this point.

9 CESR agrees that there may be less of an issue where commission levels are tiered (that is one rate applies to sales up to a certain level and another rate to sales beyond that level), than situations such as that described in example VIII of the April Consultation paper, where a distributor receives a one-off bonus payment for having exceeded a certain sales volume. CESR nevertheless recommends that with respect to tiered commission, the circumstances of each case would have to be considered: CESR (2007a), p. 17.

10 From a commercial perspective, economies of scale in fund management and distribution mean that it is only logical for a fund manager to offer more favourable terms to distributors who channel greater volumes into the manager's funds.

undeniable that tiered commission structures present greater risks than flat-rate commission arrangements, because they could be deliberately designed to incentivize, or inadvertently lead, distributors to reach or exceed set thresholds of sales volumes, possibly to their clients' detriment.

While CESR has not banned tiered commission outright, it has issued an unfavourable view on so-called 'bonus over-rides':

> [where] the investment firm receives an additional one-off bonus (or 'over-ride') payment once sales of a particular product reach an agreed level . . . it is doubtful that Article 26(b) can be satisfied. As sales approach the target level it becomes more likely that the firm's advice will become biased towards that particular product, in breach of the duty to act honestly, fairly and professionally in accordance with the best interests of the client.

That CESR takes a neutral view on tiered commission, while discouraging bonus over-rides (which in the minds of many observers amount to the same practice) seems to be inconsistent. It also unhelpfully reduces the policy debate to a question of semantics on the definition of, and difference between, tiered commission and one-off bonus over-rides.

The absence of more detailed guidance beyond the general declaration made on tiered commission, and the apparently inconsistent approach with respect to bonus over-rides, has left many distributors nervous. In addition, product providers have, to date, remained noticeably absent from the debate, leaving distributors to wonder whether or how they can change existing commercial models of distribution without the cooperation of the former. Yet some product providers have moved towards standardizing commission structures across the board, removing the tiering, but it is clear that other fund groups are not convinced they must abolish the practice. It will therefore be essential for product providers and distributors to come to a joint agreement on what is acceptable under MiFID, especially as distributors are not always in a position of strength in negotiating with product providers.

A good example is the case of top-performing managers of heavily oversubscribed closed-end funds, which occasionally open briefly to new investments. Such managers are in a position to dictate the terms on which they will allow investors to access their funds. They may insist on a tiered commission structure. In cases such as these, MiFID investment firms will have to determine whether the balance of risks is in the client's favour (i.e. balancing the risk of missing out on an excellent investment opportunity with the risk of possible mis-selling by employees or agents of the distributor, in the hopes of reaching the thresholds where higher commission rates accrue to them). Regulators must surely recognize that it is for firms to make this assessment in line with the culture of fair treatment of customers they have implemented.

This section has highlighted the considerable uncertainty and confusion among firms about whether tiered commission arrangements amount to 'volume over-rides', which CESR has explicitly rejected as a valid form of remuneration arrangement between providers and distributors under MiFID art. 26.

3.1.1 Making tiered commission arrangements MiFID-compliant

There are several ways distributors might justify a tiered commission arrangement. For example, and as described above, if top-performing managers only offer access to their funds on these terms, distributors could argue that offering their clients access to these investments is an 'enhancement of the quality of service'.[11]

However, making a determination that an inducement 'enhances the quality of the service' is not enough to ensure MiFID compliance. The second clause of art. 26(b)(ii) additionally requires firms to ensure that the inducement does not 'impair compliance with the firm's duty to act in the best interests of the client'. With respect to tiered commission, there are two main ways firms can satisfy this clause.

First, they should recognize that tiered arrangements warrant greater attention than flat commission structures, especially so that they are not seen to be advising a product or allocating it to a discretionary managed portfolio simply to trigger the threshold that propels it into the next (higher) commission bracket. This will require engagement with the front office, in order to ensure proper compliance with the sales process governance policy, and engagement with portfolio management teams, to ensure that products are not selected for inclusion in a portfolio based on the remuneration accruing to the firm.

Second, commercial negotiation teams will have to be careful not to enter into agreements where there is a total disconnect between the levels of remuneration distributors receive in the different commission brackets.

[11] This argument could also be presented in the following terms: if a fund manager only offers access to distributors on these terms, distributors might determine that granting their clients access to these investment opportunities outweighs the potential conflict arising from the structure of the remuneration they receive (so long as selling these funds via the distributor's network genuinely 'enhances the quality of the service', e.g. if these funds fill a strategy gap in the firm's offering, or if the managers in question deliver considerable outperformance).

For example, distributors should not negotiate agreements where they receive a trail commission of 20 bps for the first £100 million of assets they can source into a product, and where the next £100 million would trigger a trail of, say, 85 bps, and the final commission bracket (over £300 million) yields 95 bps. Such a structure could be seen to be designed to encourage a firm to break the £200 million barrier, whereas the firm has relatively little economic incentive to break the £300 million barrier in comparison. It is therefore essential for tiered commission arrangements which seek to be MiFID-compliant to display some kind of proportionality in the step increases. One way to approach the question is to ensure that the step increases in commission are constantly proportional (e.g. 20 bps for each threshold, or a 10 per cent increase in trail for each threshold).

3.2 Whether the inducements disclosure applies retrospectively to existing clients

Because MiFID requires firms to obtain a number of representations from their clients (e.g. express prior consent to off-exchange trading, prior consent to a firm's execution policy, choices on the frequency of client reporting, etc.), many firms decided to issue new (MiFID-compliant) terms and conditions to their clients prior to 1 November 2007. Issuing new terms and conditions is both an expensive and a labour-intensive task, from their drafting to their mailing out, to tracking which clients have not returned the requisite two-way consent forms.

Discretionary-managed clients present a particular challenge, because the investment firm inevitably has less frequent contact with them than with clients who sign up to advisory mandates. This challenge extends to inducements disclosure. Ideally, a firm would enclose its MiFID-compliant inducements disclosure in the investment management mandate, in order to comply with the MiFID provision of art. 26(b)(i)[12] that such disclosures are made prior to the service being delivered to the client.[13] This would be the most logical and easiest manner to

[12] Art. 26(b)(i) of the MiFID Implementing (Level 2) Directive reads: 'The existence, nature and amount of the fee, commission or benefit, or, where the amount cannot be ascertained, the method of calculating that amount, must be clearly disclosed to the client, in a manner that is comprehensive, accurate and understandable, prior to the provision of the relevant investment or ancillary service.'

[13] This could be done, for example, in the form of a schedule containing the commission taken on products, which are allocated to discretionary portfolios. But as pointed out below, it remains unclear what exactly is the form these disclosures must take, and how detailed they must be.

comply with the requirements, since the disclosures are embedded in the mandate of the service to which a client signs up. In fact, this is indeed the vehicle which firms have adopted to implement the inducements disclosure provisions for discretionary managed clients who sign up to an investment managed mandate any time after the 1 November MiFID implementation deadline.

Firms had more difficulty with clients who were already signed up to such a service prior to 1 November 2007. Because of the delay in the level 3 work on inducements as a result of CESR's second consultation, the inducements rules were decided at national level quite late in the day. They were only finalized in the UK in late July 2007, leaving only three months for firms to introduce the requisite inducements disclosures prior to 1 November. By this time, most firms' MiFID projects had already been budgeted for a long time and were already well underway. The main vehicle for firms' complying with new MiFID requirements on up-front disclosures to clients (i.e. prior to the service being delivered), namely the issuance of new terms and conditions, were already drafted and ready to be sent off to clients, in the hope that all the necessary two-way consents would be received from clients before 1 November. This would allow firms to continue to deal with clients in a business-as-usual manner from 1 November.

The late transposition of the inducements rules, and the continued uncertainty in the UK over whether the FSA's super-equivalent disclosures under its packaged products rules would be accepted by the European Commission as necessary to address a jurisdiction-specific market failure,[14] meant that firms were placed in the impossible situation of either having to delay the issuance of their new terms and conditions (and face the consequences of not being able to deal with their clients post-1 November), or rely on inducements disclosures which had to be drafted prior to the finalization of the inducements rules at national level. Many decided to opt for the latter as the only viable solution from a project management and risk perspective.

Yet it is not completely clear whether MiFID even requires such disclosures to be made retrospectively to existing clients. Certainly, there would be little justification for such a reading of MiFID, in that the whole point of the inducements rules is to enable an investor to make an

[14] This is the only argument which can be invoked by national regulators when attempting to introduce super-equivalent measures around a maximum-harmonization EU directive such as MiFID.

'informed decision' *prior* to the service. In addition, the firm is contractually bound by its existing agreement with its clients. If the existing agreement only specified a need to make a generic disclosure that commission may be taken, and the client signed up to that service with full knowledge that that level of disclosure is all that could be expected, then there seems little point in retrospectively advising clients of the exact amounts of commission taken. In addition, clients could have little cause to complain if the firm complies with its obligations under the existing terms of the service.

The dilemma is further complicated by questions of whether firms would have to disclose the exact amount (i.e. monetary sum) of commission taken in respect of a client's portfolio, and whether the firm would be allowed to retain commission that it had not disclosed to clients in a MiFID-compliant manner. Because there is a regular turnover of products in client portfolios, the difficulties of (1) measuring when certain products were allocated and what trail rate accrues to them (and when), (2) deciding whether or not to smooth the quarterly payment of trail commission over the course of the investment or to consider the quarterly payment as a lump sum at a given point in time, and (3) calculating the exact sum on a client by client basis of commission a firm receives in respect of discretionary managed portfolios, mean that these requirements would surely be very difficult, if not impossible, to implement in practice.

One way to get around the problem may be to stop taking trail commission on products allocated to discretionary portfolios. Yet this is hardly realistic. Nor would it be in clients' interests, as the firm would either have less of an incentive to look after its clients' interests, or would have to charge higher investment management fees to cover costs which are subsidized by trail commission. In some cases investment managers have tried to encourage managers of funds to set up an institutional share class, which are cheaper than retail share classes. Where institutional share classes exist, best practice suggests that firms should invest in those when acting on behalf of their clients (so as to avoid double-dipping). Yet there are clearly situations where managers do not issue institutional share classes, or where investing in a retail share class may be justified, for example, if the investment opportunity to which a client is being offered access is very rare or of an exceptional quality.

The dilemma presented in this section highlights just one of the examples where MiFID seems to have been drafted with a bias towards advisory relationships, without sufficient regard to the particularities of discretionary portfolio management, and the associated challenges of implementing the inducements provisions to investment management mandates established and agreed pre-MiFID.

3.3 The form of inducements disclosure – what is required?

Under MiFID, firms are required to disclose inducements in a manner that is 'comprehensive, accurate and understandable' (art. 26, Level 2), which CESR has interpreted in Level 3 as 'adequate information to enable the investor to relate the disclosure to the particular investment or ancillary service'.[15] Considerable controversy has surrounded the policy debate on what constitutes 'adequate information'.

It will immediately strike any careful reader that there is an apparent inconsistency in the wording around the form of inducements disclosure in art. 26. If the inconsistency is only apparent, regulators have not done enough to explain the logic behind it. The contradictory requirements on how exactly firms must disclose inducements to clients (especially around the level of detail required) have left many firms – and their compliance departments – puzzled. On the one hand, art. 26(b) states that a firm must disclose the 'existence, nature and amount of the [inducement] . . . in a manner that is comprehensive, accurate and understandable'. On the other hand, the final paragraph of the same article allows firms to disclose just the 'essential terms' of the inducement provided that it will make available the full details upon request.

The Commission's subsequent attempt to respond to the industry's concerns was anything but clear, largely avoiding a concrete answer to the question.[16] Nor did the Level 3 work on inducements carried out by CESR do much to clarify the situation. In fact, the contradictory requirements laid out in the Level 2 Directive are now reflected at Level 3. Paragraphs 21

15 CESR (2007b), p. 11.

16 The European Commission established a website where firms can submit questions in relation to the precise nature of their obligations under MiFID. The Commission answer to a question on the form of inducements disclosure reads as follows: 'Under the second paragraph of Article 26, the firm may disclose the "essential terms of the arrangements relating to the fee, commission or non-monetary benefit in summary form, provided that it undertakes to disclose further details at the request of the client and provided that it honours that undertaking". At the least, the essential details of the existence, nature and amount of the inducement, where the amount can be ascertained, should be provided. The goal of the summary disclosure is to enable the client to understand readily how the firm is incentivised to act. The disclosure should be fit for that purpose.' European Commission (2007), p. 59.

and 22 in CESR's second consultation paper on inducements (CESR 2006) likewise seem to contradict each other. Paragraph 21 refers to firms' publishing explicit schedules of disclosures, while paragraph 22 refers to a 'summary disclosure'. Likewise, in the culmination of CESR's initial Level 3 work on inducements (CESR 2007a), which lays out the common interpretations of MiFID rules on inducements to its members (i.e. the national regulators), recommendation 6(b) states that a generic disclosure which explains merely that a firm will or may receive or pay an inducement is not sufficient to enable a client to make an informed decision and therefore will not be considered as providing the 'essential terms of the arrangements' referred to in art. 26.

The contradiction probably arose as a consequence of political negotiations in the Council of Ministers. In all likelihood, principles-based regulators preferred an approach which discloses the 'essential terms' of the inducements, whereas the more prescriptive continental regulators may have pushed for the more detailed requirements to disclose 'the existence, nature and amount of the fee, commission or benefit, or, where the amount cannot be ascertained, the method of calculating that amount'.[17]

While it is clear that making generic statements to the effect that 'we may take commission on this investment' do not satisfy MiFID requirements, firms are left with next to no guidance on how they are to comply with the requirements in practice. The potential costs of not clarifying the requirements could be significant. It would hardly seem fair that, after the rules are established – and after regulators have repeatedly refused to give any kind of clarification or guidance as to the nature of the requirements – regulators would decide they are not satisfied with the way firms have implemented the inducements disclosure requirements. By making their expectations known only ex-post, after firms have adopted different approaches to disclosure, regulators would impose significant costs on firms, including the updating of product termsheets, ratecards and other client documentation, such as investment management mandates, and the costs of mailing these out to clients.

There is clearly little added benefit in making such detailed disclosures, over taking a range of funds and disclosing to clients something along the lines: 'for this family of funds, commissions will range between X and Y'. It could be sensibly argued that what a client needs more than knowing

[17] Oddly, the UK FSA, known to be one of the most staunch defenders of principles-based regulation in the EU, had stricter and more detailed rules on the disclosure of inducements pre-MiFID than almost any other European regulator.

the exact amount of commission a firm takes on a product is knowing the maximum commission the firm will take on that range of products, or the typical rate of commission that would apply for such a product. That should constitute 'adequate information' to satisfy the requirement to present the client with sufficient information to make an informed investment decision, since it gives the client a full appreciation of the scope for a firm to possibly give biased advice.[18] Knowing that the trail commission a firm receives for distributing a third party fund is 77 bps per annum instead of 82 bps per annum will do little to meet the objectives underlying the rule.

Without issuing any further clarifications, regulators may well identify best practices in the industry, which they would establish as benchmarks for all other firms to meet. Yet such an approach would seem to go counter to the very *raison d'être* of principles-based regulation, which is to establish the policy objectives of a legislative act at a high level, and allow firms to implement those objectives as they see fit.

It is therefore very possible that a wide variety of different approaches to the disclosure of inducements will emerge across the European Union. Whereas some firms may opt to disclose only ranges of commission by broad product type, others may decide that the legal risks of such a strategy are too considerable, prompting them to make very detailed disclosures. For large fund supermarkets, some of which have over 5,000 funds on their platforms, the prospect of mapping commissions attached to over 5,000 funds and presenting a commission 'telephone book' to their clients with details on commissions received on each fund on their platform is daunting.

Such a divergent set of practices will lead to an unhealthy equilibrium where firms which take a more legalistic approach to the rules are disadvantaged with respect to firms that either take a looser interpretation of the rules by relying on the vaguely-defined 'summary details' clause to satisfy their MiFID obligations. It goes without saying that such an outcome would yield an uncompetitive and uneven playing field

[18] It could additionally be argued that a firm would only need to go down the detailed disclosure route – i.e. disclose more than the 'essential terms' of the inducement – if it feels it is not managing the potential conflicts of interest generated by the inducement (e.g. biased investment advice) appropriately. MiFID's rules on conflicts of interest (art. 18, level 1) require a firm clearly to disclose the general nature and/or sources of conflicts of interest to the client before undertaking business on its behalf, where organizational or administrative arrangements to manage conflicts of interest are not sufficient to ensure that risks of damage to client interests will be prevented.

among firms. In the end, it is very likely that political pressure and the appearance of diverging interpretations by national regulators will force CESR to issue clearer guidance on what it expects to see from firms on inducements disclosure.

3.4 Renegotiating commission arrangements – do they need to be re-disclosed and agreed by clients?

Although MiFID requires firms to disclose at a minimum the 'essential terms' of inducements prior to a service being delivered, there is no corresponding obligation on firms to obtain explicit client consent to such arrangements, or to re-disclose the inducements to clients who are signed up to an ongoing service, if the terms of the inducements change after the initial disclosure has been made to clients. Both MiFID and the CESR Level 3 work remain completely silent on situations where the rates of commission agreed between a provider and distributors would change after an initial disclosure has been made to clients.

This is odd, given that the occasional renegotiation of distribution agreements is a commercial necessity and reality. It is yet another sign that MiFID was drafted largely with advisory services in mind.[19] There are several valid reasons why distributors may occasionally renegotiate the commercial terms on which they grant product providers access to their distribution networks. First, the initial terms that were negotiated might no longer be an accurate reflection of existing market conditions or in line with industry practices (some contracts with product providers may be decades old). Second, the initial terms that were negotiated might no longer be an accurate reflection of the ongoing costs to the provider of offering the service to clients, or indeed a fair price for the added value the firm provides to clients via the service. For example, if the take-up by a distributor's clients on a third party fund far exceeds what the distributor originally envisaged, the distributor may not be remunerated in a manner that is commensurate with the benefit its

[19] It would be easy enough to re-disclose the terms of a distribution agreement to clients with whom a firm has an ongoing advisory relationship, since the new terms of the inducement could be disclosed at the next point of contact with the client. This, however, does not address the question of whether, a very strict legal reading might even suggest that renegotiating trail commission or other fee-sharing agreements after disclosing them to clients would be prohibited under MiFID. This is not a realistic interpretation, and to suggest it would be the admission of a failure by regulators properly to understand the nature of the industry they are regulating.

clients derive from having access to this investment opportunity or with the associated costs.

Such situations mean that the regulatory regime should allow distributors, at their discretion, occasionally to renegotiate one-off changes to commercial arrangements with third-party product providers. In theory, regulators do not deny distributors their right to renegotiate higher trail commission. However, they do object to distributors doing so without their clients' knowledge (and possibly consent).

Ongoing services which require little contact between a firm and its clients, such as discretionary portfolio management, make it very difficult to obtain client consent with short turnaround times, and mail-outs to clients every time there is a change of even a couple of basis points to a distribution agreement seems to place a disproportional cost on firms, for the supposed benefits it would give clients. This leads to the question of how to adopt a pragmatic approach to MiFID implementation, but one which nevertheless remains purposeful. Possible approaches might include:

1. Where a firm has decided to make explicit disclosures on the amount of commission taken on each product, advised clients can simply be handed new product literature, such as termsheets with revised figures on commission. Firms should not have to issue new product literature for inconsequential increases in commission taken on a product. A materiality threshold of a few percentage points should therefore be established, and only if commission rises above this would the firm have to incur the significant costs associated with re-disclosing the new rate of commission to all clients subscribed to the service in question. However, such an approach would have to restrict the commission increases to one-off situations, so as to avoid progressive increases over time, which could amount to a material difference in comparison to what was initially disclosed to clients.
2. Where a firm has disclosed the ranges of commission it may receive, and any increase in commission would still lie within the range disclosed to clients, there should be no need to disclose to clients the exact increase in commission, unless the client specifically asks to be told the exact amount of commission the firm takes on a product.

The UK FSA's rules on packaged products are super-equivalent to MiFID, and directly address situations where commission rates are renegotiated subsequent to client disclosure. They unambiguously require a firm not only to disclose any increase in commission beyond the maximum range disclosed to clients, but also to obtain the client's explicit consent to the new arrangement.[20]

4. Conclusion

This chapter has highlighted the main policy objectives driving the MiFID rules on inducements, the practical implications of these rules, and the uncertainties that arise due to the lack of regulatory guidance issued around some provisions in the rules, particularly around the disclosure of inducements to clients.

To conclude, while the policy objectives underlying the rules are worthy, their formulation presents several key risks.

4.1 The lack of clarity could lead to an uneven playing field on a pan-European level

A central theme of this chapter has been that the uncertainty surrounding some of the key provisions of art. 26 would lead to diverging interpretations at national level. Over time, it will be particularly interesting to see how the national regimes around inducements emerge, especially around the interpretation of the obligation to disclose the 'essential terms' of an inducement prior to an investment service being delivered. There are already indications that, in the absence of a common European interpretation, interpretations of MiFID by national courts will lead to divergent implementations of MiFID, ultimately leading to an uncompetitive and fragmented market at European level. In Germany, for example, a ruling by the Federal Supreme Court (*Bundesgerichtshof*) in December 2006 judged that a bank was in breach of its obligations to a client by not disclosing the amount of the rebates taken from an asset manager.[21]

This is a problem which is more deeply rooted than MiFID alone. It relates to fundamental principles underlying single market law. Even if CESR were to issue more precise guidelines, the non-binding nature of its

[20] The FSA's *Conduct of Business Sourcebook* (FSA 2000), in point 6.3.18G reads: 'In accordance with the client's best interests rule and the fair, clear and not misleading rule, a firm which has started to provide a retail client with services in relation to packaged products following the provision of information on inducements required under COBS 2.3.1 R or a menu should not (at least until the completion of those services) arrange to retain any commission which exceeds the maximum amount or rate disclosed without first providing further appropriate inducements information or menu and obtaining the client's prior informed consent to the proposed alteration in a durable medium.'

[21] BGH, Urteil vom 19. Dezember 2006 – XI ZR 56/05 – OLG München, LG München I.

recommendations and the lack of any enforcement powers for CESR at present mean that national regulators are under no obligation to be bound by them.

4.2 Too detailed inducements disclosure may paradoxically result in worse outcomes for clients of firms with large distribution channels

Whereas much emphasis has been placed on the need to make the existence, nature and amount of commission publicly available as a necessary measure for the protection of investors, legislators seem to have overlooked the fact that disclosing the exact terms of commission will not always and everywhere be in the interests of consumers.

A prime example is the case of investors who are clients of firms which are large distributors. Just as firms which enjoy long-term relationships with top-performing fund managers are able to negotiate favourable terms of investment for their clients through side-letters, so also firms with large distribution networks are able to negotiate aggressive terms with managers, who are prepared to sacrifice margin for the volume of business such large distribution networks could generate. Such favourable terms might include the initial service charge (ISC) being waived for clients of large distributors. Also, the negotiating power of large distributors may help them to receive higher rates of commission than other distributors.

It is unlikely that in the environment of greater transparency which is likely to emerge in the post-MiFID world, such differentiated and preferential agreements are likely to survive, as distributors who face less favourable terms are sure to complain to fund managers about discriminatory pricing. The latter may be afraid of losing the business from all the smaller distributors, which collectively could comprise a sizeable portion of their business. There is already preliminary anecdotal evidence that some large fund management groups may be standardizing the commission and fee-sharing agreements they sign with distributors, as a result of MiFID.

4.3 The way the disclosure requirements are formulated may actually increase the risk of commission bias

While the logic underpinning one of the policy objectives underlying the inducements rules – namely, removing commission bias from the sales process – appears sound, the consequences of the requirements, as formulated, do not appear to have been considered carefully enough.

Both the Commission and the CESR have stated as one of the main drivers behind the MiFID inducements rules the removal of commission-driven bias from investment advice. However, as a consequence of the MiFID requirement to disclose inducements to clients, there will actually be far more transparency to bankers, relationship managers, advisers and salesmen on the different levels of commission their firms take on various products, than in the pre-MiFID world, where generic disclosures were made.

Unless firms dedicate resources to setting up entire teams of support staff who can draw up data on the rates of commission received from product providers subsequent to MiFID – an unlikely prospect – it is logical that the individuals who act as the interface between the firm and its clients – i.e. front-office sales staff or advisers – would be the ones addressing and answering client queries about the existence, nature and amount of commission taken by the firm on various products.

Yet by complying with the MiFID requirements on inducements disclosure and having to obtain information on the exact amount and nature of inducements taken on various products in response to client requests, front-office staff paradoxically face an increased risk of being incentivized to sell products for which higher commission accrues to the firm.

The second point, which legislators do not seem to have sufficiently emphasized, is that MiFID firms are under an obligation to identify and manage their conflicts of interest, and only to disclose them to clients as a last resort, if the controls put in place around them are deemed insufficiently robust.[22] Apart from inducements disclosure, an additional, or perhaps more effective, mechanism to align the interests of an adviser and his client, is to ensure that the remuneration schemes which the firm employs to reward front-office sales staff are blind to the amount of commission revenue generated by the sales of the products in question, or are neutral to sales volumes in a particular product.

[22] CESR did recognize this, but does not seem to agree that robust conflicts of interest management is sufficient to mitigate the risks to client interests: 'CESR agrees that the application of conflicts of interest management procedures may reduce the extent to which there is incentive to act other than in the best interests of the client. The application alone of such procedures however will not act as a safe harbour in respect of Article 26(b) nor will it affect the firm's duty of disclosure under Article 26(b).' (CESR 2007a), p. 15.

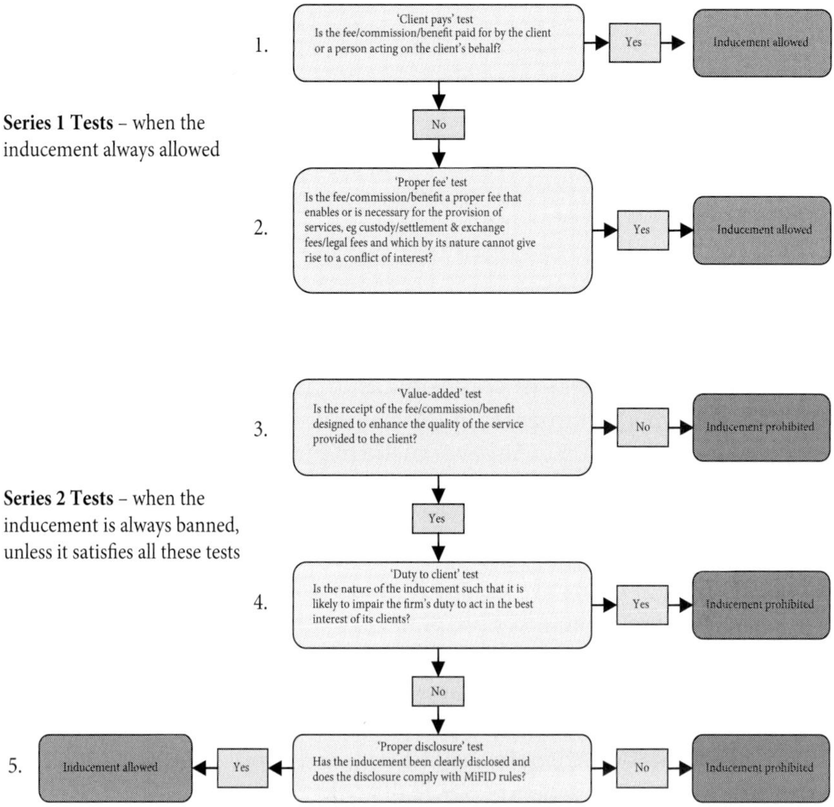

Annex I Making inducements MiFID-compliant

References

CESR 2006. *Inducements under MiFID.* Public Consultation, Ref: CESR/06-687. December. Paris: Committee of European Securities Regulators.

2007a. *Level 3 Recommendations on Inducements under MiFID: Feedback Statement,* May. Paris: Committee of European Securities Regulators.

2007b. *Inducements under MiFID – Recommendations,* Second Consultation, Ref: CESR/07-228b, May. Paris: Committee of European Securities Regulators.

European Commission 2007. MiFID Questions and Answer: http://ec.europa.eu/internal_market/securities/isd/questions/index_en.htm.

FSA 2000. *Conduct of Business Sourcebook.* Consultation Paper No. 45, London: FSA.

2006. *The Overall Impact of MiFID.* November. London: FSA.

8

MiFID's impact on the fund management industry

1. Introduction

There remains considerable confusion as to how exactly the MiFID and UCITS Directives will interact in the long run. This uncertainty reflects the growing pains of a regulatory transformation that represents nothing less than a tectonic shift from intense and prescriptive product regulation to a more flexible, principles-based regulation of management functions. Unlike UCITS, MiFID is a horizontal directive that cuts across the entire financial services industry (except for insurance). Precisely because the two directives are rooted in diverging regulatory philosophies, they are not natural partners, and the exercise of trying to fit the two together is likely to be neither effortless nor seamless.

This confusion can be traced to apparently contradictory – or, at the least, ambiguous – wording in the MiFID as to how its provisions relate to collective investment schemes. In reality, the UCITS–MiFID nexus is a web of dizzying complexity, on which this chapter attempts to shed more light. On the one hand, MiFID Recital 15 and art. 2(1)(h) state that collective investment schemes (whether or not coordinated at EU level), their management companies and depositaries are excluded from the scope of MiFID provisions. Since UCITS are collective investment undertakings that are coordinated at Community level, they, their managers and depositaries do not come under MiFID rules.

On the other hand, UCITS are listed in Section C of MiFID Annex I as MiFID financial instruments. Therefore, in their dealings with clients involving transactions in UCITS, all MiFID firms must apply conduct of business rules, which include best execution and suitability.[1] Yet conduct of business rules do not apply to eligible counterparties, otherwise

[1] The classification of UCITS under art. 19(6) as a 'non-complex' financial instrument by default means it can be exempted from the appropriateness test in art. 19(5) for execution-only transactions.

Table 8.1 MiFID provisions that apply to UCITS

MiFID provisions that apply to UCITS management companies	• Dealings as counterparty to public authorities (art. 2.2) • Cross-border takeover of a company (art. 10(4)) if it leads to a qualifying holding in that firm • Capital requirements (art. 12) • Organizational requirements (art. 13) (in particular conflicts of interest) • Conduct of business obligations (art. 19) (in particular suitability and best execution)
These MiFID provisions only apply to UCITS management companies when the latter provide the following services:	
	• Discretionary portfolio management • Investment advice • Custody and administration

known as '*per se* financial institutions'. And MiFID art. 24(2) binds member states' competent authorities to recognize as eligible counterparties UCITS and their management companies, meaning that, in their transactions with investment firms, they are by default not afforded conduct of business protections. However, investment managers (including UCITS) can request under the same article to have their transactions protected by MiFID's conduct of business rules, including best execution.

In addition, despite the art. 2(1)(h) exemption, MiFID art. 66 brings some UCITS management company functions under the scope of MiFID (see Table 8.1). Thus, UCITS management companies are subject to both the UCITS and MiFID directives: when providing ancillary investment services (investment advice, individual portfolio management, etc.) they are governed by MiFID, whereas the UCITS directive covers the designation of management companies. Under the original UCITS Directive, management companies could only provide collective investment services. But under the 'product directive' component of UCITS III, the services management companies could provide were extended to cover individual portfolio management, allowing them to compete directly with portfolio managers, who carry out these activities under a MiFID licence.[2] The decision to apply certain conduct of business rules to UCITS

[2] FSA (2006), which cites art. 5(3) of the UCITS Directive, as amended by Directive 2001/107/EC.

management companies that are undertaking individual portfolio management was a necessary consequence of the wider powers managers of UCITS were given under UCITS III: its purpose was to ensure that a level playing field emerges in the management of individual portfolios, whether by MiFID-authorized investment managers or UCITS management companies.

The interaction between UCITS and MiFID is further complicated by the art. 3(1) exemption that leaves discretion to the individual EU member states to decide whether to apply MiFID to legal persons that only receive/transmit orders in UCITS, that do not hold any clients' funds, and that only transact with certain counterparties. Because these various options and possible exemptions raise serious concerns for a level playing field at the pan-European level, it would be sensible for the European Commission to clarify to what degree UCITS funds would potentially be affected by the art. 3(1) carve-out.

The various layers of interaction, options and carve-outs described above paint a complex picture of the MiFID–UCITS nexus. Its more precise articulation over time will result in a robust learning-by-doing exercise for market participants and regulators alike. It is likely to involve hiccups along the way. The Asset Management Sector Leader of the FSA, Dan Waters, playing on a phrase coined by the former US Secretary of Defense, has described the interaction between the UCITS and MiFID Directives as being 'full of both known unknowns and unknown unknowns'.[3] His is a not so subtle recognition that regulators, just as much as market participants, have yet to come to a better understanding of how the two directives will fit together in practice.

At the same time, these differences are in many respects technical, they only touch a few areas, and they do not mean that UCITS and MiFID are fundamentally incompatible. At a very high level, and overlooking some of the technical points where the fit is not perfect, the boundary between UCITS and MiFID is fairly clear. While UCITS governs the constitution, management, administration and process around the launch of a fund, MiFID governs commercial agreements between providers and distributors, as well as services related to distribution (e.g. brokerage and advice). As mentioned above, there are however a few important exceptions from this stylised picture, notably:

[3] 'Opening up European markets for fund distribution: the impact of MiFID on UCITS distribution', speech by Dan Waters, Asset Management Sector Leader, FSA, City & Financial Croup Conference, London, 18 January 2007.

Table 8.2 Provisions that apply to UCITS: MiFID or member state discretion

UCITS funds	MiFID	Member state discretion
Fund distribution undertaken by an investment firm	X	
Fund distribution undertaken by fund management company		X
Fund distribution undertaken neither by a UCITS management company nor a MiFID investment firm		X
Investment advice on collective investment scheme given by investment firm	X	
Advice exclusively relating to collective investments given by fund management company		X
Advice on collective investments combined with other instruments given by the fund management company	X	
Advice on collective investment that is part of a package or 'wrap'	X	
Reception/transmission of orders relating to collective investments only		X
Self-managed UCITS, distribution and advice		X (?)

1. where UCITS market their own funds or delegate this activity to an agent;
2. execution – the boundary between UCITS and MiFID is not explicitly clear with regard to rules surrounding execution: the subscription/redemption of units in UCITS is governed by the UCITS directive, while the reception/transmission of client orders in UCITS is governed by MiFID;
3. where UCITS management companies carry out individual portfolio management in addition to their core activity of collective investment management.

The importance of getting these points resolved quickly should not be underestimated. If – as the current legislative framework seems to suggest – UCITS management companies can market and sell their funds cross-border under the UCITS rules, without being subjected to the MiFID regime which applies when MiFID investment firms distribute those same funds, there is a fundamental incoherence in the regulatory architecture governing the marketing and selling of UCITS. In addition, there is evidence that member states are moving to address this disconnect in an uncoordinated manner, which could fragment the UCITS market. While some member states are deciding to impose MiFID rules on their own management companies or on foreign ones when they sell cross-border into their jurisdictions, others do not.

2. Uneven playing fields?

The degree of confusion prevailing among both regulators and market participants is worrisome to the extent that it could bring about further compliance, administrative and IT costs upon the industry, as well as stifle innovation in both product development and in the evolution of the industry architecture (models of distribution, outsourcing, etc.) through continued regulatory uncertainty. In addition, the same options and exemptions mentioned above, which are the source of the confusion as to how MiFID and UCITS will interact, raise serious concerns about whether a level playing field will exist in the European investment management business post-MiFID.

Broadly speaking, there are five areas where MiFID impacts most on the asset management business: best execution, outsourcing, product fact disclosures, conflicts of interest and inducements. The fact that some actors in the UCITS market face MiFID best execution rules that are considerably stricter than those under the UCITS Directive governing actors in the same market raises legitimate concerns about a distorted playing field.

2.1 Best execution

Concerning best execution, the investment management industry does not come under a harmonized set of rules, since some entities will fall under the light-touch UCITS regime for execution (taken from ISD art. 11 on conduct of business, which sets out only very high level principles), and others will be subjected to MiFID's more detailed rules on execution.[4]

4 Specifically, the requirements to: implement an execution policy and obtain client consent to it prior to dealing with clients and conduct ongoing monitoring of execution quality delivered by the various regulated markets, MTFs and brokers used, based on the execution factors which the firm prioritizes. In order to make the review of execution policy effective, firms will have to come up with metrics to quantify, or at least make a credible qualitative assessment of, execution quality. This exercise is particularly difficult for execution factors which are not easily quantifiable, such as likelihood of execution, market impact, etc.

More precisely, management companies executing transactions in the process of managing collective investments do not come under MiFID's onerous best execution rules. They do when providing individual portfolio management services. The European Commission has clearly stated that where a UCITS management company outsources the management of a UCITS to an investment firm under art. 5(g) of the UCITS Directive, the investment firm must give the UCITS conduct of business protections and treat it as a professional or retail client.[5] However, where the management company retains investment management functions and transacts with investment firms, it is to be considered an eligible counterparty, in line with MiFID art. 24(2).

Broadening the debate beyond UCITS, the French market regulator (Autorité des Marchés Financiers – AMF), has already declared its misgivings about the uneven application of best execution requirements among management companies: 'As regards the best execution requirement, non-uniform treatment of management companies subject to MiFID in respect of all or part of their business and management companies not subject to MiFID (those that manage only non-UCITS or only UCITS, for example), seems hard to justify.'[6]

2.2 Outsourcing

The emphasis on fund management companies in the various MiFID exemptions and UCITS revision leaves one to wonder where and under what conditions self-managed UCITS fall under the MiFID umbrella. Under the UCITS Directive, both fund management companies and self-managed funds (e.g. SICAVs) may delegate investment management, administration and distribution functions to third-party service providers. In the case of delegation of the distribution, which set of rules prevails, those of UCITS or of MiFID?

2.3 Fact disclosures

Under UCITS art. 28, UCITS management companies must disclose entry and exit commissions as well as other expenses or fees. The Commission's 2004 recommendation encouraged member states to require UCITS to publish in the simplified prospectus total expense ratios

[5] See the European Commission's FAQ on MiFID, Question 97: http://ec.europa.eu/internal_market/securities/isd/questions/index_en.htm.

[6] AMF (2006).

(TERs) in order to better reflect the total operating costs of the fund.[7] However, the non-binding nature of the recommendation means that member states have introduced different forms of TERs, making cross-border comparisons of costs difficult. MiFID also requires disclosure of costs and associated charges under art. 19(3). To the extent that art. 34(2) of the MiFID Implementing Directive[8] considers the simplified prospectus to be sufficient information for the purposes of MiFID art. 19(3), MiFID firms which distribute UCITS will import the uneven application of disclosure of costs and charges that result from the patchy implementation of the Commission's 2004 recommendation. In addition, level playing field issues are raised by Recital 55 of the MiFID Implementing Directive. Notwithstanding art. 34(2) of the same directive, Recital 55 requires investment firms distributing units in UCITS to additionally inform their clients about all the other costs and associated charges related to their provision of investment services in relation to units in UCITS. It is unclear how these disclosures are to be made, or what information precisely is required, leaving scope for divergent interpretations at the national level.

2.4 Conflicts of interest

As with best execution, the UCITS requirements on conflicts of interest use a lighter touch than those of MiFID. The core duty of care to clients that is the backbone of MiFID conduct of business rules is given in art. 19(1), which requires investment firms, when providing investment services and/or, where appropriate, ancillary services to clients, to 'act honestly, fairly and professionally in accordance with the best interests of its clients'. Similarly, the UCITS Directive sets forth comparable requirements for collective investment management.[9] Notably, Directive 2001/107/EC, art. 5h lists a set of principles a management company shall respect (take from the ISD), i.e.: (1) acting honestly and fairly in conducting its business activities in the best interests of the UCITS it manages and the integrity of the market; (2) acting with due skill, care and diligence, in the best interests of the UCITS it manages and the integrity of the market; (3) trying to avoid conflicts of interests and, when they cannot be

7 Commission Recommendation 2004/384/EC of 27 April 2004.

8 Directive 2006/73/EC.

9 See UCITS I, Directive 85/611/EEC, art. 10(2): 'The management company must act independently and solely in the interest of the unit-holders'; and Directive 2001/107/EC, art. 5h.

avoided, ensuring that the UCITS it manages are fairly treated, and (4) complying with all regulatory requirements applicable to the conduct of its business activities so as to promote the best interests of its investors and the integrity of the market. To give effect to these provisions, a UCITS management company must be 'structured and organized in such a way as to minimize the risk of UCITS' or clients' interests being prejudiced by conflicts of interest between the company and its clients, between one of its clients and another, between one of its clients and a UCITS or between two UCITS'.[10]

MiFID, on the other hand, requires firms to 'maintain and operate effective organizational and administrative arrangements with a view to taking all reasonable steps designed to prevent conflicts of interest from adversely affecting the interests of its clients'.[11] Where firms are not satisfied that the controls they have put into place around a conflict are sufficient to manage it, they must disclose the conflict to clients. In addition, they must maintain a register of those conflicts of interest, including potential conflicts, which they have identified as giving rise to potential client detriment. Those registers of conflicts, as well as their attendant controls, must be reviewed occasionally by the firm. This all means that the administrative requirements around the management of conflicts of interest are significantly more burdensome for MiFID authorized firms, as opposed to those authorized under UCITS. While this will not necessarily lead to inefficiencies (given the stylized picture given above of MiFID as regulation distribution and UCITS the manufacturing and management of funds), it could lead to arbitrage where firms conduct activities which are caught in the UCITS–MiFID grey zone.

2.5 Inducements

MiFID takes a very tough stance on inducements, with a view to forcing more transparency in the market for the distribution of retail investment products, and to removing biases in investment advice that arise from product providers paying distributors a commission. The starting point is that inducements are banned, unless they meet the strict criteria laid out in art. 26 of the MiFID Level 2 Implementing Directive. Firms can only receive fees, commission or non-monetary benefits in relation to services provided to clients in the following cases:

[10] UCITS Directive 2001/107/EC, art. 5f(1)(b).

[11] See MiFID, art. 13(3).

1. When the commissions/benefits are paid or provided to or by the client (or by a person acting on his behalf).
2. When the commissions/benefits are paid or provided to or by a third party (or by a person acting on his behalf) if two cumulative sub-conditions are fulfilled: disclosure of such commissions/benefits to the client plus need for enhancing the quality of the service through the payment of the commission.
3. When the commissions are necessary for the provision of the services and cannot give rise to conflicts of interest for ensuring acting in the best interests of the client.

These provisions might create difficulties for widely accepted distribution practices in the fund management industry, namely the retrocession of fees from product providers to distributors. In particular, in some instances product providers and intermediaries (which are not in the same immediate parent company) may be contemplating significant up-front payments as a condition for the provider's products being placed on, or even considered for, the intermediary's panel or recommended list. These payments would be unconnected with, and additional to, conventional commissions which would be paid on the sale of particular products. Such payments would not be consistent with the standards of conduct for firms – irrespective of whether they will be 'whole of market' or 'multi-tied'. Such introductory payments are thus incompatible with the fundamental principle that a firm must not conduct business under arrangements that might give rise to a conflict with its duty to customers.

Where UCITS are distributed by MiFID firms, the latter will have to comply with the rules on inducements. Because UCITS management companies are allowed to distribute third-party funds under the Management Company Directive (at least according to CESR's interpretation), it was considered necessary to extend MiFID rules on inducements to cover the remuneration agreements struck between UCITS management companies and the fund management groups whose funds they may distribute in addition to their own, precisely in order to ensure that the playing field would be level.

How exactly the complex interaction between the UCITS and MiFID Directives plays out in practice will therefore have an important impact on the European fund industry, not least because UCITS constitute the vast majority of funds in the EU. This interaction is further complicated by the very real possibility that MiFID will be applied and interpreted differently in the various EU member states, meaning that the way MiFID and UCITS interact is also likely to vary from member state to member state. In reality, the potential impact of MiFID on the asset management industry, especially on distribution, could well reach far beyond what anyone had anticipated, or indeed, the European Commission intended.

3. Further impact of MiFID on the asset management sector

The practical consequences of the application of the MiFID regime to UCITS might become very burdensome for UCITS management companies: as soon as they develop the MiFID services mentioned above, they will have to comply with a comprehensive set of rules regarding their organization and functioning, and will still have to comply with the UCITS Directive provisions regarding their core activity of UCITS fund management. One can at least identify six areas of impact for those services apart from collective portfolio management.

1. Many functions have to be organized in an independent way (e.g. compliance function; risk management; internal audit). Although MiFID provides that this requirement can be softened or exempted with a proportionality test (i.e. for SMEs in particular), some of these exemption cases will be offered only if the management company is able to prove that it fulfilled the conditions to be exempted.
2. The restrictions and internal disclosure of personal transactions of management companies' staff is regulated in detail by MiFID. This might raise concerns because, for example, the scope of relevant persons is now extended to relatives (including partners for instance) and professional relations. Regarding relatives, we do not know yet how member states will be able to strike the right balance between this requirement and the European and national obligations on data protection (which have to be applied for the MiFID transposition – see Recital 43 of level 1 MiFID). In addition, those transactions will have to be disclosed 'promptly' (art. 12(b)), which might create some difficulties of organization in the daily work of compliance officers of management companies.
3. The management companies will have to deal not only with actual conflicts of interest but also with potential ones (art. 21 level 2 MiFID). It might raise difficulties as by nature some potential conflicts of interest are not always easy to anticipate.
4. The files of clients of management companies will have to be reclassified as MiFID introduces a distinction between eligible

counterparts, professional clients and retail clients. But the question of a grandfathering clause for the treatment of existing clients' files (requiring or not new information today for already existing clients' files) is not answered by MiFID.

5. Regarding best execution, even though this full requirement is only imposed on investment firms executing the transactions themselves (in general, the brokers), management companies will have to comply with it in the following way. When management companies provide individual portfolio management services or for the service of reception/transmission of orders, they have to transmit the orders to brokers for execution. MiFID requires that the management com-panies have to provide for a 'transmission policy' which ensures that brokers have been selected by the management companies among those presenting the objective criteria of offering a high probability of best execution of orders. It means that management companies will not be responsible for the best execution of orders in practice, as those orders are executed by the brokers, but that they will have to justify the way they have established their 'transmission policy'.

BOX 8.1 SUBSTANTIVE REFERENCES TO UCITS AND COLLECTIVE INVESTMENTS IN MiFID AND THE IMPLEMENTING DIRECTIVE

Recital 15 and art. 2(1)(h) – Collective investment undertakings, whether coordinated at the EU level (i.e. UCITS) or not, together with their managers and depositaries do not fall under the scope of MiFID.

Article 3(1) – Member states can decide whether or not to apply MiFID to legal persons that only receive/transmit units in collective investment undertakings and that do not hold any clients' funds and that only transact with certain counterparties.

Article 10(4) – Cross-border acquisitions by UCITS management companies that would result in a 'qualifying holding'[12] are subject to art. 60[13] subject to certain conditions.

[12] As defined in MiFID art. 4 (27).

[13] MiFID art. 60 relates to the consultations among the different competent authorities of the member states prior to the authorization of cross-border business.

Article 19(6) – Because UCITS is qualified as a non-complex instrument, investment firms do not need to apply the appropriateness test mentioned in art. 19(5) when on an execution-only basis.

Article 24(2) – UCITS and their management companies must be recognized as eligible counterparties by member states' regulatory authorities, which means MiFID's conduct of business rules do not apply for these transactions. However, this does not preclude them from requesting to opt-down (higher standard of investor protection) to a lower classification for the purposes of seeking protection under conduct of business rules.

Article 66 – Certain MiFID articles will apply to UCITS management companies, including capital requirements, organizational requirements and conduct of business rules (see Table 8.2 above).

Recital 55 (Implementing Directive 2006/73/EC) – Although art. 34 of Directive 2006/73/EC states that the simplified prospectus is enough for the purposes of Directive 2004/39/EC, investment firms distributing units in UCITS should additionally inform their clients about all the other costs and associated charges related to their provision of investment services in relation to units in UCITS.

Article 34(2) (Implementing Directive 2006/73/EC) – The simplified prospectus is sufficient information for the purposes of MiFID art. 19(3) on disclosing costs and charges associated with investing in a fund.

4. MiFID and the distribution of non-harmonized products

Much of the debate surrounding the Commission's work on the Green and White Papers has focused on eligible assets – i.e. which instruments could eventually be regarded as suitable for inclusion in a UCITS portfolio and which can not. The advantage of having a product that is harmonized at the European level like UCITS is that these funds can be marketed across the EU on the basis of a single offering document, the simplified prospectus, and under a single set of rules, which is not the case for non-harmonized funds.

With the proliferation of financial instruments, there has been significant pressure on the Commission (and CESR by extension) to widen the definition of eligible assets (which is the only way to widen the range of products that can be included in a UCITS without necessitating changes to the existing legislative framework). This pressure also arises from the fact that the market for UCITS, while originally designed essentially for retail investors, is today permeated with institutional players who seek to piggy-back on the passport for a 'retail' product as the only means to efficiently market a fund cross-border, even in the institutional space. In this respect, there have been and continue to be attempts to 'shoe-horn' various alternative products into UCITS, even though they may not be a particularly good fit for retail investors. This reality will necessitate a careful balancing act for regulators between, on the one hand, preserving the standard of investor protection for which UCITS is known and, on the other hand, making the brand flexible enough to respond to ever greater competitive pressures in the global fund market – at least until a pan-European private placement regime or a light-touch harmonized regime for the treatment of unregulated funds, is in place.

The problem with trying to shoe-horn different products into the UCITS framework is that the exercise of defining eligible assets for UCITS is outdated. It is neither sustainable given the existing institutional framework, nor does it adequately take account of the lessons of modern portfolio theory.[14] Critics will contend, however, that it is precisely this measured consideration of eligible instruments that has contributed to the reputation of the UCITS brand as ensuring a high degree of investor protection.

On the other hand, from an industry perspective, the accelerated pace of financial innovation means that the exercise of reconsidering which instruments are suitable for UCITS is handcuffed by the slow legislative machinery and therefore not conducive to facilitating a competitive EU fund market. The industry sees a distinct possibility in MiFID to by-pass this bottleneck. The Commission's expert groups on alternative investments have recommended that alternative investment funds (e.g. hedge funds) be distributed to retail investors on a cross-border basis on the basis of MiFID's distribution framework without imposing any additional product or management regulation at EU level.[15] In other words, this suggestion would amount to a pure mutual recognition regime for alternative investment funds without any minimal level of harmonization at EU level of the product. This is rather wishful thinking in light of the forty years' EU experience with single market legislation (historical precedent shows that without a minimum degree of harmonized legislation at EU level, a single market cannot emerge).

14 See Casey (2006).

15 See Recommendations 1 and 4 of European Commission (2006).

In addition to the unrealistic ambition of a pure mutual recognition regime (i.e. one where there is no minimal product harmonization at EU level), one has to consider whether regulators would really agree to passport an alternative investment fund across the EU without any form of pan-European product regulation. The answer from CESR is very clear: impossible.[16] CESR's objections are based upon two grounds. First, retail investor protection: in CESR's view, distribution rules are simply too lax under MiFID for alternative investments to be marketed to retail investors without any further product regulation. Second, the competitive effect: if alternative investments can be marketed to retail clients only on the basis of MiFID suitability/appropriateness tests, the playing field in the European fund market would be severely distorted to the advantage of alternative funds.

UCITS is widely seen to be a major success story in Europe, the only example of a truly successful pan-European retail market for financial services to date. Today, it is a globally recognized brand that is synonymous with investor protection and sound product quality. This success should be built upon, rather than undermined. No doubt markets move fast and the existing regulatory framework ought to reflect these changes. It is necessary, for example, to examine whether the quality of UCITS is indeed consistently superior on average (in terms of risk-return profiles) to that of alternative investment funds, on which no clear-cut answer has been given so far, although inclusion of some portion of derivative instruments seems to have had a positive impact (European Commission 2008). If not, there would be little reason to object to the wider inclusion of complex instruments in UCITS. But, at the same time, one must be aware that confidence in the widely recognized UCITS label could be easily destroyed: building the trust and confidence of (international) investors in certain products takes years, and clumsy action by regulators could destroy this confidence overnight.

The continuing uneven playing field between various savings products is therefore very worrying. Relying on MiFID alone for the distribution of alternative investment funds to a retail market audience without any additional product regulation would only exacerbate the problem. Indeed, the possibility for distributors to market an alternative investment fund across the EU under the MiFID distribution passport but without the attendant UCITS product passport would undermine the very *raison d'être* of the UCITS brand – a high level of investor protection

[16] For a more detailed view, see CESR (2006).

through a combination of product regulation and management regulation – effectively driving UCITS out of the market. As a consequence, vigilance and careful reflection are required on the part of regulators as they determine how exactly the MiFID distribution passport will apply to alternative investment funds, and whether this application is compatible with the UCITS Directive.

Currently, there is significant confusion in the marketplace as to how alternative investments will fit into the already tense MiFID–UCITS interaction. Under MiFID, it is not certain that a product has to be harmonized at the European level to enjoy pan-European distribution. All that is required for the (advised) sales of MiFID financial instruments is the suitability test and an appropriateness test for execution-only transactions (except under certain conditions). This looser regulatory framework (in the sense that MiFID does not regulate products) might apply not only to alternative investment funds, depending on how MiFID is ultimately interpreted, but also to structured product wrappers around these investments.

The probability that cross-border sales of alternative investment funds will be done under MiFID without any kind of pan-European sales framework is less probable than for structured products. This is because structured products are already widely available in the retail market in many European countries, mostly due to the capital protection at maturity built into many of them. As a result, even if some national regulators in the EU were to prevent the cross-border distribution of non-harmonized funds into their jurisdictions under a MiFID distribution licence only, it is quite possible that investment firms could offer structured notes around a portfolio of hedge funds to retail investors cross-border under MiFID. To the extent that structured products, or a portfolio which includes complex financial instruments such as options and other derivatives, might successfully replicate the risk-return profiles of UCITS funds, and might be marketed cross-border under MiFID without any form of product regulation, they will have a significant advantage over UCITS in terms of the regulatory framework. So long as these products can be considered 'transferable securities' under MiFID, they qualify for pan-European distribution under a MiFID license. This composite portfolio of structured products could be built through the (advised) sales of individual products that together form a portfolio akin to a fund in terms of diversification, etc. To the extent that composite portfolios made up of a combination of structured products or complex MiFID financial instruments can replicate UCITS risk-return profiles, and advised sales of these individual products (or as a package) can be done on a cross-border basis without any further product regulation, they have a significant advantage over UCITS in terms of the regulatory framework. So long as these products can be considered 'transferable securities' under MiFID, they qualify for pan-European distribution under the MiFID passport without further product regulation.

For the reasons stated in the paragraph above, without a more precise definition of the term 'transferable securities', the UCITS market faces a severe threat from a new range of structured products with alternative investments as underlying. This definition could potentially include CDOs, CLOs, and various derivatives thereof. Without a more precise definition of the term 'transferable securities', the UCITS market faces a severe threat from a new range of structured products.

Another important question in the debate on the 'MiFID-ization' of alternative investment funds and products relates to whether financial advisers are truly competent enough to handle complex instruments and non-harmonized funds without the end-investor enjoying any kind of additional protection in the form of product regulation. There are good reasons to doubt this to be the case. Additionally, one must consider whether Independent Financial Advisers or ill-trained personnel at the point of sale in bank branches will really be capable of keeping pace with and understanding the vast influx of complex new products sufficiently well to act as the ultimate safeguard of investor well-being in a world devoid of product regulation. Will there not be a significantly enhanced risk of mis-selling under such circumstances? For this reason, any move away from product regulation must be accompanied by rigorous exercises to ensure sales forces are trained and competent to advise these products and are treating customers fairly.

In our opinion, MiFID should not be seen to grant a passport to the cross-border distribution to retail investors of any or all non-harmonized collective schemes and structured products with alternative investments as underlyings. But as it currently stands, it remains very unclear whether or how regulators will prevent alternative investments from being distributed cross-border to a retail audience under MiFID. It is therefore essential that a proper articulation of how MiFID applies to the cross-border sales of non-harmonized products be developed as soon as possible. How broad a reading of MiFID is adopted by the Commission and national regulatory bodies will be critical to determining the future success of UCITS as a brand.

It is also useful to highlight how insurance products, some of which (e.g. unit-linked) can compete directly with UCITS without a similar degree of harmonized regulation, also (currently) enjoy a skewed playing field. One of the main causes of the unequal playing field between products is the differing conditions for the oversight and control over marketing documents for 'financial products' and 'insurance products'.[17] In view of the above discussion, the exclusion of insurance products from the scope of MiFID does not make any sense, and should be urgently addressed. The comparable rules under the EU's Insurance Mediation Directive (2002/92/EC) are not comparable to the regime which MiFID has put in place.

In this vein, the conclusions of the May 2007 EU Council of Finance Ministers are very welcome. The Council emphasized the importance of consistency between MiFID and UCITS, and insisted: 'to ensure, in the context of retail distribution of, and advice on, UCITS, that all steps are taken by the Commission and the Member States in enforcing the conduct of business rules provided for in the MiFID . . . and stresses the need for clearly ensuring the coherence of application of the MiFID and the UCITS directives.' The Council further invited the Commission 'to review the consistency of EU legislation regarding the different types of retail investment products (such as unit-linked life insurance, investment funds, certain structured notes and certificates), so as to ensure a coherent approach to investor protection and to avoid any mis-selling possibilities'.[18] The European Commission has opened a consultation on the subject, but it is clear that, in view of the discussion in this chapter, the answer will not be easy.[19]

References

Autorité des Marchés Financiers (AMF) 2005. *Rapport relatif à la commercialisation des produits financiers* (rapport Delmas-Marsalet): www.amf-france.org/documents/general/6383_1.pdf.

2006. *Consultation on Enforcing the Best-execution Principles in MiFID and its Implementing Directive*, 25 July: www.amf-france.org/documents/general/7274_1.pdf.

Casey, Jean-Pierre 2006. *Eligible Assets, Investment Strategies and Investor Protection in Light of Modern Portfolio Theory: Towards a Risk-based Approach for*

[17] See AMF (2005), p. 18. [18] See Casey and Lannoo (2008), p. 28.
[19] See European Commission (2007).

UCITS, ECMI Policy Brief No. 2, September. Brussels: Centre for European Policy Studies.

Casey, Jean-Pierre and Karel Lannoo 2008. *Pouring Old Wine in New Skins? UCITS and Asset Management after MiFID*, Task Force Report, April. Brussels: Centre for European Policy Studies.

CESR 2006. *Reaction to the Reports of the Commission Expert Groups on Market Efficiency and on Alternative Investment Funds*, CESR/06-46id: www.cesr.eu.org/index.php?page=contenu_groups&id=28&docmore=1.

European Commission 2006. *Report of the Alternative Investment Expert Group: Managing, Servicing and Marketing Hedge Funds in Europe*, July.

2007. *Need for a Coherent Approach to Product Transparency and Distribution Requirements for Substitute Retail Investment Products, Call for Evidence*, 26 October: http://ec.europa.eu/internal_market/finances/docs/cross-sector/call.en.pdf.

2008. *Investment Funds in the European Union: Comparative Analysis of Use of Investment Powers, Investment Outcomes and Related Risk Features in Both UCITS and Non-harmonised Markets*, February: http://ec.europa.eu/internal_market/investment/other_docs/index_en.htm#studies.

Financial Services Authority 2006. *Implementing MiFID's Best Execution Requirements*, DP06/03. May: www.fsa.gov.uk/Pages/Library/Policy/dp/2006/06_03.shtml.

9

MiFID and bond market transparency

The most important outstanding issue of MiFID is the application of pre- and post-trade transparency requirements to non-equity markets. Although the general conduct of business provisions apply to all financial instruments, the pre- and post-trade transparency requirements apply only to equity markets for the time being. Article 65.1 tasked the Commission with conducting a study to report by 31 October 2007 on whether the transparency requirements ought to be extended to classes of financial instruments other than shares.[1]

This chapter presents the pros and cons of introducing greater transparency into non-equity markets, especially bonds. It highlights the insufficient level of data available to market participants and regulators on volumes and aggregate bond market activity, as well as the lack of appropriate information made available to retail investors, suggesting that dealers may have little time to come up with a solution, and that an industry code of conduct may be an appropriate avenue to introduce more transparency, preferable to legislative initiatives.

1. Introduction

The debate on bond market transparency is a difficult one, owing to the complex interaction and possible trade-offs between the policy objectives of market liquidity, transparency, stability, efficiency and investor protection. All of these are valid policy objectives; the critical challenge becomes one of finding the appropriate mix.

Pre- and post-trade transparency may equally enhance or harm market liquidity and efficiency, depending on how they are applied, by whom, for what instruments, in which markets and at which latency.

[1] Recital 46 of MiFID states that member states have the option of applying the pre- and post-trade transparency requirements to non-equity securities. In that case, this applies to firms established and transactions carried out in that state.

Likewise, transparency does not necessarily need to enhance investor protection, depending on how it is carried out and what the consequences of these measures are likely to be for various market actors, and since investor protection in fixed-income markets depends on many other (perhaps more important factors) than price transparency alone.

This all means there are many nuances to be explored in the debate on bond market transparency, and that it is therefore important not to become trapped in an ideological mindset. Rather, one should put one's prejudices aside and seriously consider in an objective manner how to arrive at an optimal level of transparency.

2. Why regulate transparency?

The normative question of whether transparency ought to be regulated derives from the concern that the level, type and distribution of information prevailing in bond markets might be sub-optimal from the point of view of meeting the policy objectives of market efficiency and retail investor protection. If transparency is found to be deficient, it means that both market efficiency and retail investor protection could suffer, raising the spectre of a twin set of market failures. At least, this has been the FSA's rationale for looking into the possibility of further regulating secondary bond markets in the UK (FSA 2005).

On the one hand, opacity as regards essential trade information can damage the speed and quality at which new information is impounded into prices, causing the efficiency of the price formation mechanism to be compromised. Overall market efficiency will suffer as a result, since prices are that invisible hand that Adam Smith described to explain the miracle of efficient resource allocation; price formation (also known as price discovery) – generated by trading – is the mechanism by which market participants arrive at a consensus on the fundamental value of a security, enabling them better to determine how it fits in their portfolio of assets.

On the other hand, regulators are concerned that the lack of transparency prevailing in fixed-income markets can breed a culture where execution results for clients are not considered a priority by securities dealers. Trading activities in the B2C (business-to-consumer) space are especially fraught with information asymmetries that are characteristic of principal–agent relationships: the client who submits an order is at the mercy of the broker who routes or fills it. Thus, transparency is a powerful instrument in better aligning the interests of the principal and the agent: it allows the client to verify the quality of execution his broker delivered. The pressure on brokers to obtain the most favourable execution result for their clients by routing their orders to the venue that will best satisfy the client's interest – rather than to the one that will yield the most kickbacks for the broker – is clearly a positive function of market transparency.

Faced with the possible market failures associated with opacity, e.g. inefficient price discovery and the failure of brokers to execute under conditions favourable to the client, the regulator's dilemma is to consider whether introducing greater transparency into markets can solve these actual or perceived deficiencies.

A first step is to consider in which cases statutory regulation is warranted. Broadly, there are two different approaches to this kind of assessment, the first we can call the economic approach to regulation. Proponents of this school will want to ask certain questions prior to introducing new regulations (e.g. is regulatory intervention warranted?), and prior to developing a regulatory strategy once a course of action has been decided (e.g. will the proposed regulation(s) be able to overcome the perceived market failure(s) in a way that minimizes compliance costs and foregone external competitiveness?).

With respect to bond market transparency, the economic approach to regulation will encourage regulators to entertain questions such as: is there a market failure? If so, can market-led initiatives or technological improvements substitute for new regulation? Will increased transparency improve overall market efficiency/liquidity? Will transparency improve investor protection (investor protection being one of the main policy objectives for which transparency is seen to be an effective policy instrument)? Will greater transparency lead to overall welfare gains for the economy (i.e. have a net positive, not a merely redistributive, effect)?

On the other hand, what might be called the 'dirigiste' approach to regulation proceeds from the assumption that statutory regulation is preferable to self-regulation and that some degree of statutory regulation is better than none. As a result, like justice under the Code Napoléon, the '*dirigiste*' approach to regulation assumes guilt until innocence is proved by the accused. The burden of proof lies on market participants to demonstrate that there is no market failure with regard to transparency when regulators suspect there must be one based on whatever circumstantial evidence they have collected or mere suspicions they may have. Regulators adhering to this school will concentrate their attention on questions such as: are liquidity providers making excess profits? Is transparency a mechanism for redistributing some of these gains to investors?

Is the balance of power in the principal–agent relation skewed towards the service provider, and must regulation redress this asymmetry in favour of the consumer?

In our view, the key point to address is whether statutory measures aimed at enhancing transparency will generate net welfare improvements for the economy as a whole. If they do not, they will amount to a pure redistribution of rents from the dealer community to investors. Though dealers may be loathe to accept such an approach to regulation, there is nothing intrinsically wrong with it in principle. As public authorities, regulators can reserve the right to effect such redistribution of rents; yet if they choose to do so, they should not pretend to have an economic rationale for regulation – theirs would be a purely political decision. In addition, they would have to anticipate how private actors who provide liquidity would respond to such a move – and whether it would verifiably enhance market quality (although market quality is not likely to figure high on the priority list for such a regulator).

3. Arguments in favour of more transparency

A more cautious regulator will seek to balance the perceived benefits of introducing greater transparency with the costs that the economy is likely to incur as a whole from whatever approach he adopts. In terms of the benefits of market transparency, one can think of several reasons, discussed below, why more transparency in the bond market would be beneficial.

3.1 Achieving and verifying best execution

Pre-trade transparency is an important component in achieving best execution, whereas post-trade transparency helps verify best execution. Though originally a concept designed for equity markets, the obligation for investment firms to assure best execution for their clients applies equally to bond markets in the EU from 1 November 2007 under MiFID. To the extent that post-trade transparency is an important element in verifying the quality of trade execution, it would not be very consistent if the European Commission did not mandate stricter and harmonized (post-trade) price transparency rules, or at least encourage the latter through an industry code of conduct, if it already imposes strict best execution requirements. The European Commission was mandated by the Council and the Parliament under MiFID art. 65.1 to decide a course of action on regulating bond market transparency by 31 October 2007. However, if the legislative option is at all pursued, it could well be some time before a uniform degree of transparency is imposed on European bond markets due to the slowness of the EU legislative process. This will create an awkward situation whereby best execution requirements are harmonized across European bond markets where different levels of price transparency prevail in different member states, leading one to question the enforceability or practicability of harmonized best execution rules. However, this discrepancy would only affect a minority of traded bonds (in volume terms): in government bond markets, about 70 per cent of trading volume is carried out on the MTS system, which is a trading platform common to all sovereign issuers in the EU, and on which pre- and post-trade transparency requirements are virtually the same across the system; and in corporate bond markets, 70 per cent of secondary market activity is carried out in London, and thus is regulated by a single authority, the FSA.

3.2 Valuation and asset allocation

Calculating net asset values (NAVs) has become increasingly important with the explosion of bond funds and ETFs. Yet without timely, consistent, accurate and widely accessible data on bond prices, it is difficult to arrive at the NAVs, which bond funds typically calculate on a mark-to-market basis. Greater post-trade transparency would facilitate the calculation of NAVs. It would also facilitate the valuation of illiquid instruments through better proxies, e.g. matrix pricing. In the pre-trade space, more transparency would enhance the efficiency of asset allocation, with important implications for asset management.

3.3 Lowering transaction costs

By enhancing the competition between market-makers, more transparency should unleash competitive forces and lead to lower transaction costs. Opacity in prices makes it easier for liquidity providers to retain pricing power over their clients because it increases search costs for investors. High transaction costs can frustrate the development of vibrant secondary market activity and thereby reduce market liquidity. It must be noted, however, that spreads are paper-thin (and sometimes even negative) in EU cash government bond markets and are reported to be lower than those in the US market for cash corporate bonds.

3.4 Essential non-price information captured in bond prices

In corporate debt markets, price movements are critical inputs in modelling default probabilities. Price transparency can therefore be an important element of retail investor protection, especially if ongoing disclosure by issuers is not as rigorous as in equity markets, and since credit ratings often respond with a considerable lag to critical corporate information that should trigger ratings changes. This lag is due both to the nature of the ratings business, whereby reputational risk is incurred every time an agency moves ahead of others with a rating downgrade – leading to a certain inertia in ratings changes – and to the way ratings rely heavily on historical data, making them backwards-looking. Default probabilities, on the other hand, are forward-looking and thus are more reliable and more up-to-date predictors of corporate defaults. The problems associated with the lack of price transparency in EU corporate bond markets have certainly been dampened by the rapid rise of the credit default swap (CDS) market, but one cannot say it has been entirely resolved. Because the CDS market is more liquid and CDS prices are driving price discovery in the underlying cash market, modellers use prices on CDS contracts as references in the calculation of default probabilities. Nevertheless, there are sometimes situations where spreads widen in the CDS market and do so for no apparent reason that is linked to default probabilities, but rather arise due to market imperfections or the occasional market squeeze, for example, a shortage in the supply of deliverable underlying cash bonds. Improving price transparency in the cash bond market can help to increase the accuracy of calculated default probabilities by allowing one to gauge the quality of those derived from CDS prices against those derived from cash prices. Perhaps because the number of corporate defaults in the EU has been very low in recent years, insufficient attention has been drawn to the argument of improving price transparency to better capture the valuable non-price information that is implicit in the price of an asset. With a downturn in the credit cycle, this argument is sure to take on more weight.

3.5 Data consolidation

Since bond markets are characterized by a radical decentralization compared to equity markets, efficient pricing would normally require that the various trading venues be interconnected. Interconnectedness is of course very difficult if not impossible to achieve in markets that are voice-brokered, as the bond market has traditionally been. However, because the percentage of trading volume that is conducted electronically is steadily rising in fixed-income markets, the potential for interconnectedness increases. Technological advances such as electronic trading, along with the development of multi-dealer-to-client (B2C) platforms, have allowed for more transparency in a telephone-brokered market than in the past. A B2C platform, for example, can bring competing quotes of up to five market-makers simultaneously on a single screen, based on an inputted request-for-quote (by an institutional investor).[2] Ideally, in an integrated market, the same security will trade at the same price at the same point in time on multiple trading venues. In a decentralized trading environment, connecting the various trading spaces through data consolidation, such that the prices and volumes traded on some venues are visible on trading screens in other venues, will contribute materially to the quality of price discovery in the overall market. In the single market, similar transparency requirements would ideally be applied across all trading venues to facilitate data consolidation. While this is already the case for equity markets under MiFID (exchanges, internalizers and MTFs alike facing similar trade reporting rules), there is currently no such framework for bond markets. If trade information cannot be easily consolidated due to a lack of transparency or due to divergent transparency requirements across different markets, overall price efficiency will suffer because search costs will be higher. High search costs damage the quality of price discovery by either discouraging investors from trading, or by reducing their willingness to search for better prices than those they are offered by their regular broker(s). If bond transparency requirements were harmonized across the EU, it would be far easier to consolidate bond data, leading to a more efficient bond market and to the development of more and higher-quality indices.

3.6 Levelling the playing field

Large institutional investors can probably obtain all the transparency they want out of dealers due to their value to dealers as important and regular clients, who probably generate fees for dealers in other areas beyond trading. However, smaller players cannot exercise this kind of leverage over dealers. Unless standard transparency rules are applied

[2] Retail investors cannot get access to B2C platforms, which are designed for wholesale market transactions.

across the market, large players have an important information advantage. Smaller buy-side firms and retail investors suffer from the current lack of transparency in the market, while large buy-side firms and dealers benefit from opacity at the expense of the former group, who can trade profitably on their information advantages. An industry code of conduct, or mandated transparency requirements (designed in close consultation with the industry) could help to close the information gap between various classes of market participants, contributing to market confidence.

3.7 Index construction

Indices can only be as good as their inputs. Good indices rely on high-quality and consistent price data. The TRACE reporting system provides just that in the US corporate bond market, presenting post-trade data in a consistent format that allows data consolidation and thereby affords a view of overall market activity. In the European corporate bond market, the iBoxx index covering liquid investment grade credits is a good start to more transparency, since it consolidates prices from the eleven investment banks who market-make in iBoxx-eligible bonds and publishes them in real time. These real-time quotes, along with the daily closing prices freely available on the International Index Company website, are already a significant step in the right direction. iTraxx does the same for the credit derivatives market. MTS indices and (recently launched) index futures provide a similar function in the European government bond market, enhancing the quality of price discovery. Nevertheless, prices on Bloombergs and other terminals that rely on iBoxx feeds are occasionally several basis points off mark, undermining the quality of market data. Greater transparency of bond prices and volumes will also improve the accuracy of index-tracking. If greater transparency brings more traders with active trading strategies to the market, it will increase the regularity of trading. By leading to more continuous pricing rather than price movements characterized by sometimes significant discrete jumps as in the past, a smoother stream of orders will also have positive knock-on effects on the quality of bond indices.

3.8 Improving liquidity

The more homogeneous the liquidity needs of the trading community, the more likely it is that liquidity will freeze over in the markets, since market movements will largely be uni-directional. Fixed income markets have traditionally been dominated by institutional investors who pursue buy-and-hold strategies for asset-liability matching purposes. While retail investors are also largely buy-and-hold investors, their liquidity needs fluctuate more regularly than those of institutional investors, so greater retail investor participation in the bond market should lead to more regular trading. Other players with heterogeneous trading strategies are also likely to come into the market as transparency increases, such as hedge funds which thrive on arbitrage plays on default, event, interest rate, inflation and liquidity risk. The presence of these groups of heterogeneous traders should lessen the volatility in price movements. Greater pre-trade transparency in particular is also likely to improve liquidity by tapping into unfulfilled liquidity demand (potential orders that are not executed because bond investors are unaware of existing trading opportunities).

3.9 Enhancing disclosure of financial risks

There is a marked tendency today to move towards fair-value accounting, witnessed by the requirement for all listed firms in the EU since January 2005 to present their accounts in IFRS, which is based on fair value, rather than historical cost, accounting. At the same time, owing to concerns about systemic risk in the economy and a preference for pre-emptive action to stave off financial crises, regulators are pushing for more disclosure of financial risk on a more regular basis for credit institutions and insurance firms alike. More recourse to, and more accurate, mark-to-market accounting can contribute to systemic stability by highlighting weak points in the financial system as they emerge. Greater transparency in bond markets can contribute to systemic stability: price transparency helps market-makers value their inventory and credit institutions and helps institutional investors and hedge funds to more accurately and regularly value their portfolio holdings. More transparency in bond and credit derivatives holdings can contribute to financial stability by helping financial market supervisors trace the path of risk as it cascades through the financial system.[3]

[3] For a more detailed exposition of the latter argument, see Laganá, von Koppen-Mertes and Persaud (2006).

4. Arguments against more transparency

Although in preparing this chapter we found more arguments in support of transparency than against it, this is not to suggest that pros necessarily outweigh the cons in terms of total economic impact.

4.1 Could damage liquidity

Unlike equity markets, where liquidity is brought to the market by orders from investors – the exchange merely providing a service of facilitating the matching of orders in a consolidated limit order book – liquidity in the bond market depends critically on the willingness of market-makers to risk their capital in proprietary trading to buy and sell blocks of bonds from their clients as a service to them. This activity is not without a certain risk: bonds tend to be illiquid, and the market is quite concentrated. As a result, if greater pre-trade transparency is imposed through regulation, traders could exploit the service market-makers provide to their clients by hitting or lifting bids or offers posted on a continuous basis in opportunistic fashion, especially if greater transparency is combined with market-making obligations (as under MiFID for equities dealt by systematic internalizers or for EU government bonds traded on MTS platforms). In these cases, the profits of opportunistic traders would come at the expense of the market-maker and of the overall market, since it will discourage a dealer from providing liquidity, a public good.

If introduced in a haphazard fashion, mandated post-trade transparency could increase the costs to dealers of providing liquidity, since real-time disclosure on large blocks of illiquid securities can lead other market participants to anticipate the need to rebalance or hedge inventory by taking exploitative positions in the swap market that will increase the costs of hedging to the dealer or by increasing the market impact of dealer trades by anticipating a dealer's need to offload some inventory and front-running the inventory reshuffling.

The regulatory debate on bond market transparency has largely focused on the need to provide greater protection to retail investors. The law of unintended consequences always portends caution on the part of the regulator who seeks to alter existing market structures. Paradoxically, retail investors could even be worse off if market-makers withdraw their capital from liquidity providing activities if the costs/risks of providing this service are too great; the same can be said if greater transparency would erode the profitability of market-making to such an extent that dealers no longer find it a worthwhile activity for certain types of credits.

4.2 Other instruments better suited for retail investor protection[4]

Although one of the pillars of retail investor protection in any marketplace is transparency, it is important to highlight that regulatory attention ought not to focus solely on transparency, as a number of more important variables can impact on the level of investor protection in the bond market.

Fixed-income investments are associated with a wide array of risks, which retail investors may either not understand or remain completely oblivious to. Bonds are often presented as relatively simple financial instruments compared to equities. They typically offer annual or semi-annual coupon payments that represent interest on the principal one has loaned to the issuer until maturity, whereupon the principal is recovered. However, to present bonds so simply is to mislead investors as to the true nature of risks they are undertaking when purchasing a bond. Not only does an investor face the risk of not recovering his invested principal, known as default risk, but also the value of his investment can be negatively affected by interest rate risk, inflation risk, event risk and liquidity risk. These risks are largely unknown to the average retail investor.

This is not to say that transparency is not an important component of investor protection. Transparency ought to be improved. But besides mere transparency, there is an array of flanking measures that should be considered in earnest by regulators if retail investor protection is their primary concern in the regulation of bond markets. These include: suitability of instruments ('know your client' principle); addressing conflicts of interest in, and ensuring principled distribution (e.g. in remuneration schemes), thereby reducing the risk of mis-selling; improving bond documentation; protecting invested principal against default and event risk; educating investors to the particularities of fixed income investments; and encouraging indirect investments through diversified funds for risky products.

An interesting related question is: how is it that retail investors are allowed by regulators to buy individual credits but are often not allowed to buy e.g. a diversified fund? It shows there is an odd bias in the regulatory framework that makes little sense from an economic or indeed consumer-welfare viewpoint. This dilemma is primarily relevant to countries, such

4 For a more complete exposition of auxiliary measures/instruments that are more relevant for investor protection in fixed income markets, see Casey and Lannoo (2005), ch. 4.

as Italy, Denmark and Spain, where bond markets are populated by a large retail presence. In the European bond market as a whole, retail-investor participation only accounts for a miniscule percentage of trading activity in volume terms. Yet this fact is not a good argument in itself for not regulating: people's savings are at risk, and these investments, though small in macroeconomic terms, can be large in terms of the invested wealth of a retail investor. The question is rather one of how to preserve the integrity and efficiency of the wholesale market while adopting a regulatory scheme that contributes to more retail investor protection.

4.3 No clear evidence of a market failure

One of the principal arguments that has been touted by market participants against introducing greater transparency in the bond market is the lack of evidence of a market failure significant enough to warrant regulatory intervention. This argument has found some backing, not least from the FSA, which found no compelling case of market failure in UK secondary bond markets. Because London accounts for up to 70 per cent of secondary market activity in European corporate bonds, the FSA's analysis ought to be treated with considerable weight. Others regulators, however, are not likely to be satisfied with this approach. The Italian market regulator, Consob, has consistently been pushing for greater transparency, owing to the large presence of retail investors in the Italian bond market and the losses they suffered in the recent past (Parmalat, Argentina) – close to 30 per cent of the Italian bond market is held by retail investors, a total that is often a multiple of the same figure for other EU countries and the US (see figure 9.1).

5. Lessons from TRACE

Industry representatives have often argued that the TRACE experience ought not to be the starting point for European regulators for the following reasons: there is greater pre-trade transparency in Europe than in the US; spreads are lower in Europe; the structure of the two markets is not directly comparable and the two markets operate quite differently; the conclusions of academic studies on the effects of TRACE which show enhanced liquidity in the US corporate bond market are not convincing because NASD does not want to share TRACE data with any independent researchers and the models used have their limitations. Some other positive aspects of TRACE are less frequently mentioned, but are

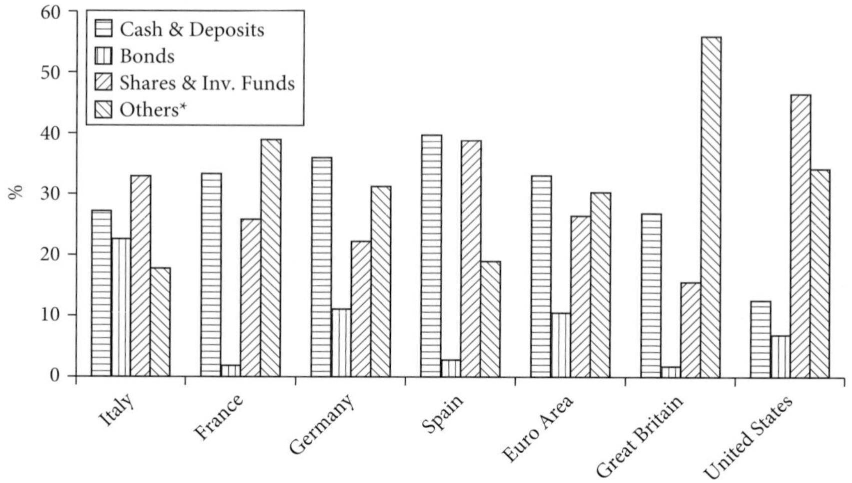

Note: * Insurance, technical reserves, pension funds (families)

Source: Bank of Italy.

Figure 9.1. Bond market household savings structure: international comparison (2004)

nonetheless important and relevant for the European corporate bond market.

Though the bond market is characterized by decentralization, it is little short of inexcusable that neither regulators nor market participants, whether institutional or retail, are able to obtain aggregated information on bond market activity in a given day in the European bond market. Although asset allocation is typically driven by price considerations, the information captured in traded volumes, with breakdowns by type of securities, is undoubtedly of economic value and could improve market efficiency if available to all. It is impossible to do so without a common reporting engine akin to TRACE, or at least without interlinked reporting systems whose post-trade inputs can be consolidated. Table 9.1 shows activity in the US corporate bond market on 29 February 2008.

The TRACE engine allows one to verify on a daily basis the total number of corporate bonds traded in the US market, with a breakdown into three sub-categories: investment grade, high-yield and convertible. It also documents the number of bonds that gained in price over the previous market closing as well as those whose price declined or remained

Table 9.1 Trading activity in the US corporate bond market, 29 February 2008

	All issues	Investment grade	High yield	Convertibles
Total issues traded	3,731	2,606	900	225
Advances	1,812	1,450	313	49
Declines	1,492	844	494	154
Unchanged	110	57	45	8
52 Wk high	298	282	13	3
52 Wk low	212	105	83	24
Dollar vol*.	14,931	8,018	4,149	2,765

* Par value in millions
Source: NASD website: www.nasd.com.

unchanged. It provides fifty-two-week high/lows. And the total dollar volume of trades is recorded. By any measure, this aggregated market information is a valuable resource for all market participants, dealers, asset managers, retail investors and regulators alike. While TRAX offers a similar service for Eurobonds and for bonds traded in the City of London, the service is neither comprehensive nor aggregated. Currently, the TRAX engine only enables one to obtain end-of-day data on individual securities, but volumes are often excluded. The same applies to 'BondMarketPrices.com', which was launched in December 2007 by the International Capital Markets Association (ICMA) to provide retail investors with direct access to that day's traded and quoted pricing information at the end of the day. Both initiatives do not represent an aggregate picture of bond market activity.

Likewise, TRACE enables market participants to collect information on traded volumes, which is a useful proxy to gauge the liquidity of certain bonds. Tables 9.2 and 9.3 show the outputs that can be produced with TRACE data. One can compare the dispersion in liquidity among US corporate bonds by issuer, coupon, maturity and rating. In 2007, the most liquid corporate bond, a GE 5 per cent 2013 bond, registered almost 13,000 trades. The liquidity in the high-yield issues declined importantly as compared to previous years, which is related to the market circumstances. In 2005, a GM 8 per cent 2033, registered nearly 60,000 trades. The data also suggests that liquidity in the corporate bond market is concentrated in a few issues and that it quickly trails off subsequently.

Table 9.2 Top 50 publicly traded investment grade issues by number of trades executed in 2007 (excluding convertible bonds)

Rank	SYMBOL	ISSUER NAME	COUPON	MATURITY	RATING	TRADES
1	GE.ADF	GENERAL ELECTRIC COMPANY	5.000	2/1/13	AAA	12,857
2	MS.QP	MORGAN STANLEY	4.750	4/1/14	A	12,333
3	GS.OU	GOLDMAN SACHS GROUP, INC. (THE)	5.700	9/1/12	AA	11,573
4	C.HEF	CITIGROUP INC.	5.000	9/15/14	AA	11,212
5	GE.AAD	GENERAL ELECTRIC CAPITAL CORPORATION	6.000	6/15/12	AAA	11,085
6	BLS.HW	BELLSOUTH CORPORATION	6.000	11/15/34	A	10,450
7	WMT.HN	WAL-MART STORES, INC.	4.550	5/1/13	AA	9,681
8	GE.WB	GENERAL ELECTRIC CAPITAL CORPORATION	5.875	2/15/12	AAA	9,468
9	GS.WL	GOLDMAN SACHS GROUP INC	5.625	1/15/17	A	8,108
10	JPM.QP	J.P. MORGAN CHASE & CO.	5.750	1/2/13	A	8,051

Table 9.3 Top 50 publicly traded high-yield issues by number of trades executed in 2007 (excluding convertible bonds)

Rank	SYMBOL	ISSUER NAME	COUPON	MATURITY	RATING	TRADES
1	GM.HB	GENERAL MOTORS CORPORATION	8.375	7/15/33	B	10,166
2	GMA.GY	GENERAL MOTORS ACCEPTANCE CORPORATION	7.750	1/19/10	BB	10,020
3	F.IF	FORD MOTOR CREDIT COMPANY	7.375	10/28/09	B	8,966
4	GMA.HF	GENERAL MOTORS ACCEPTANCE CORPORATION	8.000	11/1/31	BB	8,801
5	F.GY	FORD MOTOR COMPANY	7.450	7/16/31	CCC	8,582
6	CPN.GJ	CALPINE CORPORATION	8.500	2/15/11	D	7,756
7	F.IT	FORD MOTOR CREDIT COMPANY	7.250	10/25/11	B	7,651
8	F.IB	FORD MOTOR CREDIT COMPANY	5.800	1/12/09	B	7,620
9	GM.GM	GENERAL MOTORS CORPORATION	7.200	1/15/11	B	6,706
10	GMA.HSF	GENERAL MOTORS ACCEPTANCE CORPORATION	5.125	5/9/08	BB	6,529

Source: FINRA: www.finra.org/web/groups/reg_systems/documents/regulatory_systems/p038013.pdf.

Overall, TRACE provides three essential benefits to the US corporate bond market that must be considered seriously by European bond market SROs and regulators. These benefits are:

1. As described above, TRACE gives all market participants and regulators useful information on aggregate activity in the bond market and on individual credits.
2. Enabling retail and institutional investors to verify the quality of execution no later than fifteen minutes after a trade.[5] This possibility puts pressure on brokers to ensure that they are consistently making efforts to place their clients' needs over any professional arrangements or proprietary trading activities.
3. By making post-trade information available to all, TRACE levels the playing field between various categories of market participants as regards access to information. Without a system like TRACE, large dealers, large institutional investors and active hedge funds have a clear advantage over smaller players because they will have a much better idea of what constitutes a good price for a given credit, which are the most liquid securities and where to find them – and they can trade on this informational edge to their advantage.

6. What kind of transparency is warranted?

Who will argue that more information is worse than less? That more information made available to market participants will damage market quality? Hardly anybody. Markets thrive on information. The quality of a marketplace in any sector of the economy depends critically on the intangible assets and preconditions for a successful market economy that are publicly disseminated information and contract law. The critical question, therefore, is not so much whether more transparency is needed, but rather how it should be introduced, by whom and under what conditions.

[5] Some will argue that the notion of best execution is a pure theoretical construct that can only apply in perfect markets where there are no frictions, all information is available to all market participants, etc. The concept is difficult enough to apply to equity markets where trading typically is concentrated on a handful of trading venues, but in fixed income markets, it is a matter of great controversy over how exactly best execution can be applied and enforced. The vigorous debate surrounding the FSA's suggested benchmarking approach attests to this.

The all-encompassing notion of transparency as applied to bond markets can mean a variety of things. It could mean price transparency – and even price transparency can be broken down into its pre-trade and post-trade components, each of which can be calibrated to the nth degree in their implementation by regulators. It could mean more data on volumes in addition to mere price transparency – without information on the quantity of bonds traded, prices are not as informative as they ought to be: comparing the price on a block trade of 5,000 bonds to the price of trading an individual security makes little economic sense. It could include the direction of trade (i.e. whether the trade was a 'buy' or a 'sell'). It could mean a certain delay in the dissemination of post-trade information to other market participants. This delay can also be calibrated to the nth degree, depending on the relevant market or instrument. It could mean different ways to publish the disseminated post-trade information: ought it to be consolidated? Should trades over a given size be given abstract representations so as to protect liquidity providers from opportunistic behaviour that moves the market against them as they attempt to hedge or unwind the positions they have built up in dealing with their clients?[6]

Clearly, there is no right or wrong answer. Different forms of transparency can be implemented and considered appropriate for different instruments, which highlights the importance of regulatory flexibility as opposed to an established blueprint. The European Commission seems to have appreciated this nuance in its ongoing review.[7]

7. Will market-led initiatives improve transparency?

The key question then is whether market-led initiatives will be sufficient to satisfy the needs of retail investors, smaller buy-side firms and regulators. Markets need to be given a chance. But this chance has to be couched

[6] This will especially be important if the dissemination delays for illiquid securities are for very short periods of time.

[7] '[T]he provision does not require consideration only of two options: full MiFID-style transparency for each instrument class or nothing. We believe the "extension" referred to includes the possibility of adapting that regime to the characteristics of a particular instrument market, the nature of the instrument market concerned and the characteristics of the investors who typically use that market. Therefore, one possible outcome would be to have more than one transparency regime (for example, more than one set of post-trade publication deferrals for large transactions) for different instrument classes.' European Commission (2006).

in terms of a limited window of opportunity after which regulators will be forced to act, either through an industry code of conduct (preferable) or through legislation.

Encouragingly, some positive developments in market-driven initiatives to enhance transparency could recently be noticed: the dealer community, whether pushed by greater competition or pulled by technological improvements, has moved towards providing greater transparency to the marketplace than was available to investors in the past. Initiatives include ICMA's TRAX and TRAX2, MTS indices, the Iboxx/iTraxx indices and the development of B2C multi-dealer-to-customer platforms, which have greatly increased the degree of both pre- and post-trade transparency in the bond market (although to a lesser extent for the latter). In addition, a consortium of sixteen investment banks launched LiquidityHub, an initiative aimed at consolidating liquidity and market data for electronic trading in the fixed-income market, in November 2007.

Are these initiatives enough? We would argue not. Retail investors still lack good information access to the bond market; and all market participants along with regulators lack volume data and an aggregated view of the European bond market, both government and corporate, on a daily, weekly or other latency – a considerable shortfall. In addition, no consolidated tape exists post-trade to verify whether best execution has effectively been delivered.

Are market-led efforts to overcome these deficiencies credible? The problem with a market-led initiative regarding post-trade transparency is whether it will ever materialize – its development is rendered more difficult by the classic collective action problem: unless all dealers implement post-trade transparency together and in the same way, nobody will do it. No dealer has the incentive to move ahead with the introduction of greater transparency with respect to his dealing if others do not all move with him. Otherwise, he exposes himself to risks from which the others will benefit. In addition, unless all join in on the industry-led initiative, whatever consolidation is arrived at will not be representative of the whole market. The first-mover disadvantage that characterizes collective action problems makes it somewhat unlikely that market-led solutions to introducing greater transparency can work unless SROs take a strong lead and impose such measures equally on all their members. Their potential role in pushing their members towards an effective industry-led solution in this important debate cannot be underestimated.

It is evident that dealers have a commercial incentive to prefer less, rather than more, transparency, since it will enhance competition and probably squeeze margins as a result – as well as costing dealers resources in terms of inputting the data (the large share of bonds are voice-brokered as opposed to electronically traded). But nobody ever said the data have to be made available to all market participants for free! Revenues from the sale of data would allow dealers to recoup at least in part the 'losses' generated by higher post-trade transparency and possibly to profit from it if they move towards consolidating liquidity and data in a cost-effective manner through more joint efforts such as LiquidityHub.

This brings us back to the paradox of market information: the market information is proprietary, and the dealer feels it belongs to him for commercial purposes. But information is not generated in a vacuum. A 'market-maker' is less of a liquidity 'provider' than a liquidity 'facilitator': market liquidity is also brought about by the counterparty who makes a RFQ – it takes two to tango! Without a demand for liquidity, the supplier of liquidity would earn no revenues and generate no profits from liquidity provision. In addition, trade information is a public good in a market economy. Information on bond prices, volumes and yields has value that goes far beyond that created in the bilateral deal struck between counterparties: this information is used to price other assets (estimate discount rates), to mark portfolios to market and to assess inflationary expectations. So to the extent that dealers operate within a given market structure and rely on it to derive profits from dealing, they have a responsibility to sustain and enhance the efficiency of that structure. Also, to the extent 'proprietary' information can be a public good, dealers should make it available to the wider marketplace, but obviously should be allowed to charge for it.

Will dealers overcome the existing coordination failure in markets? Will they ensure consistent pricing across a wide range of assets? Will they consolidate data to allow a pan-European view on debt markets? Regulators should give dealers and bond market SROs a chance to develop market-led solutions to the unsatisfactory level of post-trade transparency in particular that prevails in the European bond market today. Alternatively, an industry code of conduct or mandated set of transparency requirements (designed in close consultation with the industry) could help to bring more information to the marketplace on volumes on individual credits – a good proxy for liquidity – and on aggregate bond market activity. In addition, more information that is relevant for retail investors in particular ought to be made available by dealers, not least because doing so could preclude the need for mandated transparency requirements on wholesale market operations – requirements that are designed with the retail investor in mind and thus are ill-suited to wholesale transactions. Finally, increasing the level of available market information can serve to close the information gap between various classes of market participants, thereby contributing to market confidence.

The legislative option currently hangs over dealers' heads as a sword of Damocles that could drop at any time. Because of their flexibility and their proximity to the business, market-led solutions are preferable to legislative alternatives. But they have to be credible, and time is running short. That means the ball is in the dealers' court. Now the key question is: are they up to the challenge?

References

Casey, Jean-Pierre and Karel Lannoo 2005. *Europe's Hidden Capital Markets*, Brussels: Centre for European Policy Studies.

CESR 2007. *Response to the Commission on Non-equities Transparency*, Ref CESR/07-538: www.cesr-eu.org/data/document/07_538.pdf.

European Commission 2006. *Call for Evidence, Pre- and Post-trade Transparency Provisions of the Markets in Financial Instruments Directive (MiFID) in Relation to Transactions in Classes of Financial Instruments other than Shares*: http://ec.europa.eu/internal_market/securities/does/isd/call-for-evidence_en.pdf.

FINRA, *2007 Trace Fact Book* 2008: www.finra.org Regulatory Systems/TRACE/TRACEFactBook/index.htm.

FSA 2005. *Trading Transparency in the UK Secondary Bond Markets*, FSA DP05/5, September.

Laganá, Marco, Martin Perina, Isabel von Köppen-Mertes and Avinash D. Persaud 2006. *Implications for Liquidity from Innovation and Transparency in the European Corporate Bond Market*, ECB Occasional Paper Series No. 50. Frankfurt: European Central Bank.

10

The division of home and host country competences under MiFID[1]

1. Introduction

The provision of services by investment firms and banks is subject to matters covering prudential, contractual and conduct of business rules. Prudential rules regard the minimum licensing and capital requirements; contractual rules apply to the conclusion of agreements between intermediaries and their clients, and conduct of business rules relate the norms of behaviour firms have to respect (Tison 2002). This was the case under the first European directive covering investment services – the 1993 Investment Services Directive (ISD) – and also applies to the directive currently in force – the Markets in Financial Instruments Directive (MiFID).

Policy intervention in these areas is necessary to ensure that firms perform their crucial economic role without endangering financial stability or hampering investor confidence. To be effective, legislative requirements should be accompanied by appropriate supervisory and enforcement powers – respectively powers to control the rules are respected and to intervene in case these are breached. When firms extend their operations beyond national borders, the allocation of rule-making, supervisory and enforcement powers becomes critical to avoid regulatory arbitrage and to ensure that misconducts are readily detected and controlled. If illicit acts are not identified and prevented promptly, they risk spilling over into other national markets.

Against this background, a regulatory level playing field, a proper allocation of responsibilities and coordinated supervision are crucial elements for the smooth functioning of the market. In addition, by responding to firms' need for legal certainty, a well-designed regulatory and supervisory architecture lowers compliance costs and fosters cross-border activities.

[1] This chapter was prepared in cooperation with Giulia Gobbo.

The aim of this chapter is to assess the way in which MiFID allots rule-making, supervisory and enforcement powers between home and host member states in case of cross-border activities. We also assess the extent to which the new regulation levels the playing field and promotes coordination among member states. The starting point of our analysis is the 1993 ISD, but we continue to refer to it when necessary to assess MiFID's attempt to smooth the provision of investment services throughout the EU. Overall, we believe the new directive represents a considerable step forward for the purpose of fostering the cross-border provision of investment services. It simplifies the previous regime and strengthens its efficacy for the benefit of firms and investors. Indeed, applicable rules are of the full harmonization type; their supervision and enforcement are clearly allotted among states, and the duty of cooperation among national authorities is made more stringent.

2. The ISD

The 1993 ISD[2] aimed at creating a single European market in investment services. For this purpose, it allowed firms to perform services across Europe with or without the establishment of branches, on the basis of a unique authorization issued by the home state.

The unique authorization regime was necessary but not sufficient to achieve the objective of market integration. This shortcoming of the ISD resulted from three factors: the possibility for member states to impose more stringent rules on foreign firms; the lack of a clear allocation of rule-making, supervisory and enforcement powers between home and host states; and the use of ambiguous wordings, which left the application of the directive to discretionary national interpretations.

To obtain authorization, firms had to comply with the home state's prudential rules, which had to be devised in such a way as to meet the directive's minimum requirements.[3] From a prudential point of view, the home state had to verify the coherence between the organization and the envisaged cross-border activities after the firm had notified its intention to provide services abroad. Further, home states were entrusted with monitoring ongoing compliance with prudential requirements.

[2] Directive 93/22/EEC of 10 May 1993, OJ L 141, 27.

[3] See arts. 3, 4, 6, 8, 9, 10, 14, 17 ISD. Among the minimum requirements, art. 3 prescribes compliance with Directive 93/6/EEC of 15 March 1993 on the capital adequacy of investment firms and credit institutions.

Host states were not allowed to make the provision of services on their territory conditional upon additional rules. In other words, states could not refuse to mutually recognize the rules adopted by other states and apply more stringent requirements in the interest of the general good (Tison 2002, p. 90).

All in all, the ISD framework could be labelled as 'mutual recognition of authorization and of prudential supervision' (CESR 2006, p. 3). This system was beneficial insofar as it allowed firms to provide services without duplication of binding prudential provisions and with a clear identification of the applicable rules as well as of the authority entrusted with their enforcement. Moreover, the regulator aimed at granting investors a minimum level of protection as a means to foster confidence and promote financial activities. To this end, the ISD contained provisions on firms' conduct of business, allotting rule-making powers on this matter to the state 'where the service is provided' (art. 11).

States were free to enact their conduct of business rules at the condition of reaching the directive's minimum requirements: firms were to act loyally and fairly with competence and diligence, in the interest of clients and market integrity; they had to maintain adequate resources and procedures to be used in an effective manner; they had to acquire information on the clients' experience, financial situation and investment objectives and they had to provide investors with due information; finally they had to avoid conflicts of interest and, where not possible, to ensure clients' fair treatment. Lastly, firms had to comply with all (other) 'regulatory requirements applicable to the conduct of . . . [their] business activities' (art. 11(1)).

As a result of this flexibility, member states' implementation of these principles could vary considerably in the light of the 'interest of the general good' (arts. 17(4) and 18(2), second subparagraph). In this way, they ended up hindering firms' free provision of services and burdening firms with high compliance costs. Investors across Europe were also unevenly protected, depending upon whether their state enacted additional rules and how these rules were devised. Finally, the obscure wording of art. 11(2) exacerbated such drawbacks: 'without prejudice to any decisions to be taken in the context of the harmonization of the rules of conduct, their implementation and the supervision of compliance with them shall remain the responsibility of the Member State in which a service is provided'. Such a concept could be interpreted as referring to the state where the investor resides or to the state of the market where the transactions are executed, to the detriment of legal certainty and simplification (Herbst 2003, p. 212).[4]

In the absence of deeper harmonization, allocating rule-making powers to the host member state was the only viable possibility (Köndgen 1998, p. 127). Bestowing these competences on the home state would have triggered a race to the bottom, with firms establishing themselves in states with the most lenient rules, irrespective of where they would perform services. Host states were given the tools to supervise compliance with conduct-of-business rules: after firms notified the intention to provide services across borders, but before they actually commenced their business, host states could impose additional conditions. Moreover, host states could require information and conduct on-site inspections (arts. 17(3), 18(2), 19(2) and 24(3)). Nevertheless, enforcement of conduct-of-business rules was, in practice, shared between the home and host state: the latter could take measures against breaches only after the home state's intervention proved ineffective (art. 19(3), (4), (5)).

The ISD attempted to coordinate the supervisory activities of national authorities: states were to exchange information on request and carry out on-the-spot verification on behalf of other states (arts. 23 and 24). Despite these efforts, the way it allocated rule-making, supervisory and enforcement powers between home and host states was not optimal.[5] In addition, an EU Securities Committee to decide on implementing legislation and common interpretations of conduct of business rules could never be created because of a procedural disagreement with the European Parliament (Lannoo 1999, p. 17). The rapid growth in the cross-border provision of services increasingly emphasised the problem of the proper allocation of regulatory and supervisory powers in the EU (Pacces 1999, p. 6; OECD 2000; European Commission 2000). The November 2002 Commission proposal for a new directive on investment services concluded that the existing framework for undertaking investment business on a cross-border basis in the EU was no longer effective. In particular, the ISD failed to 'provide sufficient harmonisation to allow effective mutual recognition of investment firm licences' (European Commission 2002, p. 64).

[4] Conduct of business rules were not included in the first draft for the directive: OJ C 43/7 of 22 February 1989, and were only later proposed in an Opinion of the Economic and Social Committee, OJ C 298/6 of 27 November 1989. This aspect of MiFID was enacted in a rush, as Cruickshank (1998, p. 131) recognizes.

[5] See also Köndgen (1998, pp. 124–5).

3. MiFID's rule-making

MiFID (Directive 2004/39/EC) and its implementing measures (Regulation 1287/2006 and Directive 2006/73/EC) aim at overcoming the shortcomings of the ISD by introducing a 'new' system for the cross-border provision of services.[6] The four-step Lamfalussy approach dramatically changes the terms of the relation between home and host states on the matters of rule-making, supervision and enforcement. This new approach gives CESR a central role in ensuring that the Level 1 and Level 2 rules are uniformly interpreted and applied throughout the Community.[7] Where the Level 1 and Level 2 measures do not provide for a complete set of rules, member states retain a margin of manoeuvre, albeit following CESR coordination.

3.1. Prudential rules

At first sight, the basic prudential rules of MiFID almost perfectly mirror those of the ISD. Despite these resemblances, the current European rules differ dramatically from their forerunner: the Implementing Directive translates MiFID's stated objectives into specific obligations. Prudential rule-making powers are exercised in a framework of full harmonization, obtained through the Lamfalussy approach, which ensures that implementation does not vary across Europe.

MiFID allows firms to operate and set up branches throughout Europe solely on the basis of their home state's authorization (MiFID arts. 5, 6(3), 31 and 32).[8] To obtain the authorization, firms have to comply with the initial and operating conditions (i.e. the prudential rules) laid down by the home state in the Directive's implementation. In a similar fashion to the ISD, such conditions relate to: capital adequacy requirements (Directive 2006/49/EC[9]); the repute and experience of management; the

[6] Directive 2004/39/EC of 21 April 2004, OJ EU L 154/1 of 30 April 2004; Regulation and Directive of 10 August 2006, OJ EU L 241/1 and L 241/26 of 2 September 2006 (Level 2 Regulation and Level 2 Directive). We refer to these three pieces of legislation collectively as MiFID or the 'European rules'.

[7] For this purpose, CESR issues administrative guidelines, interpretative recommendations, common standards, peer reviews, comparisons of regulatory practice recommendations which do not form part of the European legislation and do not require any legislative action on the part of member states.

[8] What will be said applies to both investment firms and banks, but the latter are excluded from the application of MiFID arts. 31(2)–(4), 32 (2)–(6) and (8)–(9) and 48–53 .

[9] Directive of 14 June 2006 on the capital adequacy of investment firms and credit institutions (OJ EU of 30 June 2006 L177/201) replacing Directive 93/6/EEC of 15 March 1993.

suitability of the shareholders for sound and prudent management; and the appropriateness of the organizational requirements.

MIFID art. 13 contains a number of paragraphs perfectly mirroring those of ISD art. 10 on matters of administrative and accounting procedures, employees' personal transactions, clients' assets and funds defence and record-keeping. As under the ISD, firms shall communicate to their home state the intention to operate abroad together with details about the envisaged services. If they are to establish branches, the information required is more extensive: the home state shall be satisfied that setting up branches does not entail prudential concerns, and that the administrative structure as well as the financial situation are adequate (MiFID arts. 31 and 32).

In both the establishment of branches and the provision of cross-border services, the home-state authority has to inform the host state, which, however, cannot impose additional prudential requirements. The European Commission has clarified that the information addressed to the host state only serves the practical purpose of 'enabling the effective cooperation among the authorities of home and host member states' (European Commission 2007a, p. 1).

3.2 Transactional rules

Under MiFID, firms acting abroad without establishing branches are bound by the home country's conduct-of-business rules. Conduct-of-business rules are also known as transactional rules, which regulate the behaviour firms should maintain vis-à-vis their clients. Host states are prohibited from imposing additional requirements (arts. 31(1), second subparagraph and 32(1), second subparagraph). However, in case investment services are provided through branches, the host country's conduct-of-business rules apply, as stipulated in art. 32(7).[10]

In this way, a proper balance is struck between three needs: the need to reduce the multiplication of the number of applicable rules when a firm is acting in different states; the need to make the applicable rules clearly identifiable; and the need to allot rule-making powers to the state which is closer to the entity and therefore on a better footing for

[10] Article 32(7) mentions the rules contained in MiFID arts. 19, 21, 22, 25, 27 and 28. These articles refer to the duty to act honestly, fairly, professionally; to information duties; to suitability and appropriateness; best execution; reporting obligations; to the client-orders' handling rules; and the pre- and post-trade disclosure duties for systematic internalizers.

intervening.[11] Indeed, when a firm acts abroad without establishment, only the home state's regulation is applicable; when a firm sets up branches, the rules of each state where it has branches apply. Unlike ISD, the problem of identifying the state 'where the service is provided' is overcome. Moreover, thanks to the Level 2 legislation, member states' conduct-of-business rules should be comparable all across the EU, alleviating fears of an un-level playing field.[12]

Not only does MiFID regulate in a detailed way conduct-of-business matters, it also contains clear definitions, providing that each rule can effectively achieve its objectives. For example, it identifies three categories of clients (retail, professional and eligible counterparties), their boundaries, and the conduct of business rules applicable to each of them. On the contrary, ISD art. 11(1) only required states to devise and apply conduct of business rules 'in such a way as to take account of the professional nature of the person for whom the service is provided'. Lacking a clear client categorization regime under the ISD, clients could fall into different categories depending upon the applicable national rules. Therefore, firms contracting similar clients in different member states could be confronted to comply at the same time with different obligations.[13]

Article 4 of the Level 2 Directive allows states to address specific risks to investors' protection or market integrity by retaining or imposing objectively justified and proportionate additional requirements ('super-equivalent rules'), in case those risks are not addressed by community provisions and are of particular importance in the light of the market structure of that state.

The super-equivalent rules can relate to transactional matters, to the prudential matters or to matters covering both fields (CESR 2006, pp. 9–12). The European Commission has explicitly stated that only the

[11] CESR (2006, p. 3) clearly states: host states are 'closest to the branch and . . . better placed to detect and intervene in respect to infringements of rules governing [its] operations'. This is also likely to happen because 'violations of rules of conduct are frequently referred to the competent authorities only on complaint by investors who have been defrauded or abused' (Köndgen 1998, pp. 125–6).

[12] States benefit from a limited margin of manoeuvre in the implementation of the client-order handling rule for limit orders (art. 22), of the transaction-reporting rule for instruments not admitted to trading on a regulated market (art. 25), and of the post-trading transparency rule (art. 28): see CESR (2007a).

[13] For example, in the UK all companies had to be treated (and protected) as non-sophisticated clients, unless having called up share capital or net assets of £5 million; in Italy the same companies could be treated as professional (sophisticated) clients; for this purpose it was sufficient for their legal representatives to state the company's specific experience and knowledge in the field of financial instruments transactions.

home state can apply *prudential* super-equivalent requirements (European Commission 2007a). France, the UK and Ireland have applied additional *transactional* requirements only to branches acting within their territories. Hence, super-equivalent requirements covering prudential and conduct of business issues are always applied by the home state, except in the case of a firm providing services abroad through a branch. In this case, the host state will be competent for applying the general conduct-of-business rules together with its conduct-of-business super-equivalent requirements.

Despite art. 4, the level of harmonization brought about by MiFID is much higher than the one under the ISD to such an extent that it appears legitimate to talk about full harmonization, in contrast with the minimum harmonization brought about by MiFID's forerunner.[14] Whereas the ISD only identified the objectives states had to pursue, today the EU rules pre-determine the specific rights and obligations that should arise to parties, as well as the conditions that clients and firms have to comply with to enjoy these rights, or to be considered compliant with these obligations.[15] MiFID is deemed to be comprehensive for all the conduct-of-business issues, and no space is left for goldplating;[16] the vague concept of the general good cannot be invoked – as it was under the ISD – to more tightly regulate foreign firms. Article 4 was drafted for this purpose: to clearly limit member states' margin of manoeuvre by identifying the conditions for it, as well as its object and extent. Lastly, the mechanism following which all additional requirements should be transmitted to the Commission before their application (art. 4(3) of the Implementing Directive) is a substitute for the European Court of Justice's *ex post* control over national requirements, which applied under the minimum harmonization of the ISD.[17] Unlike the previous system,

[14] *De facto* maximum harmonization, given the lack of an 'explicit reference in the legislative text . . . that officially qualifies MiFID as a "maximum harmonisation" directive' (Casey and Lannoo 2006a, p. 2).

[15] For example, clients have the right to be warned if the firm esteems that the service is not appropriate to their need. Nevertheless, for this purpose, clients should put firms on the footing of understanding those needs by providing the exact type and amount of information required by MiFID art. 19 ; firms are only compliant with the rules on the proper management of conflicts of interest if they draw up a 'conflicts of interest policy' whose content is identified by art. 22 of the Level 2 Directive.

[16] Article 11(1) of the ISD included among firms' obligations that of complying 'with all regulatory requirements applicable to the conduct of . . . [their] business activities'.

[17] Under the ISD the ECJ could evaluate the national rules adopted and hold them for illegitimate where they amounted to an unjustified restriction of the Treaty freedom to provide services, as translated in the ISD.

this mechanism conveys the idea that even national rule-making for the transposition of the European rules directly involves the Community.

Despite the above, investors are not necessarily granted the same level of protection throughout Europe. This is because member states are free to decide how to implement the conduct-of-business obligations. They can choose the legal status of the rules implementing them, which influences the rights conferred to clients when the rules are breached. Not all types of rules confer clients the right to bring a judiciary action against the firm in case of breaches and to benefit from court redress. Indeed, under MiFID arts. 51 and 53, states only have to ensure that national authorities can take administrative measures or sanctions against breaches, and to encourage the setting up of extra-judicial mechanisms for investors' complaints. No reference is made to court proceedings for the benefit of investors.

3.3 Contractual rules

Contractual rules are the rules applicable to the firm–client relationship in the provision of services. They govern the pre-contractual obligations, i.e. the duties the parties owe each other in the course of the negotiations, as well as the contractual obligations, i.e. the duties of the contractual links. These rules are contained in national rules and are further elaborated by national courts, notably when they are called to specify general terms such as those of 'fairness' and 'loyalty'.

Contract law and conduct-of-business rules overlap to a non-negligible extent, although the former still exceed the latter. EU policy-makers have for a long time shown interest in the harmonization of contract law to improve the functioning of the internal market, but without result so far. MiFID was not meant to achieve the harmonization of contractual rules, hence contract law and consumer protection remain national competences.

Although MiFID does not provide harmonization for all national contractual rules,[18] it nevertheless impacts them. Under MiFID art. 19, firms shall provide clients with 'information about financial instruments and proposed investment strategies', which is to be understood as a duty to provide generic information. In Germany, however, courts requested intermediaries to supply instrument-specific financial information

[18] For example, national rules on how a contract is concluded, amended, terminated, and renewed are not touched upon, as recognized by CESR (CESR 2005, p. 61).

(Mülbert 2006, pp. 301 and 317). According to some, this approach may have to be abandoned as a result of MiFID, since it may amount to a restriction of the freedom to provide services.[19] But it is also possible to argue that where conduct-of-business rules are enacted by means of administrative (public) rules, they should remain distinguished from – and not interfere with – the contractual (private) rules, since the two give rise to different rights and are supervised by different authorities.[20]

By virtue of two European regulations, the parties to a contract for the provision of investment services can freely decide which national contractual rules should apply to their transaction: Regulation 593/2008 (Rome I)[21] governs contractual obligations, and Regulation 864/2007 (Rome II)[22] states that the national law chosen to regulate the contractual obligations shall also apply to the pre-contractual obligations. In absence of an agreement, contractual obligations are governed by the law of the country where the client has his habitual residence, provided that the firm pursues its activities in – or directs its activities to – the same country (recital 26 and art. 6 of Rome I).

The question can be raised how the interaction between MiFID and these two 'Rome' regulations will function. Let us take two examples. When state A's firm freely provides services without establishment to a client resident of state B, Rome I makes the contractual rules of state B applicable, whereas under MiFID the applicable conduct-of-business rules should be those of state A. State B's contractual rules should nevertheless take into account MiFID's rules of conduct (as shown in the example of Germany), as their level of detail should ensure that states A and B's implementation of the conduct-of-business rules does not differ. Hence, despite the application of two different national laws, there should be little risk that the applicable rules contradict each other. Still, the issue of enforcement arises. MiFID allots this power with respect to conduct-of-business rules to state A, whereas the Rome Regulation, referring to Regulation 44/2001[23] allows clients to bring action against firms before the courts of the state of their domicile, supposedly state B. Thus for the same breach both states might acquire enforcement powers, with

[19] Mülbert (2006, p. 302) finds in the European regulation the source of 'substantial amendments to existing provisions and rules'.

[20] Financial markets' authorities for the former, judges for the latter.

[21] Regulation of 17 June 2008, OJ EU of 4 July 2008 L 177/6.

[22] Regulation of 11 July 2007, OJ EU of 31 July 2007 L 199/40.

[23] Regulation of 22 December 2000 on jurisdiction and the recognition and enforcement of judgments in civil and commercial matters (OJ EU of 16 January 2001 L 12/23).

the risk that the same conduct is evaluated in different proceedings and gives rise to different forms of redress.[24]

Imagine the case of a firm established in member state A which provides services through a branch in member state B to a client resident of member state C. Pursuant to Rome I, parties can agree to apply the contractual rules of a non-EU state, even where it features a lower degree of clients' protection. Problematically, this would frustrate MiFID's efforts to level the playing field among European jurisdictions. The following interpretation of art. 3 of Rome I might help overcome this problem. Article 3 states that when all the elements relevant to the contract point to a country other than the one whose law has been chosen, parties should respect the mandatory[25] rules of that other country. In the case above, all the elements point to three different states; nevertheless, upon closer inspection, one can argue that they all point to Europe and to the uniform system of conduct-of-business rules introduced by MiFID. If we further admit that MiFID's rules become mandatory once transposed in the national legal systems, we can conclude that despite the parties' choice of the applicable law, clients cannot be denied the level of protection brought about by member states in implementation of the European rules. Still, this interpretation can be rebutted: one could argue that national borders are relevant for the purpose of art. 3, that art. 4 of the Level 2 Directive contradicts the existence of a true uniform European system for conduct-of-business rules and that at least some MiFID rules are not mandatory.[26] Hence, the interaction between MiFID and Rome I remains controversial.

Two conclusions emerge: a level playing field in contractual rules would facilitate cross-border provision of services and grant clients the same degree of protection throughout Europe. Its realization is nevertheless hampered by member states defending the peculiarities of their legal tradition and opposing a complete convergence of contractual rules. The interaction between Rome I and Rome II, and MiFID further complicates the issue of clients' protection.

[24] See above, where we point out that states can choose the legal status of the regulations implementing the conduct-of-business rules.

[25] The rules which cannot be derogated by agreement.

[26] For example, if the client does not provide information on his financial needs, firms do not have to assess the adequacy of the investments.

4. Supervision and enforcement under MiFID

MiFID regulates the supervision of firms and the enforcement of applicable rules more accurately than the ISD. First, MiFID confers supervisory and enforcement powers to the state with rule-making powers. Second, it gives due response to the problems faced by home states' authorities in supervising services provided abroad under the free provision of services, without establishing a branch. Third, it only applies the system of dual supervision (supervision by both home and host states) to branches, and ensures its proper performance by dealing more in depth with coordination issues arising among national authorities.

Under the ISD, a host state detecting a breach of rules for which it is competent could merely ask firms to put an end to the illicit practice. However, the home state is the sole authority able to apply sanctions against non-compliant firms. The host state's authority was residual in the sense that it had the possibility to intervene exclusively in case of emergency or after the home state's measures had proven inadequate.

By contrast, MiFID allocates supervisory and enforcement powers to the same authority entrusted with rule-making. Therefore, the home state supervises and enforces the application of prudential rules in all cases and of conduct-of-business rules in case of companies providing cross-border services or in case their branches operate in third countries. On the other hand, the host state supervises and enforces the conduct-of-business rules applying to branches providing services within its territory. Thus the host state can take the necessary measures to sanction illicit behaviour, after having informed the home state.

This system is far more practical and effective than the one previously in place, but implies that national authorities trust each other and that supervisory practices across Europe converge. To this end, MiFID arts. 48 *et seq.* identify the powers which all jurisdictions shall grant to their national authorities: the power to access documents and records; to demand information; to carry out on-site inspections; to require the cessation of prohibited practices; to request the freezing or the sequestration of assets and the temporary prohibition of professional activity; and the right to issue administrative sanctions.

MiFID greatly expands home states' responsibility. In effect, home states supervise their national firms acting abroad without establishing a branch. This raises concerns that authorities may be overloaded and encounter difficulties in detecting breaches outside their territory (CESR 2006, p. 9). Enriques (2005) argues that the expansion of home states' competences means that supervisors will choose to focus on detection of breaches in national markets rather than in foreign markets, not only for lack of information but also for 'political reasons'.

To counterbalance the possible negative effects on the quality of supervision, the European rules contain measures reinforcing the collaboration mechanisms and assigning host states an auxiliary role in supporting home states' supervision. Under the ISD, host states' authorities were mandated to inform home states' supervisors only on the measures taken against breaches they were competent for, that is breaches of the conduct-of-business rules. Other information was exchanged on request. On the other hand, MiFID mandates that where host states believe that firms acting within their territory are in breach of duties for which the home state is competent, they shall refer their findings to the home state. If the measures adopted by the home state are inadequate, the host state itself can take action to protect investors and the proper functioning of the market. Thus the host state may acquire supervisory and enforcement powers that would normally fall under home states' competence.

Overall, authorities have to cooperate by exchanging information and performing on-the-spot verifications; they cannot refuse cooperation maintaining that the investigated conduct does not breach any national regulation; they should guard against misconducts, even those conducted outside their territory and for which they are not competent, and inform the competent national authority thereof.

MiFID restrains dual supervision to branches, which are subject to their home state's authority for prudential matters and to the host state's authority for transactional matters. Under the ISD framework, firms were subject to the supervision of both home and host states any time they performed services abroad, regardless of whether they acted with or without establishment. The current regulation mirrors the ISD in some respects. Home states are empowered to conduct on-site inspections on branches abroad (MiFID art. 32(8)). Host states can require information from branches set up in their territory (MiFID art. 61(2)), ask for variations to business arrangements before the branch starts operations if they are not satisfied with the proposed arrangements (MiFID art. 32(7), second subparagraph), and ask to put an end to breaches of conduct-of-business rules when branches are already in place (MiFID art. 62(2)). In addition, unlike the ISD, MiFID allows host states' authorities to take direct measures against detected breaches, even though they are not explicitly bestowed the power to conduct on-site verifications.

Dual supervision is a particularly sensitive matter. It implies that the home state's authority exercises control in another state's jurisdiction and that the host state applies measures to a firm which is not national. From a legal point of view, this might be problematic, unless explicit provisions confer specific powers upon states. The ISD identified these powers, but MiFID adds to those powers and reduces the cases of dual supervision, thereby ensuring more stringent supervision with less complexity.

The last feature distinguishing MiFID from its forerunner is the attention devoted to the need for cooperation among national supervisory authorities. Cooperation can take different forms, for example exchange of information, collaboration in the performance of on-site inspections and other investigations. MiFID spells out the core principles guiding states' cooperating with each other (arts. 56–58). Nevertheless, they can define how to implement the collaboration concretely. Following CESR's guidance, states can agree on joint supervision, and they can delegate or 'outsource' supervision under the condition that each retains its responsibility (CESR 2007c). Concretely, this might take place under two forms: the 'Common Oversight Request' through which a state requests an agreement on a common oversight programme; the 'Standing Request for Assistance' used to solicit the assistance of another authority on certain supervisory matters. Both cooperative measures are subject to the principles contained in CESR's 'Protocol on the supervision of branches'.[27] However, the margin of manoeuvre shall not result in member states refraining from acting and frustrating any concrete result. Therefore, art. 59 of MiFID makes clear that states can refuse a request for cooperation for investigation, on-the-spot verification or supervisory activity only on limited grounds: where the activities could adversely affect the sovereignty, security or public policy of the state; where the matters which should be investigated are already being evaluated in judicial proceedings or a decision thereon has already been taken with a final judgment.

5. Access to regulated markets and clearing and settlement systems under MiFID

The passporting system established by MiFID can only enhance cross-border activities and promote the internal market when coupled with the firms' right to participate in a host country's regulated markets and clearing and settlement systems. Indeed, this participation is necessary to

[27] To date, thirteen bilateral standing requests for assistance have been concluded, as well as a common oversight programme between the UK (FSA) and Germany (BaFin): see CESR (2008).

finalize the financial transactions. Under MiFID,[28] member states shall allow foreign firms to be member or have access to their regulated markets, and are prohibited from enacting additional requirements for this purpose. Additionally, all firms authorized by their home state to execute clients' orders or to deal on own account benefit from this access right, which can be exercised under two forms: directly, by setting up branches in the host state and remotely, i.e. without any presence in the host state.[29]

Markets can establish rules governing access or membership, but they should be transparent, non-discriminatory and based on objective criteria. Moreover, the rules should directly derive from the principles governing the transactions on that market and pertain to firms' professional standards or organization. The right to remote access by investment firms to regulated markets in other member states was missing under the ISD: art. 15 allowed only for direct access (by means of branches) and indirect access, obtained 'by setting up subsidiaries in the host member state or by acquiring firms in the host member state that are already members of regulated markets'. The ISD also authorized states to impose additional capital requirements (but only on matters not covered by the directive).

Clearing and settlement systems ensure the smooth finalization of both domestic and cross-border investment activities, in that they ensure that payment and transfer of financial instruments take place safely. Unlike domestic transactions, the finalization of cross-border transactions requires participation in clearing and settlement systems located in different states. A cross-border investment activities regime should therefore provide for the broadest possible participation in these systems across the EU. The ISD regulated participation in a restrictive fashion: it made participation to a national clearing and settlement system conditional upon participation in the regulated market of the same state. This heightened the costs for participation, and thus discouraged cross-border activities. By contrast, MiFID allows firms to freely designate a clearing and settlement system throughout the Community irrespective of where the transactions have been concluded;[30] direct participation can only be subject to the 'same non-discriminatory, transparent and objective criteria as apply to local participants', unless the participation is refused 'on legitimate commercial grounds'.

[28] Arts. 33, 34 and 42.

[29] Under the condition that the trading procedures and systems of the regulated market do not require physical presence: MiFID art. 33.

[30] MiFID arts. 34 and 46.

Nevertheless, MiFID neither identifies the criteria for determining whether access has been granted, nor does it define the terms 'clearing and settlement', leaving considerable room for national interpretations. Further, MiFID does not harmonize the framework for the authorization and ongoing supervision of entities providing clearing and settlement activities. Thus national authorities can impede the participation of foreign users on reasons connected to the orderly functioning of the national market.

6. MiFID's weaknesses and shortcomings

Although MiFID is a clear improvement on the ISD, some weaknesses remain. First, the boundaries between what is prudential and what is transactional are partially blurred. 'Whilst on paper "organisational requirements" are reserved to the home regulator, the distinction between the system and controls environment for a branch and the way in which the business is conducted may not be a clear one' (CESR 2006, p. 9). In some cases, therefore, it is difficult to determine whether a home or host state's rules apply. CESR suggested that national authorities should agree on where to draw the line between organizational and conduct-of-business requirements; that the home regulator can inquire on behalf of the host regulator on organizational matters; and that firms provide a defined set of common information on organizational matters to both regulators (CESR 2006, pp. 11–12).

Second, while MiFID treats conflicts of interest as a pure home state competence,[31] it could have split the competences between the home state (for the management of conflicts by means of organizational arrangements) and the host states (for the management of conflicts by means of disclosure) to better achieve its objective. Although the first safeguard against conflicts of interest lies with organizational requirements – a home state competence – disclosure represents another possible means of control. Disclosure belongs to conduct-of-business rules, which are a host state competence. Specifically, firms should be aware of the conflicts which might arise and identify the way of managing them. What shall be pursued for this purpose is 'an appropriate level of independence from the part of the relevant persons engaged in different business activities involving a conflict of interest' (art. 22(3) of the Level 2 Regulation). As the European regulator admits, this level of independence – despite being the maximum possible given the size and complexity of the business – may well not be sufficient to ensure that clients' interests are not damaged. If this is the case, firms shall disclose the general nature or the

[31] Art. 32(7) does not include conflicts of interest among the matters which should be regulated by the host state when services are provided through branches.

sources of conflicts to the clients. Thus, the safeguard provided by disclosure goes hand in hand with that provided by organizational requirements. Accuracy in the information provided is therefore important, and should be attentively monitored. The host state, where the branch is located, should be better placed for this purpose.

Third, the wording of art. 32(7) retains some ambiguity: the principle of host state responsibility applies to the services provided by the branch *within its territory.* Which rules apply to a branch offering services to clients located in the territory of a third state? The European Commission has made clear that 'any cross-border operation through a branch outside the territory of the member state in which this branch is located is a provision of services by the investment firm and not by the branch as a separate legal entity'. Therefore, it is considered a provision of services without establishment from the part of the firm itself (European Commission 2007a). As a result, the home state acquires rule-making powers on activities performed by the branch. However, the host state where the branch originating the services is physically located would be better placed to exercise rule-making and supervisory powers.

This solution would also level the treatment between branches and subsidiaries. Subsidiaries are autonomous legal entities, incorporated as such and owned by firms incorporated elsewhere in Europe.[32] The parent company 'owning' the subsidiary can perform cross-border services through them, as it would through a branch. Nevertheless, when branches provide services abroad, they are subject to conduct-of-business rules of the home state, which is not the state where they are located. By contrast, when subsidiaries provide services abroad, they are subject to the rules of the state where they are located, which is considered their home state. From the viewpoint of clients' protection and of application of conduct-of-business rules, the different legal status between branches and subsidiaries should not play any role (CESR 2007d, p. 6).

Fourth, MiFID does not solve the problem of conduct-of-business rules overlapping with national contractual rules and, presumably, the latter have to be amended to take the European regulation into account. Moreover, its interaction with the Rome I and II Regulations is perfectible: in some cases it results in more than one state having enforcement powers with respect to the same conducts; in other cases it does not adequately protect clients against firms choosing the (least protective) non-EU national regulation to rule their relationship.

Lastly, the lack of a passporting system in the domain of clearing and

[32] On the contrary, branches are not autonomous legal entities, in that the rights and obligations they acquire refer back to the company which set them up.

settlement might frustrate MiFID's aim of fostering financial markets' integration. No matter how easily investors can choose their investment services' provider among all the European firms and how easily firms can access markets, if firms are not granted smooth access to clearing and settlement systems, transactions may not take place at all. This could be detrimental for the economy, diminishing the efficient allocation of financial resources and raising the cost of capital.

7. Conclusion

The aim of this chapter was to analyse MiFID's architecture with respect to the home/host state's competence for the regulation and supervision of cross-border provision of investment services. The proper allocation of competences is crucial in order to ensure that markets are duly protected, firms are not discouraged from acting abroad and investors' confidence is fostered. This promotes sound, safe and integrated financial markets.

The novelties brought about by MiFID can be summarized as follows. MiFID lays down a full harmonization framework, which prevents states from enacting more or less stringent rules. This applies to both prudential and transactional regulations, save for the exceptional and proportionate additional requirements states can apply pursuant to art. 4 of the Level 2 Directive. Hence, the conditions for obtaining the authorization to conduct business are levelled throughout Europe; firms are subject to comparable conduct-of-business rules, irrespective of where and under which form they perform services. Therefore, member states are not allowed to relax rules to put their national firms at a competitive advantage with respect to foreign firms; nor can they burden incoming firms with more stringent obligations. Moreover, firms cannot arbitrate among jurisdictions in search of the less stringent regulation irrespective of where they perform services.

The new directive does not level the playing field on contractual matters, but makes a step forward in this direction. The harmonization of conduct-of-business rules will have some impact on the obligations to which firms are subject when acting vis-à-vis their clients.

MiFID also achieves the worthy objective of legislative simplification: where the service is provided without establishment, only the home state's law applies; in case of branches, prudential matters are regulated by the home state, and transactional matters by the host state, which is on a better footing for this purpose because of vicinity to the business. For branches performing services abroad without establishment, MiFID derogates to the host state's competence on transactional rules, but still avoids the multiplication of competences by entrusting the home state with conduct-of-business supervision.

Supervision and enforcement are duly allocated to the state having rule-making powers without exceptions and branches' supervision is managed effectively, since host states have the power to intervene directly against misbehaviours. The duty of cooperation among national authorities is made more stringent: they shall monitor breaches occurring both within and outside their territories, irrespective of their rule-making, supervision and enforcement powers.

MiFID features other provisions fostering cross-border business, namely those giving firms the right to access regulated markets as well as clearing and settlement systems abroad. Whereas the access to regulated market can take place under a number of different forms, firms' freedom to participate in clearing and settlement systems is still incomplete. Future steps therefore need to be taken in this respect, in order to further foster cross-border activities, for the benefit of firms and their clients.

References

Casey, Jean-Pierre and Karel Lannoo 2006. *The MiFID Implementing Measures: Excessive Detail or Level Playing Field?* ECMI Policy Brief No. 1, May, available at www.ceps.be.

CESR 2006. 'The Passport under MiFID. Public consultation', December, CESR 06-669, available at www.cesr.eu, accessed September 2008.

2007a. 'Overview of national options and discretions under MiFID Level 1 – Dir. n. 2004/39/EC', CESR/07-703, October, available at http://tinyurl.com/ skrhs, accessed September 2008.

2007b. 'Protocol on MiFID passport notifications', May, CESR/07-317b, available at http://tinyurl.com/3vqzk3, accessed October 2008.

2007c. 'Protocol on the supervision of branches under MiFID', October, CESR/07-672, available at http://tinyurl.com/3taj53.

2007d. 'The Passport under MiFID. Recommendations for the implementation of the Directive 2004/39/EC. Feedback Statement', May, available at www.cesr.eu.

2008. 'Press Release. MiFID: CESR Members enhance supervisory co-operation for branch supervision', September, CESR/08-675, available at http://tinyurl.com/5kjfyh.

Committee of Wise Men 2001. 'Final Report of the Committee of Wise Men on the Regulation of European Securities Markets', February, available at http://ec.europa.eu.

Cruickshank, Cristopher 1998. 'Is there a need to harmonise conduct business rules?', in Guido Ferrarini (ed.), *European Securities Markets. The Investments Services Directive and Beyond*, Kluwer Law International: London, the Hague, Boston.

Enriques, Luca 2005. 'Conflicts of interest in investment services: the price and uncertain impact of MiFID's regulatory framework', available at www.ssrn.com.

European Commission 2000. 'Retail financial services: overcoming remaining barriers. a legal analysis', March, MARKT/C/PT available at: http://tinyurl.com/5fm5xu.

2001. 'Comunicazione della Commissione al Consiglio e al Parlamento Europeo sul diritto contrattuale europeo', July, COM(2001) 398 def, available at http://tinyurl.com/5a5n3v.

2002. 'Proposal for a Directive of the European Parliament and of the Council on investment services and regulated markets, and amending Council Directives 85/611/EEC, Council Directive 93/6/EEC and European Parliament and Council Directive 2000/12/EC', COM(2002) 625 final, November, available at http://eur-lex.europa.eu/LexUriServ/LexUri Serv.do?uri=OJ:C: 2003:071E:0062:0125:EN:PDF.

2004. 'Communication from the Commission to the Council and the European Parliament. Clearing and Settlement in the European Union. The Way Forward', COM(2004) 312 final, April, available at http://tinyurl.com/5vnx7b.

2007a. 'Working Document ESC/21/2007' rev1, May, MARKT/G/3/MV D(2007).

2007b. 'Working Paper ESC/06/2007', available at http://tinyurl.com/64vwlf.

France (2007) 'Transposition de la directive MIF', available at http://tinyurl.com/29x2vo.

Herbst, Jonathan 2003. 'Revision of the Investment Services Directive', 11(3) *Journal of Financial Regulation and Compliance.*

Ireland 2007. 'Justification for Retention under Article 4 of 2006/73/EC', available at http://tinyurl.com/29x2vo, accessed May 2008.

Köndgen, Johannes 1998. 'Rules of conduct: further harmonisation?', in Guido Ferrarini (ed.) *European Securities Markets. The Investments Services Directive and Beyond*, Kluwer Law International: London, the Hague, Boston.

Lannoo, Karel 1999. 'Does Europe need an SEC?' European Capital Markets Institute (ECMI), Occasional Paper No. 1, November 1999.

OECD 2000. 'Cross-border trade in financial services: economics and regulation', 75 *Financial Market Trends*, available at www.oecd. org.

Pacces, Alessio Maria 1999. 'La disciplina europea dei servizi finanziari al dettaglio. Prospettive di armonizzazione di concorrenza tra ordinamenti nella tutela del consumatore', *Ente Einaudi*, Quaderni di ricerche No. 47.

Tison, Michel 2002. 'Conduct of business rules and their implementation in the EU Member States', in Guido Ferrarini, Klaus J. Hopt, Eddy Wymeersch (eds.), *Capital Market in the Age of the Euro*, Kluwer Law International: The Hague, London, New York.

United Kingdom 2007. 'Notification and justification for retention of certain requirements', available at http://tinyurl.com/29x2vo.

11

MiFID and Reg NMS: a test-case for 'substituted compliance'?

This chapter compares the EU MiFID and the US Regulation National Market System (Reg NMS) and explores whether they could be accepted as equivalent by regulators on both sides of the Atlantic. Apart from many similarities, the most important one being that the main purpose of both measures is to enforce best execution in equity trading, there are also many differences in the definition of best execution, the structures of the markets, and the role and powers of supervisory authorities. It calls upon the European Commission to make a detailed comparison between both measures and to take the opportunity to negotiate a mutual recognition agreement on securities trading with the US.

1. Introduction

Two substantive pieces of legislation came into force on both sides of the Atlantic at roughly the same time – MiFID in the EU and Reg NMS in the US. Both aimed at updating regulation to reflect technological changes and market developments. Should this coincidence be taken as a sign of a well-functioning regulatory dialogue or of capital market integration? At the heart of each regulation is the introduction and specification of the best execution concept in securities transactions. MiFID intends to complete the process started with the 1993 Investment Services Directive (ISD) and further liberalizes Europe's capital markets, by abolishing the monopoly of exchanges. Reg NMS aims to modernize and strengthen the National Market System (NMS) for equity securities trading. Although the latter is more limited in scope than MiFID, a closer look reveals substantial differences in the regulation of equity trading on both continents. With the establishment of the first transatlantic exchange and the significant activity of several large firms in both markets, the question emerges whether a managed convergence approach is feasible and desirable, or whether this will come about as a result of market forces.

In comparing these two pieces of regulation, one needs to keep the substantial differences in the market and regulatory structure on the two sides of the Atlantic in mind. The US has a much longer tradition of securities markets regulation than the EU, but at the same time it has kept elements that Europe has abandoned in the meantime. Reg NMS is a further adaptation of the 1934 Securities Exchange Act, which laid the basis of the US structure as we know it today, with a powerful regulator, the Securities and Exchange Commission (SEC), at the centre, but with important powers assigned to self-regulatory organizations (SROs). EU efforts to create a single capital market started in the 1980s, with the Investment Services Directive as the centrepiece. This happened against the background of limited experience with capital market regulation at member state level, a heterogeneous supervisory structure and a high degree of self-regulation. The Financial Services Action Plan (FSAP) succeeded in streamlining this structure, but largely eliminated self-regulation.

This chapter starts with an overview of the key points of both measures. In a second step, a closer analysis is made of the definition of best execution as provided for in each measure, and the effects it will have on the market. In a third part, we analyse whether and how both pieces of regulation could become part of the regulatory dialogue between the EU and the US and ask whether the new approach of 'substituted compliance' could be applied.

2. MiFID and Reg NMS in a nutshell

Although *omnis comparatio claudicat* (every comparison is to some extent flawed), the similarities between the two regulations are too great to simply chalk them up to coincidence. Reg NMS is based on the 1934 Securities Exchange Act, which requires that investors receive financial and other relevant information concerning securities being offered for public sale; and prohibits deceit, misrepresentations, and other fraud in the sale of securities. To enforce these stipulations, the Act created the Securities and Exchange Commission (SEC) and endowed it with large rule-making powers. Many of the current US securities laws are based upon this Act. The ISD and MiFID are based upon the EU Treaty, and their objective is to create a single market. EU directives or regulations flesh out and detail the relevant freedoms set forth in the EU Treaty, namely the free provision of services and the free movement of capital.

2.1 MiFID

The ISD, which was adopted in 1993, introduced the freedom to provide services for exchanges, i.e. licensed regulated markets, and broker dealers in the EU. Although the directive clearly had a liberalizing effect, the harmonization of conduct of business rules was insufficiently detailed, with the effect that free provision of services did not work effectively on a cross-border basis, especially for retail clients. To correct this shortcoming, MiFID introduces a far-reaching degree of harmonization of conduct of business rules, aimed at achieving a single rule in the EU. In addition, it abolishes the option provided by the ISD for the concentration of trades on the regulated market, the local exchange, and allows systemic internalization of equity trading by banks.

The key provisions of MiFID are as follows:

1. A far-reaching harmonization of conduct of business rules for securities trading, including strict rules on best execution of trades, client categorization and client reporting.
2. Rules on the internal governance of investment firms, requiring them to tackle conflicts of interest, maintain good governance and ensure continuity of their services.
3. Abolition of the concentration rules of the ISD, by which member states could require equity trades to be executed on the main exchange or the 'regulated market'.
4. Systematic internalization of equity trades, subject to strict pre- and post-trade transparency requirements within certain thresholds, or less limited above that.
5. A European passport for Multilateral Trading Facilities (MTFs), which can be created by investment firms and exchanges.
6. The extension of the single passport regime to some other services (investment advice and non-discretionary portfolio management) and some other markets (commodities, more derivative instruments).

MiFID is also one of the first EU financial regulation directives to assign extensive scope for implementing measures, i.e. secondary (or 'Level 2' in Lamfalussy parlance) legislation, to the EU Securities Committee, which is composed of Ministry of Finance officials of the member states and chaired by the European Commission. Some twenty of the seventy-three articles of the Level 1 (or Framework) Directive assign implementing powers to this committee, shielded from direct parliamentary scrutiny.

Implementing measures, consisting of a directive and a regulation, were adopted in September 2006 (see reference in Table 11.1), and almost double the total size of the Level 1 Directive.

The ISD is credited with having allowed trading in stocks to concentrate on the home market of the listed companies, and hence to enhance liquidity, reduce spreads and improve the price discovery process. It also brought increased competition between financial centres and more concentration of business in certain places.

2.2 Reg NMS

While the core issue of the debate generated by Reg NMS was similar to that of MiFID – i.e. to what extent one needs to concentrate securities trading for the sake of liquidity and an orderly price formation process – the outcome was radically different in each case. Reg NMS protects the incumbent stock exchanges against competition from 'alternative' markets, whereas MiFID increases the competition to exchanges. Unlike in Europe, which had seen a concentration of blue chip trades on the home stock exchanges, the US had experienced a much stronger growth of alternative execution venues, such as internalizers, ECNs, ATSs and crossing networks, raising concerns with regulators that it reduces market liquidity, diminishes the price discovery process and dampens the appetite of investors to display limit orders. But the SEC's solution was certainly not uncontroversial, as illustrated by the formal and open dissent of Commissioners Paul S. Atkins and Cynthia A. Glassman to the adoption of Reg NMS (Glassman and Atkins 2005).

Reg NMS builds upon the establishment of the National Market System (NMS) from 1975. The latter was intended to connect the different individual markets that trade securities, through a unified system that links the different buy and sell orders in a particular stock in order to give the best quote to investors. This culminated in the establishment of the Inter-market Trading System (ITS), which did not include NASDAQ. NMS aimed to stimulate competition between markets and competition for individual orders. The first should stimulate innovation of trading systems, the second efficient pricing of stocks. Unlike other national markets, which are dominated by a single public market, the SEC asserts that the US has vigorous competition between different types of markets, including national and regional exchanges with different degrees of automation, purely electronic markets, market-making securities dealers and automated matching systems.[1] In its words, the NMS has thus been 'remarkably successful' in promoting market competition, but because of growing fragmentation, this has come at the expense of competition among orders for individual stock, affecting the quality of the price discovery process, the market depth and liquidity. Hence, there is a need for tighter regulation of best execution.

Reg NMS contains the following four key provisions:

1. *Order protection rule* – Designed to enforce best execution and protect limit orders, this rule reinforces the fundamental principle of obtaining the best price for investors when such price is represented by quotations that are immediately accessible for automatic execution in trading centres. It requires that firms establish, maintain and enforce written policies and procedures in place to prevent trade-throughs for NMS stock, which occur when trades are executed without regard for immediately available and better-priced quotations in other trading centres. Trade-throughs reduce liquidity and transparency and increase transaction costs. They also discourage investors from displaying limit orders, which are seen to be the building blocks of price discovery and efficient markets. There are many exceptions to the rule, for example, for intermarket sweep orders (block transactions), flickering quotes and benchmark trades, which raise questions about enforcement.
2. *Access rule* – Establishing fair and efficient access to quotations in NMS stock, the rule enables the use of private linkages by a variety of connectivity providers. It limits the fee a trading centre can charge to access protected quotations to no more than €0.003 per share. And it requires SROs to maintain written rules prohibiting their members from locking or crossing protected quotations of other trading centres.
3. *Sub-penny rule* – This prohibits market participants from displaying, ranking or accepting quotations that are priced at an increment of less than 1 cent, unless the quotation is less than $1.
4. *Market data rules* – These amend the rules for the functioning of the single market data consolidator, changing the formula for the allocation of the revenues to provide the right incentives to those SROs that provide the most useful data for investors.

The trade-through prohibition applies to automated quotations in all trading centres, that is, displayed quotations that are immediately

[1] As drawn by the European Commission in its Working Document (European Commission 2007a).

Table 11.1 MiFID vs. Reg NMS at a glance

	MiFID	Reg NMS
Objective/scope	• Upgrade Investment Services Directive (ISD) • Further integrate Europe's capital markets through a single set of conduct of business rules	• Strengthen and modernize regulatory structure of US *equity* markets • Reflect technological and market developments
Main measures	• Abolition of concentration rule for equity trading and data • Best execution • Harmonized MTF regime • Rules on systematic internalization for equity trading	• Order protection rule • Access rule • Sub-penny rule • Market data rules
Trading venue classification	• Regulated markets • MTFs • Systematic internalizers	• Fast markets (automated quotes) • Slow markets (manual quotes)
Best execution approach	• Several parameters (price, costs, speed . . .), depending on characteristics of client, order, financial instrument and venue • Prior consent for internalization • Policy to be set by firms, to be reviewed annually	• Price precedes • Prohibition of 'trade-throughs' • Firms are requested to maintain written policies
Regulatory authorities	European Commission, ESC, CESR, national authorities	SEC, SROs
Entry into force	1 November 2007	Over a series of five dates starting in October 2006 and ending 8 October 2007
Likely market impact	• Increased competition among trading venues • Concentration on sell side	• Markets to become fully electronic • Protection of larger markets, supports liquidity

Table 11.1 (*cont.*)

	MiFID	Reg NMS
		• Further concentration, international mergers
Problems	• Compliance costs: industry needs to make important modifications to their order routing systems to obtain best price • Demand for clarifications • Request for delays • Enforceability	• Compliance costs: industry needs to make important modifications to their order routing systems to obtain best price • Demand for clarifications • Request for delays • Enforceability
Outstanding issues	• Price transparency in bond markets • Data consolidation • Impact on buy side institutions (e.g. UCITS) • Clearing and settlement	• Role of SROs • Block trading
Reference	Directive 2004/39/EC; implementing measures Commission Directive 2006/73/EC and Commission Regulation (EC) No. 1287/2006	Exchange Act Release No. 34–51808 (9 June 2005)
Size	128 pages in OJ; 67,000 words	52 pages (amendments to part 242 of the Securities Exchange Act of 1934)

accessible for execution in national securities exchanges, exchange specialists, ATSs, OTC market-makers and internalizers. Thus, according to the trade-through rule, once a best bid or offer has been posted for a stock, any order must be routed to that trading venue for execution. Unlike MiFID, the obligation of best execution thus also applies to exchanges under Reg NMS, but only for automated quotes.

At first sight, both rules are thus highly comparable. Although MiFID is wider in scope than Reg NMS, which is solely concerned with equity markets, both measures impact market structure, set and define best execution and regulate the market for market data. Moreover, both also

Table 11.2 Best execution and market data rules: MiFID vs. Reg NMS

	MiFID	Reg NMS
Best execution	Article 21 of MiFID defines best execution as not only a matter of the price of a trade, but also 'costs, speed, likelihood of execution and settlement, size, nature or any other consideration relevant to the execution of the order'. Investment firms are required to establish and implement order execution policies, including the factors affecting the order execution venue. These policies will be assessed by investment firms on a regular basis.	Rule 602 b of Reg NMS obliges trading centres to execute buy and sell orders at the best price. Rule 611 requires trading centres to establish, maintain and enforce written policies that are designed to prevent trade-throughs of protected quotations. The trading centre must perform regular and rigorous reviews to ensure the effectiveness of the required policies and procedures, and to evaluate the execution quality of markets.
Markets for financial market data	MiFID liberalizes pre- and post-trade data markets, without imposing a structure. Regulated markets (art. 45), MTFs (art. 30) and systematic internalizers (art. 28) are requested 'to make public the price, volume and time of the transactions . . . as close to real time as possible . . . [and] on a reasonable commercial basis'. The same applies for pre-trade data.	NMS instituted a single data consolidator. Reg NMS gives more freedom to SROs to disseminate their trade reports independently, but still requires them to communicate best prices to the data consolidator.

stimulated wide-ranging and polarized discussions. Both rules came into force at about the same time, and the expectation is that both measures will have a fundamental impact on market structure, as well as on exchanges and their respective broker communities.

A closer look reveals very substantial differences, however, demonstrating that each measure developed independently within its own institutional environment. There are important differences, for example, in the way each measure defines best execution: under MiFID, it is more of a principle, whereas it is a rule under Reg NMS. In defining best execution, MiFID takes a series of criteria and characteristics into account – thus allowing best execution requirements to be tailored to each investor's profile – whereas price alone matters under Reg NMS. As a consequence, there are many exceptions to best execution under Reg NMS, whereas there are virtually none under MiFID, with the proviso of eligible counterparties. In addition, Reg NMS has some elements that are seen, from a European perspective, to be alien to a liberal economic system, as the US is viewed from Europe. The regulation is seen as a form of price regulation (the access rule and sub-penny rule) and mandates consolidation of equity market data in a single consolidator, with a complex method for allocating fees, whereas MiFID just opens market data to competition.

As vividly demonstrated by the US Sarbanes-Oxley Act of 2002, capital markets are increasingly interconnected and globalized. Rules that are seen to be too burdensome or protective will turn business away to other centres. Specifically in equity trading, in the context of large broker dealers with a global presence, trading in stocks can easily be moved to other jurisdictions. Moreover, with the opening of the first transatlantic exchange and a second one in the near future, integrated transatlantic trading floors will soon emerge, facilitating the execution of trades under the most favourable regime. Should the MiFID–Reg NMS nexus therefore be discussed urgently in the context of the EU–US regulatory dialogue? Or should one expect the dictates of the market to resolve any problems? Based on our analysis of the expected effects of both measures, this subject is addressed in the next section.

3. Comparative effects of MiFID and Reg NMS

While it is still too early to assess the effects of both measures on the markets, there is broad criticism in the US that Reg NMS is excessively protectionist, prescriptive and anti-competitive. The open dissent of two SEC Commissioners to the adoption of Reg NMS is probably the clearest sign of this criticism, but there were also wide-ranging and contentious debates throughout the country prior to the adoption of the measure (which is summarized in the 437 pages preceding the text of adopted rules). MiFID has also been heavily criticized as being burdensome, excessively detailed and costly, although a timid consensus is emerging that its long-term effects could be positive for Europe's capital markets as a result of its market-opening effects, albeit with some caveats.

As with MiFID, Reg NMS is expected to provide markets with a strong incentive to innovate and to adopt technologies that allow them to be more responsive to the speed of execution and thus to market efficiency. It entices manual venues to accelerate their automation process. It places the different execution venues on a more equal footing and does away with the asymmetric regulation that existed before. It is expected to stimulate consolidation and reduce the number of alternative trading venues in the US, a trend that was already evident over the last two years (Gentzoglanis 2006). At the same time, however, it protects the dominant exchange, which has the liquidity advantage to offer the best price. But this may slow future innovation in US equity trading (Gkanitinis 2006).

The criticism expressed by SEC Commissioners Cynthia A. Glassman and Paul S. Atkins focused on the prohibition of trade-throughs, which, in their opinion, is not warranted. They claim that the figures used on trade-throughs by the SEC, which point to a degree of fragmentation, were not correctly measured, and do not point to a lack of liquidity (Glassman and Atkins 2005). They assert that Reg NMS will not achieve its goals. Current trade-through rates do not mandate the action proposed, nor will its prohibition improve best execution (pp. 20–1). In addition, they argue that narrowing down best execution to the price criterion reduces competition to the detriment of other factors of execution quality, and to the detriment of the market structure and innovation (p. 30). According to the Commissioners, the trade-through rule imposes government-controlled competition, increases barriers to competition and represents a misguided attempt to micro-manage the markets. The Commissioners also criticized the 'codification' of the single data consolidator model, which 'grants a monopoly for the consolidation of market data', constituting another barrier to competition and increasing the cost of implementation (pp. 41–2). This criticism was also voiced by academics (Blume 2007, Wallison 2006).

These critical remarks are a useful reminder in the context of the European MiFID debate. While the market environments are similar on both sides of the Atlantic, the EU has taken a radically different route, which is more in line with the criticism voiced by the two US Commissioners. The most serious criticism one could level at MiFID, and which was an important issue during the discussions of the directive, is that it would contribute to fragmentation. Hence, the last-minute addition of pre-trade price transparency for internalizers. Nevertheless, overall, regulation under MiFID goes in the opposite direction from Reg NMS. It abolishes monopolies and opens up the securities markets to more competition. Whereas exchanges have exercised a formal or effective monopoly in many EU markets until today, this changes radically under MiFID, which allows three forms of execution venues (exchanges, multilateral trading facilities and systematic internalizers), and also opens up the market for (equity) financial market data. Hence, with a restructuring of today's regulated markets, the emergence of new specialized regulated markets and MTFs, a much higher degree of competition can be expected between execution venues. Moreover, exchanges will also face challenges to their financial market data revenues. From a best-execution perspective, the biggest challenge for market operators will be to provide fast linkages between all these execution venues to allow best execution to work in practice, as exists in the US. If they fail to meet this challenge, Europe could be heading towards the same situation the SEC is trying to avoid with Reg NMS; that is, strong competition between markets, but achieved at the expense of a transparent and effective price formation process.

The jury is still out as to which form of best execution will prove to be the most effective. Even if, in theory, it may be better to have a broader set of criteria to judge best execution, this may give rise to arbitrariness and create legal uncertainty. The broad set of criteria under MiFID gives firms a large degree of flexibility and discretion in applying best execution, adapted to the wishes of their clients, but at the same time it creates uncertainty as to which interpretation supervisors will apply. This argues in favour of Reg NMS, which is one-dimensional, clearer and easier to apply for regulators (Gentzoglanis 2006). The laborious discussions surrounding the implementation of MiFID's best execution provisions in the context of the Committee of European Securities Regulators (CESR) and the concerns expressed by intermediaries about the priority of the criteria are an early warning of the possible difficulties to come in Europe. In addition, these rules can be implemented and enforced differently at national level by the EU member states, whereas the US has a single body in charge of enforcement.

4. A test-case for 'substituted compliance'?

In a remarkable change of policy direction, the SEC has recently indicated an interest in a form of selective bilateral mutual recognition to adapt to growing international portfolio diversification of US investors.[2] In the past, the SEC strictly applied the territoriality principle, which meant that foreign providers of services on US territory were asked to follow US rules. The principle was adduced, for example, as the justification for forbidding the display of screens of foreign exchanges in the US.[3] Under the new regime, the SEC would negotiate a bilateral 'substituted compliance' regime with another regime deemed to be substantially comparable to the US. This would be based on an initial agreement on minimum standards and information-sharing arrangements. Could the MiFID Reg NMS conundrum be a test case for this new regime?

The concept of 'substituted compliance', a phrase coined by Tafara and Peterson (2007), is comparable to the mutual recognition approach, bolstered by minimum harmonization, as we know it in the context of the EU's single market. It has been experimented within the context of the EU–US regulatory dialogue, which started in February 2002, between the European Commission on the one hand, and the US Treasury Department and the respective US supervisory authorities on the other. It has, for example, led to agreements on the equivalence of rules for auditor oversight (March 2004) and the equivalence of accounting standards (April 2005 and 2006). Although there are many elements of comparability and pressing market developments, MiFID and Reg NMS have so far not been discussed in detail in the context of this dialogue.[4] A possible structure for mutual recognition in the areas of trading screens and broker dealers is developed by Tafara and Peterson (2007).

[2] In theory, this change was intended to mean that firms can provide services solely on the basis of their home state rules. In practice, it is unlikely to achieve such a sweeping effect as it may be still possible for host member states to claim that certain requirements are not covered in MiFID, and therefore that the host member state is free to impose additional requirements in this regard (one example might be local language requirements). MiFID is silent on this point. Therefore, theoretically, host member states might maintain a requirement that documentation be provided in the local language. A key risk for firms to manage under MiFID is the risk that host member states may try to maintain super-equivalent requirements and apply them to businesses which the investment firm thinks are free from such requirements thanks to the approach taken by MiFID to cross-border business.

[3] Namely those provisions aimed at ensuring investor protection and market transparency. See arts. 19, 21, 22, 25, 27 and 28 MiFID.

[4] The matters reserved to the home state regulator include organizational requirements (e.g., systems and controls, client assets and conflict of interest provisions). They also appear to include conduct of business, transaction reporting and transparency requirements relating to the activities of a branch that are not conducted within the territory of the member state in which the branch is located.

The justification for substituted compliance is to bring more competition to both the US capital market and the US regulatory model as well as to reduce transaction costs. It would create more investment opportunities at a lower cost with greater protection. In this context, Tafara and Peterson (2007) draw a distinction between regulatory competition and regulatory arbitrage. Since the SEC would only be interested in concluding a bilateral agreement with a jurisdiction with a similar regulatory philosophy, involving a considerable degree of prudence and information-sharing, there would be no 'race to the bottom'. On the contrary, by setting minimum standards, poorly regulated markets would have the incentive to upgrade their regulatory system to gain access, thereby triggering a 'race towards optimality' (Tafara and Peterson 2007, p. 67). Investors would be protected by a mandatory disclosure statement informing them that trading conducted on a foreign stock exchange or through a foreign broker dealer may entail different forms of protection. This would at the same time insulate the US market from any adverse effects arising from these trades (Tafara and Peterson 2007, p. 57). Only fraud would remain fully subject to US provisions.

The proposed framework would consist of a four-step process:

1. The foreign firm would submit a request to the SEC seeking an exemption from registration.
2. Discussions would be held between the SEC and the home country regulator of the foreign entity, based initially on an assessment of the degree to which the two countries' prudential rules and enforcement capabilities are comparable. A second step would involve technical arrangements regarding enforcement, inspections and information-sharing arrangements, requiring a high degree of oversight coordination between both regulators. This could be laid down in a bilateral arrangement in the form of a memorandum of understanding (MoU).
3. A dialogue would then ensue between the SEC and the firm petitioning access.
4. A public notice of the request by the foreign firm and solicitation of comments would then be posted, followed by the final decision.

Apart from the standard assessment criteria of exchanges and broker dealers, the comparability assessment would also cover disclosure rules for securities issuers and a broader assessment of the general legal and enforcement comparability of the host country. The extension of reciprocal access to US firms in the host country would be an important criterion in granting exemption.

Tafara and Peterson (2007, p. 64) insist that exemption will only be granted to exchanges and broker dealers if 'all the objectives of the SEC's registration and oversight regime are otherwise met by the comparable regulatory regime in the . . . home jurisdiction'. They will, in addition, need to provide a clear risk disclosure statement to US investors that the orders or transactions are not subject to SEC oversight (2007, p. 65). Foreign broker dealers will need to maintain in a separate account assets in an amount that at least is sufficient to cover all their current obligations to US investors.

Will this new scheme finally provide easier access for EU exchanges and broker dealers to the US market? This is still an open question, in light of the brief comparisons drawn above between MiFID and Reg NMS. Possible problems might arise before granting exemption as a result of the following differences in the two systems:

- the definition of best execution, and the role of execution venues in applying best execution;
- the role played by data consolidators in both markets;
- the role and performance of clearing and settlement systems; and
- the supervisory set-up on both sides, with a big role for self-regulatory organizations in the US, and varying degrees of supervisory effectiveness and enforcement in the EU.

The EU has long insisted that EU companies should be granted greater reciprocal access to US capital markets. The European Commission should take this opportunity to make a detailed comparison between the requirements for exchanges and broker dealers in both jurisdictions, as a basis for a bilateral agreement between both jurisdictions. It should demonstrate how certain provisions of MiFID provide more advantageous access for US firms to the EU market than vice versa. It should also emphasize the high degree of investor protection as contained in MiFID's best execution provision and other aspects of its conduct of business rules.

5. Conclusion

Although MiFID and Reg NMS may at first sight seem comparable, because of the prominent role each assigns to best execution, the two regulations have developed independently within their respective markets and policy environments. Accordingly, they differ importantly in many regards. Seen from the EU, Reg NMS is more protective of US exchanges and execution venues providing automated execution, applies a narrower definition of best execution, contains outdated forms of price regulation and maintains a monopolistic data consolidator. MiFID, on the other hand, is more orientated towards market opening, but it may lead to a higher degree of order fragmentation, and hence reduce liquidity, if connectivity is not assured. It has a broad and flexible definition of best execution, but this raises at the same time two weak points: enforceability and precisely how it would be implemented by national authorities.

The coming into force of MiFID provides a unique opportunity for the EU to negotiate a mutual recognition agreement with the US to allow reciprocal access to exchanges and broker-dealers. With MiFID, the policy goals for regulating both sets of institutions have come much closer, as have also many of the detailed provisions. Although it is still early days to judge whether the SEC is really willing to move to some form of mutual recognition, the European Commission should seize upon this opportunity and actively start to explore the differences and similarities of the regulatory regimes governing brokers and exchanges on both sides of the Atlantic. This would give European exchanges and banks much better access to the US market, which has been on the EU agenda for a long time.

References

Becker, Brandon, Christie Farris Öberg and Brian Johnson 2007. *Overview of Regulation NMS*. WilmerHale: www.wilmerhale.com/publications/.

Blume, Marshall E. 2007. *Competition and Fragmentation in Equity Markets: The Effects of Regulation NMS*. Philadelphia, PA: The Wharton School, University of Pennsylvania.

Campos, Roel C. 2007. 'The Challenge of MiFID in the US', Conference speech, Amsterdam, May.

Engelen, Pieter-Jan (ed.) 2006. 'The Future of alternative trading systems in global financial markets', *Competition and Regulation in Network Industries* 1(4).

Dechert 2005. *Divided SEC Adopts Regulation NMS*, Legal Update from the Dechert Financial Services Group, Washington, DC, September.

Gentzoglanis, Anastassios 2006. 'Reg NMS and Competition in Alternative Trading Systems in the US', in Pieter-Jan Engelen (ed.), *Competition and Regulation in Network Industries* 1(4).

Gkantinis, Stavros 2006. *Regulation and Innovation, Comparing US and European Equity Trading Markets*, Harvard Law School, Student Scholarship Series, Paper 13.

Glassman, Cynthia A. and Paul S. Atkins (SEC Commissioners) 2005. 'Dissent to the Adoption of Regulation NMS', 70 Fe. Reg. 37633, June.

Levin, Mattias 2003. *Competition, Fragmentation and Transparency: Providing the Regulatory Framework for Fair, Efficient and Dynamic European Securities Markets, Assessing the ISD Review*, CEPS Task Force Report. Brussels: Centre for European Policy Studies.

Revue d'Economie Financière 2006. *The Future of Financial Exchanges*, Special Edition.

Tafara, Ethiopis and Robert J. Peterson 2007. 'A blueprint for cross-border access to US investors: a new international framework', *Harvard International Law Journal*, 48(1).

Wallison, Peter 2006. *Financial Services Outlook*. Washington, DC.: American Enterprise Institute.

Wohlburgh Jenah, Susan 2007. 'Commentary on A blueprint for cross-border access to US investors', *Harvard International Law Journal*, 48(1).

GLOSSARY

ATS	Alternative Trading System.
Best Execution	The principle that demands trading execution firms to be able to prove that they provided their clients with the best possible result.
CDO	Collateralized debt obligations.
CESR	Committee of European Securities Regulators.
CFD	Contract for difference.
CLO	Collateralized loan obligation.
COB	Conduct of Business, a set of rules applied to clients dealings for investment firms.
Credit Derivatives	A contract which transfers the risk of a credit asset's returns falling below an agreed level, without transferring the underlying asset itself.
CSD	Central Securities Depositary.
DMA	Direct Market Access, the ability for a buy-side firm to invest directly in financial instruments through automated systems without a requirement to use sell-side brokers for advice or, increasingly, execution.
EEA	European Economic Area
ESC	European Securities Committee
Home State	European country of registration for a financial institution's main office. In the case of investment firms: 1. if the investment firm is a natural person, the member state in which its head office is situated; 2. if the investment firm is a legal person, the member state in which its registered office is situated;

	3. if the investment firm has, under its national law, no registered office, the member state in which its head office is situated. In the case of a regulated market, the member state in which the regulated market is registered or, if under the law of that member state it has no registered office, the member state in which the head office of the regulated market is situated.
Host state	The member state, other than the home member state, in which an investment firm has a branch or performs services and/or activities or the member state in which a regulated market provides appropriate arrangements so as to facilitate access to trading on its system by remote members or participants established in that same member state.
HNW	High Net Worth individuals
IOSCO	International Organization of Securities Commissions.
ISC	Initial service charge
KYC	Know Your Customer, a key regulatory term relating to suitability and appropriateness within MiFID's conduct of business rules.
Financial instrument	See list of instruments specified in Section C of Annex I of MiFID.
Liquidity	The more an asset is bought and sold, the more liquid the asset becomes as price moves rapidly.
MiFID Connect	Formed in November 2005 to represent the major UK Financial Market Trading Associations.
MTF	Multilateral Trading Facility, a multilateral system, operated by an investment firm or a market operator, which brings together multiple third-party buying and selling interests in financial instruments – in the system and in accordance with non-discretionary rules – in a way that results in a contract in accordance with the provisions of Title II of MiFID.
NAV	Net Asset Value
NYSE	New York Stock Exchange.

Passporting	A MiFID rule allowing investment firms to be registered under one national regulator in their home state and transact business anywhere in Europe under that registration.
Project Boat	Formed in October 2006 by a group of large pan-European investment banks to aggregate trade and market data.
Project Turquoise	Formed in November 2006 by seven large pan-European investment banks to create an alternative exchange to Europe's existing national exchanges.
OTC	Over the Counter Trading.
RM	Regulated Market, a multilateral system operated and/or managed by a market operator, which brings together or facilitates the bringing together of multiple third-party buying and selling interests in financial instruments – in the system and in accordance with its non-discretionary rules – in a way that results in a contract, in respect of the financial instruments admitted to trading under its rules and/or systems, and which is authorized and functions regularly and in accordance with the provisions of Title III of MiFID.
SEC	Securities and Exchange Commission.
SI	Systematic Internalizer, a new term introduced by MiFID to describe firms that trade in an organized, frequent and systematic manner from their own book of business.
SRO	Self Regulatory Organizations.
TER	Total Expense Ratio.
Trading venue	A regulated market, MTF or systematic internalizer acting in its capacity as such, and, where appropriate, a system outside the Community with similar functions to a regulated market or MTF.
UCITS	Undertakings for Collective Investments in Transferable Securities. Transferable securities refers to those classes of securities which are negotiable on the capital market, with the exception of instruments of payment, such as:

1. shares in companies and other securities equivalent to shares in companies, partnerships or other entities, and depositary receipts in respect of shares;
2. bonds or other forms of securitized debt, including depositary receipts in respect of such securities;
3. any other securities giving the right to acquire or sell any such transferable securities or giving rise to a cash settlement determined by reference to transferable securities, currencies, interest rates or yields, commodities or other indices or measures.

Annex I

List of services and activities and financial instruments falling under the MiFID's scope

Investment services and activities

1. Reception and transmission of orders in relation to one or more financial instruments.
2. Execution of orders on behalf of clients.
3. Dealing on own account.
4. Portfolio management.
5. Investment advice.
6. Underwriting of financial instruments and/or placing of financial instruments on a firm commitment basis.
7. Placing of financial instruments without a firm commitment basis.
8. Operation of multilateral trading facilities.

Ancillary services

1. Safekeeping and administration of financial instruments for the account of clients, including custodianship and related services such as cash/collateral management.
2. Granting credits or loans to an investor to allow him to carry out a transaction in one or more financial instruments, where the firm granting the credit or loan is involved in the transaction.
3. Advice to undertakings on capital structure, industrial strategy and related matters and advice and services relating to mergers and the purchase of undertakings.
4. Foreign exchange services where these are connected to the provision of investment services.
5. Investment research and financial analysis or other forms of general recommendation relating to transactions in financial instruments.
6. Services related to underwriting.
7. Investment services and activities as well as ancillary services of the type included under Section A or B of Annex 1 related to the underlying of the derivatives included under Section C – 5, 6, 7 and

10 – where these are connected to the provision of investment or ancillary services.

Financial instruments

1. Transferable securities.
2. Money-market instruments.
3. Units in collective investment undertakings.
4. Options, futures, swaps, forward rate agreements and any other derivative contracts relating to securities, currencies, interest rates or yields, or other derivatives instruments, financial indices or financial measures which may be settled physically or in cash.
5. Options, futures, swaps, forward rate agreements and any other derivative contracts relating to commodities that must be settled in cash or may be settled in cash at the option of one of the parties (otherwise than by reason of a default or other termination event).
6. Options, futures, swaps, and any other derivative contract relating to commodities that can be physically settled provided that they are traded on a regulated market and/or an MTF.
7. Options, futures, swaps, forwards and any other derivative contracts relating to commodities, that can be physically settled not otherwise mentioned in C.6 and not being for commercial purposes, which have the characteristics of other derivative financial instruments, having regard to whether, *inter alia*, they are cleared and settled through recognized clearing houses or are subject to regular margin calls.
8. Derivative instruments for the transfer of credit risk.
9. Financial contracts for differences.
10. Options, futures, swaps, forward rate agreements and any other derivative contracts relating to climatic variables, freight rates, emission allowances or inflation rates or other official economic statistics that must be settled in cash or may be settled in cash at the option of one of the parties (otherwise than by reason of a default or other termination event), as well as any other derivative contracts relating to assets, rights, obligations, indices and measures not otherwise mentioned in this section, which have the characteristics of other derivative financial instruments, having regard to whether, *inter alia*, they are traded on a regulated market or an MTF, are cleared and settled through recognized clearing houses or are subject to regular margin calls.

BIBLIOGRAPHY

Banque de France, (2008) *Financial Stability Review*, Special Issue on Liquidity, No. 11, February. Available at www.banque–france.fr/gb/publications/rsf/rsf_022008.htm.

Casey, J.-P. 2006. *Eligible Assets, Investment Strategies and Investor Protection in Light of Modern Portfolio Theory: Towards a Risk-based Approach for UCITS*, ECMI Policy Brief No. 2, September. Brussels: Centre for European Policy Studies.

Casey, J.-P. and Lannoo, K. 2006. *The MiFID Implementing Measures: Excessive detail or level playing field?*, ECMI Policy Brief No. 1, May. Brussels: Centre for European Policy Studies.

CESR 2006. *Inducements under MiFID*, Consultation Paper, Ref: CESR/06-687. Paris: Committee of European Securities Regulators.

2007a. *CESR's Response to the Commission on Non-equities Transparency*, Ref: CESR/07-284b, July. Paris: Committee of European Securities Regulators.

2007b. *Inducements under MiFID*, Recommendations, Ref: CESR/07-228b. Paris: Committee of European Securities Regulators.

Chiu, I. 2007. 'Securities intermediaries in the Internet age and the traditional principal-agent model of regulation: some observations from the EU's Markets in the Financial Instruments Directive', *Journal of International Commercial Law and Technology* 2(1).

Ferrarini, G. and Wymeersch, E. (eds.) 2006. *Investor Protection in Europe. Corporate Law Making, The MiFID and Beyond*. Oxford: Oxford University Press.

Giraud, J.-R. and D'Hondt, C. 2006. *MiFID. Convergence towards a Unified European Capital Markets Industry*. London: Risks Books.

IBM Business Consulting Services 2006a. 'A practical guide to preparing for MiFID': www-935.ibm.com/services/uk/bcs/pdf/ibm-mifid-8pp-04–2006-f2lo.pdf.

IBM Global Business Services 2006b. 'Tackling latency – the algorithmic arms race': www-03.ibm.com/industries/financialservices/doc/content/bin/fss_latency_arms_race.pdf.

JPMorgan 2006. *MiFID Report II. Earnings at risk analysis: The threat to the integrated business model*. Available at www.lesechos.fr/medias/2006/0925//300100099.pdf.

Lannoo, Karel and Khachaturyan, A. 2003. *Disclosure Regulation in The EU: The Emerging Framework*, CEPS Task Force Report No. 48. Brussels: Centre for European Policy Studies.

Levin, Mattias 2003. *Competition, Fragmentation and Transparency; Providing the Regulatory Framework for Fair, Efficient and Dynamic European Securities Markets, Assessing the ISD Review*, CEPS Task Force Report, April. Brussels: Centre for European Policy Studies.

MiFID Connect – Clifford Chance 2007a. *Information Memorandum on the Application of the Conflicts of Interest Requirements under the FSA Rules Implementing MiFID and the CRD in the UK:* www.mifidconnect.org/content/1/c6/01/06/90/conflicts_of_interest_memo.pdf.

2007b. *Guideline on Investment Research:* www.mifidconnect.org/content/1/c6/01/02/52/Investment_Research_Guideline.pdf.

Skinner, C. (ed.) 2007. *The Future of Investing in Europe's Markets after MiFID*, Chichester: John Wiley.

INDEX